Ann G. Imlah

Britain and Switzerland 1845–60

a study of Anglo-Swiss relations during some critical years for Swiss neutrality

Longmans

LONGMANS, GREEN AND CO. LTD
48 Grosvenor Street, London W.1
Associated companies, branches and representatives
throughout the world

© Ann G. Imlah 1966
First published 1966

Made and printed in Great Britain by
William Clowes and Sons, Limited, London and Beccles

Contents

Preface   ix

List of Tables   x

Abbreviations   x

Dramatis Personae   xi

Map of Switzerland   xv

CHAPTER ONE   **Introduction**

The enigma of Swiss neutrality   1
Neutrality in the nineteenth century   3
Factors determining British and Swiss policies   4

CHAPTER TWO   **Development of the *Sonderbund* Crisis**

Switzerland between 1798 and 1840   6
Economic development before 1848   10
Swiss political agitation and the policies
  of the Great Powers before 1847   13
1847: The crisis approaches   19
Conclusions about this phase of
  Anglo-Swiss relations   22

CHAPTER THREE   **Civil War and National Consolidation**

Factors influencing the Great Powers
  at the outbreak of the Sonderbund *war*   24
Diplomatic activity during the war   25

The end of the war and Canning's mission   30
Continued threats from the Continental Powers   35
British policy toward the Sonderbund reconsidered   37
Consolidation of the new Swiss government
    and its international position   40

CHAPTER FOUR   **The Neuchâtel Question: Part I**

The problems of liberal
    and neutral Switzerland after 1848   42
1848 diplomacy over Neuchâtel   43
The Prussian threat in 1848–49   45
1849–50 attempts to negotiate   47
Revival of the question in 1851   50
Negotiation of a Great Power agreement in 1852   52
Aftermath of the London Protocol of 1852   55
Review of the Neuchâtel discussions to 1852   58

CHAPTER FIVE   **The Refugee Problem**

The nub of the problem   60
The 1848 Austro-Swiss dispute   61
Discussions with Germany in 1848–49   63
Friction between France
    and Switzerland, 1849–50   64
The French ultimatum of 1852   67
The British role in Franco-Swiss relations   73
The Austro-Swiss dispute, 1853–55   74
Comparison of French and Austrian
    policy toward Switzerland   87
Franco-Swiss discussions of 1856 and 1858   88

CHAPTER SIX   **The Swiss Position during the Crimean War**

Swiss neutrality faced with war   91
Belligerent pressures on Switzerland   92
The British Swiss Legion   94
Realism in the development of neutrality   98

CHAPTER SEVEN   **Anglo-Swiss Economic Relations**

Anglo-Swiss economic relations before 1848   100
Swiss economic growth after 1848   101
Swiss export industries   103
British participation in Swiss
     economic development   108
The Anglo-Swiss Treaty of 1855   111
Measurement of Anglo-Swiss trade   115
Organization of Anglo-Swiss trade   119
Implications of Anglo-Swiss trade   125

CHAPTER EIGHT   **The Neuchâtel Question: Part II**

Revival of the Prussian claim   127
The British attempt to find a settlement   130
British quiescence   133
The threat of war   135
Negotiation of a settlement   143
Reflections about the Neuchâtel question   149

CHAPTER NINE   **The Savoy Question**

Application of neutrality   153
Development of French annexation plans   155
French persistence and the European responses   159
Failure of Anglo-Swiss policy   168
Reconsideration of the Savoy question   172

CHAPTER TEN   **Conclusion**   176

APPENDIX I   The Canning Memorandum
     of 12 November 1847   181

APPENDIX II   TABLE VIII   186

BIBLIOGRAPHY   187

INDEX   202

Preface

SWISS HISTORY in general has been given very little attention in the English language, so that even the potential areas of exploration have not been well known in Britain and the United States. It has been very exciting to find not only that the subject is deserving of close examination, but also that an enormous amount of documentation, hitherto unused, is available on the west side of the Channel. Swiss studies of their foreign relations in the middle of the nineteenth century have been based entirely on their own or other continental sources and on a limited amount of British material, so that this study should make some addition to the research already done, as well as being written in English. Because time for research in France and Switzerland has been very limited, and because a wealth of material is available in Britain, the reader will notice that the discussion is based to a very great extent on British documents.

I should like to express my gratitude to many who have helped me with this project: to the Central Research Fund of the University of London for financing research in Paris; to the officials of the Public Record Office and the British Museum in London, of the Bodleian Library in Oxford, of the Archives d'Etat in Geneva, of the Archives of the Ministry of Foreign Affairs in Paris, and, also in Paris, to M. du Verdier of the National Archives, and especially to Professor L. Haas and Dr O. J. F. Gauye of the Swiss Federal Archives; to my friends, Dr B. W. E. Alford, Mrs H. Gould, and Miss C. Freeman, who have read some parts of the manuscript; to members of the staff of the London School of Economics and Political Science, Professor F. J. Fisher, Dr A. H. John, and very specially to my supervisors, Professor W. N. Medlicott and Dr H. Hearder. My father's steady encouragement has contributed in great measure to the progress of the study.

AGI

List of Tables

I	Swiss Poll Results on Reasons for Neutrality	3
II	Switzerland at the Great Exhibition of 1851	104
III	Course of Swiss Foreign Commerce, 1850–60	116
IV	Estimated Swiss Trade with Britain, 1848–60	118
V	Estimates of the Importance of Switzerland for British Re-export and Transit Trades, 1848–60	120
VI	Statistics related to Swiss Trade	122
VII	Comparison of the Anglo-Swiss Trade with British Foreign Trade, 1848–60	125
VIII	Anglo-Swiss Trade for 1855: Estimates and Reports related to them	186

ABBREVIATIONS

AAE	(French) Archives des Affaires Etrangères
AN	(French) Archives Nationales
BM	British Museum
BPP	British Parliamentary Papers
Clar	Clarendon Papers
FF	Feuille Fédérale de la Confédération Suisse
FO	Foreign Office
PRO	Public Record Office
RO	Receuil Officiel des Lois et Ordonnances de la Confédération Suisse
SFA	Swiss Federal Archives
EPD	Eidgenössisches Politisches Departement
EMD	Eidgenössisches Militär Departement
KD	Konsular Dienst

DRAMATIS PERSONAE

This list is intended to show, briefly, the role of some important people in Anglo-Swiss relations in the middle of the nineteenth century. It is not an attempt to give a complete résumé of their accomplishments, nor does it pretend to include all those who were important during this period.

ABERDEEN (Earl of) (George Gordon-Hamilton): British Foreign Secretary, 1841–46; Prime Minister, December 1852–January 1855.

BARMAN (Joseph-Hyacinthe): Swiss Minister to France, 1849–57.

BISMARCK (-Schoenhausen) (Prince Otto von): Prussian representative to the German Diet in Frankfurt, 1851–59.

BLOOMFIELD (Lord John Arthur Douglas): British Minister to Prussia, 1851–60.

BOIS-LE-COMTE (Count Charles Edmond de): French Minister to Switzerland, 1844–48.

BUCHANAN (Sir Andrew): British Minister to Switzerland, 1852–53.

BUOL (-Schauenstein) (Count Karl Ferdinand von): Austrian Foreign Minister, 1852–59.

BUNSEN (Christian Karl Josias): Prussian Ambassador to Britain, 1845–60.

BURNLEY (Joseph Hume): British Secretary of Legation in Switzerland, 1858–64.

CANNING (Sir Stratford): British Minister to Switzerland, 1814–20; attended the Congress of Vienna, on the committee for Swiss affairs; special emissary to Switzerland, Prussia, and Austria, 1847–48.

CAVOUR (Count Camillo Benso): Prime Minister of Sardinia, 1852–61.

CHRISTIE (William Dougal): British Secretary of Legation in Switzerland, 1851–54.

CLARENDON (Earl of) (George William Frederick Villiers): British Foreign Secretary, 1853–58.

COWLEY (Earl of) (Henry Richard Charles Wellesley): Appointed British Minister to Switzerland in 1848 but did not take up the post; Minister to the German Confederation, 1848–52; Ambassador to France, 1852–67.

DE LA RIVE (Auguste): Professor of physics in Geneva; special Swiss Minister to Britain, 1860; cousin of Cavour.

DROUYN DE LHUYS (Edouard): French Minister of Foreign Affairs, 1848–49; Ambassador to Britain, 1850; Minister of Foreign Affairs, 1851 (two weeks) and 1852–55.

DUFOUR (Guillaume-Henri): Teacher and friend of Louis-Napoleon in the 1830s; General of the Swiss army in 1847–48, 1849, 1856–57, and 1859; special Swiss emissary to Napoleon in 1856 and in 1860.

FURRER (Jonas): President of the Swiss Federal Council, 1849, 1852, 1855, and 1858.

GORDON (George John Robert): British Minister to Switzerland, 1854–1858.

GRANVILLE (Lord) (George Leveson Gower): British Foreign Secretary, 1851–52.

GUIZOT (François): French Prime Minister, 1840–48.

HARRIS (Captain Edward Alfred John): British Minister to Switzerland, 1858–67; brother of the Earl of Malmesbury, and his cousin was the wife of Lord John Russell.

HATZFELDT (Count Maximillian Friedrich Karl Franz): Prussian Minister to France, 1849–59.

HERRIES (Edward): Attached to Canning's special mission to Switzerland, 1847–48; British Secretary of Legation in Switzerland, 1850 and 1854–58.

HUDSON (Sir James): British Minister to Sardinia, 1852–63.

KERN (Johann Conrad): Swiss Minister to Paris, 1856–83; friend of Louis-Napoleon in the 1830s.

MAGENIS (Sir Arthur Charles): British Secretary of Legation in Switzerland, 1838–44; Minister to Switzerland, 1851–52.

MALMESBURY (Earl of) (James Howard Harris): British Foreign Secretary, 1852 and 1858–59.

MANTEUFFEL (Baron Otto von): Prussian Prime Minister, 1850–58.

MAZZINI (Guiseppe): Italian revolutionary.

METTERNICH (-Winneburg) (Prince von): Austrian Chancellor, 1809–48.

MINTO (Earl of) (Gilbert Elliot): Special British emissary to Switzerland and Italy, 1847–48.

MORIER (David R.): British Minister to Switzerland, 1832–47; father of Sir Robert Morier.

NORMANBY (Marquis of) (Constantine Henry Phipps): British Ambassador to France, 1846–52.

OCHSENBEIN (Ulrich): Commander of the volunteer bands attacking Lucerne, 1844–45; President of Berne, and of Switzerland, 1847–48; officer in charge of the French Swiss Legion during the Crimean War.

PALMERSTON (Viscount) (Henry John Temple): British Foreign Secretary, 1846–51; Prime Minister, 1855–58 and 1859–65.

PEEL (Robert): British Secretary of Legation in Switzerland, 1846–50; son of the Prime Minister.

PERSIGNY (Count Jean Gilbert Victor Fialin de): French Ambassador to Britain, 1855–58 and 1859–60; special French emissary to Prussia, 1849–50.

PONSONBY (Lord): British Minister to Austria, from before 1847 to 1850.

RADETZKY (Marshal): Austrian military commander in Lombardy, 1836–58.

RUSSELL (Earl John): British Prime Minister, 1847–52; Foreign Secretary, 1852–53 and 1859–65.

SALIGNAC-FÉNELON (Count): French Minister to Switzerland, 1851–58.

SYDOW (Rudolf von): Prussian Minister to Switzerland, 1841(?)–1856.

THOUVENEL (Antoine-Edouard): French Minister of Foreign Affairs, 1860–62.

TOURTE (Abraham): Special Swiss Minister to Sardinia, 1860; Minister to Italy, 1860–63.

TURGOT (Marquis Louis): French Minister of Foreign Affairs, 1851–52; Ambassador to Switzerland, 1858–after 1865.

WALEWSKI (Count Alexandre Florian Joseph Colonna-): French Minister of Foreign Affairs, 1855–60.

WESTMORLAND (Earl of) (Francis William Fane): British Minister to Prussia, 1841–51; Minister to Austria, 1851–55.

ACKNOWLEDGEMENTS

We are indebted to the following for permission to reproduce copyright material:

Lord Clarendon for extracts from the *Clarendon Papers* deposited at the Bodleian Library, Oxford, and the Controller of Her Majesty's Stationery Office for *Canning's memorandum to Palmerston (12 November 1847; FO 100/54)* (Crown-copyright).

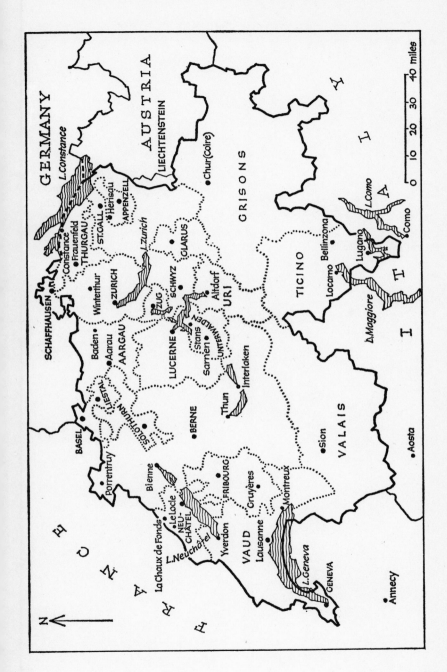

Introduction

THE ENIGMA OF SWISS NEUTRALITY

THE INQUIRING visitor to Switzerland in the mid-twentieth century is struck by a number of evident contrasts and contradictions. He finds fundamental differences in landscape and culture throughout the country and a strong pride in local institutions. Yet he is also aware of a pervasive sense of national identity, dignity, and purpose which is expressed, in Swiss foreign relations, in the policy of neutrality to which the Swiss persistently adhere.

Variety is observable in several aspects of Swiss life. Its first and most obvious manifestation is linguistic: three cantons and parts of at least three others are French-speaking; in one canton Italian is the main language; part of another is Romansch-speaking; and the remaining fourteen cantons, as well as parts of the four mixed ones, are German-speaking. A second manifestation is religious, with Protestants somewhat more numerous than Catholics; yet the predominant religion of a canton is not necessarily related to the linguistic division. A third symptom of Swiss diversity is political: the small country is composed of twenty-two cantons, three of them divided again in halves. Because these political divisions are based on deeply rooted local traditions and loyalties, sizes of the cantons vary, with some surprisingly small while others are relatively large. Economic differences exist also; although the country as a whole is very well off, some areas are much richer than others.

Intercantonal rivalry, or even conflict, has been a significant factor in Swiss political life, since some basic cultural characteristics have a separative effect. The French-speaking cantons quite naturally are very interested in events in France; their architecture is in the French style; they patronize the French theatre and read French books. Their residents would seldom go to German or Italian plays, read German or

Italian books, or be as interested in German or Italian affairs as the citizens of a German- or Italian-speaking canton. Lack of knowledge and the simple inability to communicate have contributed to many misunderstandings between cantons. However, even within a language area, disagreements have arisen because of religious irritation, political disagreement, or conflict of economic interests. In earlier centuries, before the means of communication over and around the mountains were developed, all of these sources of disagreement were more noticeable than now, but even today the tradition of rivalry and strong local loyalty remains an important force.

Despite all these divisive elements in their body politic, one may also find among the Swiss a binding sense of national purpose. Their pride in Swiss accomplishments and position in Europe, both of which are often attributed to the policy of neutrality, is at times surprisingly strong. They have developed a real sense of responsibility, as a neutral nation, to the international community: 'It is un-Swiss to be merely Swiss.'[1] In discussing the possibility of membership in the European Economic Community, one may discover that many Swiss consider their country to be the real heart of Europe, an example of what the Continent should strive to be: Switzerland, with her success as a polylingual nation, is proof that Europe as a viable unit may also be realized some day. Switzerland is the guardian of the European centre, indeed she *is* Europe. The majority of Swiss citizens believe that their country should stay aloof from any political squabbles in order to continue their good example of European community; the sanctified policy of neutrality should be maintained. Although she deviated from a strictly neutral policy to join the League of Nations (with reservations), Switzerland has not joined the United Nations. One may be surprised by the pretentiousness of these views. How could this strong nationalism have come to be?

Interestingly enough, just as the Swiss disagree now about the extent to which they should continue their policy of neutrality, their explanations of the reasons for it also vary. After the voters decided not to join the United Nations, the New Helvetian Society conducted a poll to discover the reasons for which the Swiss believed the continuation of neutrality to be necessary. Justification was significantly different in each language area.[2] For example, 28·5 per cent in German Switzerland and 24·1 per cent in Italian Switzerland, compared with none in French

[1] Edgar Bonjour, in Neue Helvetische Gesellschaft, *Neutralität und Mitverantwortung* (Berne, 1957), p21
[2] See Table I

Table I. Swiss poll results on reasons for neutrality

	German per cent	French per cent	Italian per cent
Neutrality has proved itself	28·5	—	24·1
Neutrality helps to prevent war	22·5	10·0	19·9
Neutrality facilitates the maintenance of internal peace	14·0	16·0	8·5
Neutrality allows Switzerland to fulfil humanitarian duties	13·5	34·0	9·5
Neutrality facilitates maintenance of independence	11·0	33·0	17·0
Neutrality makes possible Swiss help to other lands	5·5	—	—
Neutrality is a political necessity	—	—	21·0
Other reasons	5·0	7·0	—

SOURCE: Neue Helvetische Gesellschaft, *Die Schweiz Hält Durch* (Zurich, 1948), pp 174–5.

Switzerland, believed that neutrality should be continued because it had proved itself.

The poll also indicates some of the factors which have contributed to the evolution of the Swiss position. Because of the variety of extra-national cultural ties, the country could not maintain its integrity by aligning itself with any one of the neighbouring Powers. The only way to independence was a course apart from all of them, neutrality. Some Swiss, understandably proud of their national achievements, say that their neutrality has been determined by the peculiarities of their political existence, but insist that it has not been dictated by the neighbouring Powers.[3] How realistic is this assertion? Might not the Swiss be deluding themselves? Is it possible that a people with such diverse customs and interests could voluntarily and independently choose and develop their policy of neutrality? What answers might their history offer?

NEUTRALITY IN THE NINETEENTH CENTURY

The nineteenth century has been described as a classic period of Swiss neutrality.[4] This might imply that the nineteenth century was an exemplary and perhaps relatively static period politically for Switzerland, but such was not the case. For the Continent as a whole it was a

[3] Neue Helvetische Gesellschaft, *Die Schweiz Hält Durch* (Zurich, 1948), p19
[4] Werner Kagi, in Neue Helvetische Gesellschaft, *Neutralität* ... , p49

3

time of very dramatic political and economic change. The French Revolution had set in motion many waves of ideological ferment. Republicanism was threatening old monarchies. Patterns of commerce and communication were radically revised and their tempo much increased. Nationalistic movements gained force, with language as a primary common bond, culminating in the unification of two more strong states bordering on Switzerland. The little country could not remain unmoved by all these currents swirling about it. The Italian, German, and French language groups in Switzerland were all tempted, to some extent, to respond to the calls for help from movements outside the country, and this posed a serious threat to the neutral confederation. The nineteenth century, therefore, was a dynamic and formative time in the development of a modern concept of neutrality, a classic period in the sense that decisions made then have been used as precedents for more recent policy.

The crucial decisions which determined the survival of a neutral Switzerland were made in the middle part of the nineteenth century. These decades saw the strong national movements in Italy and Germany and, corresponding to them, a growing temptation in France, Austria, and Prussia to use military means to achieve national aims. In the midst of these conflicts, Switzerland was also struggling to find her national identity and she, too, was forced to clarify her position on the Continent.

In this potentially explosive mid-century political situation, the support of a friendly Power was of critical importance to preserve Swiss independence. The geographic separation of Britain from Switzerland made Britain much less an interested party in Swiss internal politics than France or Austria, so that the Swiss were inclined to trust Britain. Because of this special Anglo-Swiss relationship, and because British observations and analyses of the Swiss scene are often more perceptive than those of the neighbouring Powers, a study of the relations between Britain and Switzerland will permit some tenable conclusions about the development of neutrality.

FACTORS DETERMINING BRITISH AND SWISS POLICIES

Before beginning a detailed examination of the events between, roughly, 1845 and 1860, a suggestion of some of the possible policy considerations for Britain, and for Switzerland, might be appropriate. Writers agree that Britain's general aim was to maintain peace in Europe, be it for idealistic, political, or economic reasons. Some may assert that Britain as a liberal nation wanted to perpetuate liberalism elsewhere, and Switzerland was a liberal state threatened by conservative neighbours. Practically, the preservation of Switzerland's position in Europe was critical for the European peace, since her dismemberment would have radically altered the relations of France, Austria, Sardinia, and the German states. Britain, simply as a defender of the European equilibrium, would tend to support Swiss independence. On the economic side, in the early part of the nineteenth century, Swiss wealth was as yet untapped, in that her capital resources had not yet been channelled into productive enterprise at home or abroad. Her industrialization had not advanced very far or attracted much domestic or foreign capital. She had been an active trader with Britain, on a modest scale, since the sixteenth century, and as a land-locked country increasingly dependent on an export trade she could give British merchants much business. Serious disruption in Switzerland might well cause general war in Europe which would hurt British commerce with many countries. These, then, were factors arguing for the development, in the British interest, of a viable, independent, and peaceful Switzerland.

Other factors led the Powers, including Britain, to treat Swiss affairs in whatever way best suited their policy aims elsewhere, and Switzerland was at times a mere pawn in the game of power politics. Settlements of disputes involving Switzerland were sometimes incomplete or prolonged according to the exigencies of other international questions. Britain and the other Powers were on occasion quite inconsistent in their demands of the Swiss—for example, by demanding the cessation of the mercenary system and then engaging mercenaries themselves a year later.

Swiss attitudes toward Britain were varied also. The Swiss admired British economic development and sought advice for furthering their own. Although a few voices were raised to reject British advice in the political sphere as an infringement of Swiss independence, most Swiss had confidence in the policy of a liberal and remote nation. As a very small and politically rather disunited state, particularly in the early part of the century, with less than minimal diplomatic and consular services, the Swiss often relied on British guidance and sometimes expected Britain to play the role of a mediator, as well as that of a protector, in her disputes with neighbouring Powers.

Here, then, are some ingredients of the question to be explored and suggestions of turnings which the investigation may take. Swiss foreign policy was probably not dictated entirely from the outside, but it certainly was conditioned by the position of Switzerland in the centre of Europe, surrounded by larger states.

CHAPTER TWO

Development of
the *Sonderbund* Crisis

AS WITH SO MUCH of Europe, the Napoleonic period had a profound influence on Swiss political and economic development. At the time of the French invasion of Switzerland in 1798, the cantons were only very loosely confederated, each one being independent, jealous, and incapable of much political, economic, or even military cooperation, so that sustained defence was impossible. With little organized Swiss opposition to the French, the country was a European battlefield for over a year, until Napoleon gained firm control in late 1799. He took some benevolent interest in remedying the political weaknesses, by imposing on Switzerland a unitary government and abolishing the privileged positions of certain families and cantons. In 1803, when it became obvious that completely unitary government would not work, a new constitution, the Act of Mediation, was drawn up to allow some recognition of cantonal sovereignty. Despite the fact that Napoleon was forced to concede something to cantonal sovereignty, the change in the direction of a more unified national life was started and, in the long run, it was irreversible.[1]

During the next decade, with some of the social barriers to progress swept away and with the economic stimulus of Napoleon's Continental System after 1807, the Swiss economy could develop a great deal. At the beginning of the Napoleonic period, the population of less than 1·7 million was primarily agrarian. Farmers supplemented their incomes with work at home, in textiles or watchmaking, so that industrial activity

[1] For general works on Swiss history, see Edgar Bonjour, H. S. Offler, and G. R. Potter, *A Short History of Switzerland* (Oxford, 1952); Ernest Gagliardi, *Histoire de la Suisse* (translated into French by August Reymond) (Lausanne, 1925), Vol. II; or Johannes Dierauer, *Geschichte der Schweizerischen Eidgenossenschaft*, Vol. V (1798-1848) (Gotha, 1922) and Vol. VI, written by Hans Schneider (*Geschichte des Schweizerischen Bundesstaates, 1848-1918*) (Stuttgart, 1931)

was spread out and the cities were relatively small, being primarily commercial centres. Although the basic pattern was unchanged under Napoleon, small factories began to spring up, away from the cities but near sources of water power. The textile industry, which had existed for many years as a cottage industry, began to be mechanized in eastern Switzerland (St Gall) and near Zurich. The machine industry began in Winterthur, north of Zurich and nearer the Rhine and sources of imported raw materials, such as iron and coal. These beginnings of industrialization were on a small enough scale so that most workers could continue to live with their farming families. Watchmaking, still a home industry, was already well established in western villages, in the Jura mountains, near the commercial centres of Neuchâtel and Geneva. This lack of centralization in the economic sphere was a strong factor in maintaining Swiss resistance to much political centralization.

Switzerland was delivered from Napoleonic tutelage late in 1813, as the armies of the great alliance closed in on France. Nearly all the former cantonal governments were restored and the old rivalries flared up again, to the extent that there was real question as to how the Powers would deal with Switzerland in the peace settlement. At the Congress of Vienna, the committee on Switzerland was particularly influenced by two delegations, the Russian and the British. The Tsar of Russia relied heavily on his Swiss adviser, de la Harpe, whose romantic and liberal vision called for a free and independent Switzerland. The British also wanted Swiss independence, but used a more realistic argument, namely, the threat of renewed war if any other solution were attempted. Consequently, the committee decided to maintain Switzerland as some sort of viable political unit. The three cantons which Napoleon had separated from the confederation, Geneva, Neuchâtel, and the Valais, were added again. By the 1815 Acts, the Powers guaranteed perpetual Swiss neutrality; in accepting the guarantee, the Swiss declared their adherence to the European system, confirmed the existing frontiers of the cantons, and undertook not to enter into any alliance which would be contrary to the European interest. Specifically, they promised to maintain enough military force to defend themselves, and the Powers agreed to put sufficient forces at their disposal for defence in case of attack.[2] As the Prussian government described the arrangement as late as 1857, Switzerland was merely to serve as a barrier, a buffer state between Austria and France,

[2] Acts of 20 and 29 March 1815, in Sir Edward Hertslet, *The Map of Europe by Treaty* (London, 1875), i, 64-74; 'Swiss Ratification of the Act of the Vienna Treaty on Swiss Independence and Neutrality' (FO 94/321)

currently the two principal competitors for influence in the alpine country.[3]

The Congress made other provisions for Switzerland which were to cause difficulties in later years. First, while the canton of Neuchâtel again became part of the confederation, it was at the same time to remain a principality under the sovereignty of the King of Prussia. Second, as part of the system of neutrality in central Europe, a strip of land along the southern side of Lake Geneva belonging to Sardinia was to be occupied by the Swiss in the event of war between neighbouring states.[4] The third provision was not explicitly a condition of the Great Power guarantee of neutrality: before the guarantee was signed, the Swiss adopted a constitution setting up a confederate government slightly stronger than the pre-Napoleonic arrangement.

According to this constitution, or Federal Pact, as it was called, the canton was again the principal governing authority. The central government was controlled by a Diet, which was composed of two instructed delegates from each of the cantons; in most cases a simple majority vote was sufficient for binding decisions. The Diet was responsible for foreign relations and it shared military authority with the cantons. The administration of federal affairs was carried out in rotation by three directing cantons – Berne, Lucerne, and Zurich – each for two year periods. The President of the Confederation was the elected head of whichever cantonal government was administering federal affairs. No provision was made for amendment.

Swiss government machinery was thus of a very loose nature. Indeed, it was because of the minimal amount of competence accorded to the central government that Austria and France agreed to the formal treaty provisions for neutrality, since each could hope to exert more influence in the country if it lacked a strong central government. More obviously, the disunity attending such an arrangement ensured that Switzerland would not be able to adopt any aggressive or even firm foreign policy. More than thirty years later, in 1847, Metternich argued for the maintenance of complete cantonal sovereignty as 'the best security ... that no projects of ambition can be carried into effect by the Swiss'.[5] Thus, the Swiss neutrality of 1815 was merely a neutralization, an absence of coherent policy, rather than a positive policy of non-alignment directed by the Swiss themselves.

[3] Manteuffel to Bernstorff, 9 January 1857 (FO 64/448)
[4] Final Act of the Congress of Vienna, Article XCII, in Hertslet, i, 262
[5] Ponsonby to Palmerston, 30 September 1847 (FO 7/337)

8

Weakness of the central authority in Switzerland led to serious problems in foreign relations. The neighbouring Powers threatened the confederation with various kinds of action from time to time because it was unable to adopt or enforce measures to restrain the refugees who congregated within Swiss territory. The fugitives were relatively uncontrolled as they waited for an appropriate moment to return to their homelands to make revolution, in the meantime producing considerable propaganda. Sir Robert Morier, son of David Morier who was British Minister to Switzerland from 1832 to 1847, described the situation of Switzerland in the 1830s as 'either the battlefield for the rival intrigues of its big neighbours, or the green room in which political dramas, to be afterwards acted on the big European stage, have been rehearsed ...'.[6] It was little different a decade earlier. In 1822, because of the problem of the refugees, the Congress of Verona made clear that Swiss independence was contingent on the favour of the Powers. The following year, the Swiss government was forced by pressure from all the Continental Powers to adopt a 'Press and Aliens Conclusum' which greatly limited the freedom of the refugees. Yet, humiliating though this piece of legislation was for the Swiss, its passage had a hopeful aspect also, in that the government was capable of at least some action under duress. More significant were the Swiss reaction against the Conclusum and the even stronger reactions in the 1830s against similar foreign pressures.

The July revolution of 1830 in France had a twofold effect on Switzerland. It encouraged Swiss liberals to force improvements in their own political institutions, and it broke up the unity of the Continental Powers, so that France and Britain soon reached a friendly entente. Switzerland could rely on a better operation of the balance of power than in the 1820s and consequently could follow a slightly more independent course. Most of the cantons, in 1830 or soon thereafter, underwent revolutions which replaced the aristocratic with more representative forms of government. By 1832 Swiss liberal ferment had gained so much momentum that a proposal to revise the Federal Pact reached the Diet.

Despite the separation of France from the conservative eastern bloc of Powers in 1830, in 1832 all the Powers agreed in disapproval of substantial change in Swiss government. They feared having a liberal state in the heart of Europe, but they did not agree on measures to prevent it. Metternich wanted some form of intervention, while the French government took the attitude that Pact reform, however dangerous, was a Swiss

[6] Rosslyn Wemyss, *Memoirs and Letters of the Right Hon. Sir Robert Morier, G.C.B., from 1826 to 1876* (London, 1911), i, 38

9

affair. Britain obviously wanted peace in central Europe, and Lord Palmerston, then Foreign Secretary, anticipated an upsetting effect either from a strong liberal government in the midst of the conservative Powers or from any attempt to divide an uncooperative Switzerland among neighbouring Powers. To try to restrain the Swiss, he reminded them that any changes tending to destroy cantonal sovereignty and to centralize the government would be 'so much at variance with the stipulations under which the neutrality and inviolability of the Swiss territory were guaranteed that ... guaranteeing Powers would undoubtedly be entitled to object. The neutrality of Switzerland is essentially connected with the Federal system ...'. Much change in Swiss government would be very dangerous, since it might bring on civil war and the possible dismemberment of the Confederation.[7] To restrain the Continental Powers, he supported the French position and recommended that they wait to take any action until Switzerland might have 'failed in performing Her part of the Duties of Neutrality'.[8] The Swiss must have taken Palmerston's warning seriously, since the proposal for Pact reform failed in the Diet, although only by a narrow vote. The dreaded European crisis was temporarily averted.

ECONOMIC DEVELOPMENT BEFORE 1848

Underlying forces favouring change in the Swiss body politic continued to grow. The population was increasing at the rate of nearly 7 per cent per year, so that, despite improvements in farming methods, natural resources became insufficient to supply food and other necessities. The country was thus more and more dependent on imports, and it was vital to develop ways of earning them with an expanded export trade.

After 1815 Swiss industrial growth was impeded from both outside and inside the country. Napoleon's Continental System had provided a stimulus to development, but, after it ceased to function, tariff barriers imposed by neighbouring countries served to limit markets for Swiss goods. Within Switzerland, application of the principle of cantonal sovereignty to economic life restrained growth in several respects. First, the Diet was unable to effect any unified Customs system, although it was competent in foreign affairs. Each canton had its own tariff and toll rates which, however low, were cumulatively sufficient to divert traffic, especially the transit trade, from some parts of Switzerland. Cantons in

[7] Palmerston to Percy, 9 June 1832 (FO 74/65)
[8] Palmerston to Granville, June 1832, enclosed in Palmerston to Normanby, 19 January 1848 (FO 27/797)

10

the interior which were industrializing and hence increasingly dependent on imported raw materials and food, were more interested in customs unification than the border cantons. Whether the large number of local tariffs did in fact retard Swiss economic development is a matter of some discussion,[9] but they were at least a considerable annoyance which encouraged businessmen to consider plans for more centralization. A second constitutional limitation on economic development was the fact that the Federal Pact did not provide for the right of establishment for any Swiss citizen outside his canton, so that the labour force was relatively immobile, unable to respond to employment needs irrespective of location. The variety of monetary standards and the lack of a coordinated transportation or postal system were also drags on economic development. It was imperative for the Swiss to compete effectively abroad, but they were hard pressed in doing it because of these limitations on development.

The Swiss were keenly aware of their industrial potential, in spite of the paucity of domestic raw materials. They regarded their neutral position as a great advantage because war was not likely to disrupt economic growth. John Bowring, in his 1836 report to Parliament on Swiss industry, noted a general recognition among businessmen that more uniform legislation would be beneficial to commerce; but he was at the same time impressed by the progress which had been made in the circumstances, writing that 'it could not, indeed, but excite the attention of any reflecting person, that the manufactures of Switzerland – almost unobserved, and altogether unprotected, had been gradually, but triumphantly, forcing their way into all the markets of the world, however remote ...'.[10] The Swiss textile industry was again showing promising development, as was the machine industry, partially protected from British competition by poor transportation. Success in the few manufacturing ventures established since the turn of the century had given a taste of what could be ahead.

Many resources were in a position to be put to use. The demand for Swiss mercenaries in foreign countries had decreased considerably since 1815, so that more manpower was available for domestic industrial development. Also, service abroad had given many former mercenaries valuable commercial contacts which might be exploited. The growing number of refugees had the same effect of increasing resources of manpower, technical knowledge, and trade contacts. Swiss foreign trade in

[9] E. Dérobert, *La politique douanière de la Confédération suisse* (Geneva, 1926), p21
[10] BPP 1836 [60], XLV, p3

the early 1840s was probably still quite small and could not earn enough overseas credit to finance industrialization,[11] but capital was available from several other sources: from past accumulation, from some of the refugees, from earlier foreign military service pensions, and from other financial rewards for services abroad. The Swiss have a strong tradition of thrift among most classes of the population, but on the whole their savings had not as yet been invested in large-scale productive domestic enterprise. The dramatic surge of Swiss interest in economic development shows in the beginning of cantonal banks after 1830. Indeed, some of these banks were founded with the express aim of affording the working man a financially rewarding repository for his savings. Their facilities channelled capital resources into productive enterprise and generally facilitated commercial transactions. Swiss private bankers were investing at home rather than in foreign lands because 'the renascent Swiss economy ... [was] more badly in need of funds and could offer plenty of attractive investment opportunities'.[12] A growth of national pride was evident in this turning of Swiss capital toward domestic investments.

After the failure of the Pact revision proposal in 1832, increasing realization of these economic potentials and limitations kept the political issues before the public. The press discussed ways of combatting the tendency of trade to go elsewhere. Some industrial interests favoured increased centralization mainly to obtain tariff protection, but they were quite considerably in the minority. In the early 1840s several attempts were made among the cantons to form Customs unions, but the abstention of a large number of them led to further frustration. By 1844 Morier wrote of the growing 'state of depression, to which the Swiss manufacturing interests ... have been reduced,' largely because of the German Zollverein. As a result of pressure from a national association which aimed to establish a 'Common Toll-union' but not a system of protection, in 1843 the Diet appointed a commission to investigate Swiss commercial relations.[13] Railroad projects, which would require coordination of cantonal interests, were being discussed by 1837 in Zurich and by 1845 in the Diet.

[11] Information about the volume of Swiss foreign trade is not available. In 1844 Morier estimated British exports to Berne, Vaud, and Geneva to be worth more than £327,000, but he gave no estimates at all of British imports from Switzerland. Morier to Aberdeen, 27 April 1844 (FO 100/41)
[12] George Soloveytchik, *Leu & Co., 1755-1955* (Zurich, 1955), p34
[13] Morier to Aberdeen, 24 February 1844 (FO 100/41)

12

Thus it is no coincidence that the cantons with the strongest interest in economic development formed the nucleus of a second movement for Pact revision. The advocates of Pact revision were primarily concerned to improve commercial conditions. To achieve this, they would have to persuade the cantons to give up more of their sovereignty to a central government, but they did not urge any kind of unitary government, which would be contrary to deeply ingrained Swiss local loyalties. Swiss business leaders, who were often active in government too, had compelling material interest in changing the Swiss political structure, and they had much to lose if constricting forces remained predominant or if the situation disintegrated to a state of anarchy, which might well have brought intervention by one or more of the Powers. It is interesting that even within a year of the outbreak of the Swiss civil war in 1847 the less industrial cantons were voting together in the Diet irrespective of their predominant religious or political affiliation.

The divisions within Switzerland, mentioned in Chapter One, were more important factors in Swiss political life in the nineteenth century than they are today. Because of their language affinities, the French-, German-, and Italian-speaking areas felt considerable sympathy for their neighbours outside Switzerland. The Catholic Church tended to oppose any governmental centralization in fear of giving increased power to the Protestants. The principles of cantonal sovereignty and equality, which the Powers were so eager to preserve, meant among other things that the very small and economically undeveloped 'forest' cantons, all Catholic, exercised a voting power in the Diet out of all proportion to their population. The small cantons were naturally very anxious to keep their power.

In the early 1840s the conflicts of interest became sharper, immediately stimulated by disagreement between the civil authorities and the conservative clerical elements among the Catholic Swiss. Ultramontanist groups had been active politically in several cantons since the movement for Pact reform in 1832. The Jesuits had controlled the education system of the canton of Fribourg for many years, but when they increased their activity in the canton of Aargau they were not so well received. In 1841 the Aargau government decided to close the four monasteries and four convents which had been centres of Jesuit propaganda. This roused a storm of protest in many parts of Switzerland. The Ultramontanes, who were in principle against extension of federal action to reopen the convents, called for federal action to restore the convents and monasteries, because, they argued, the Federal Pact had guaranteed religious institutions. The Diet was aware that the action of the Aargau government had been taken only after considerable provocation, and its majority declared the matter settled in 1843 when the four convents, but not the monasteries, were reopened.

The Diet was able to persist in its somewhat anti-Jesuit course without concerted foreign pressure since this was again a time of Anglo-French entente. Of all the Powers, Austria was most sympathetic to the Swiss Ultramontanes; she sent several notes of protest to the Swiss, but was unable to persuade Britain or France to do the same. Britain had previously tended to recommend respect for the existing order in Switzerland, but she had no desire to encourage the spread of Catholicism, so she simply urged the Swiss to settle the matter as quickly as possible in order to avoid foreign intervention.[14]

The conservative, Catholic, and relatively poor cantons were displeased with the compromise over the monasteries and, with Austrian encouragement, their general dissatisfaction assumed larger proportions. In September 1843, worried by the liberal influence of the Radical party in the Diet, they called a special meeting to discuss the problems of maintaining their independence from Diet interference. In 1844 the cantonal government of Lucerne decided to strengthen itself against Radical encroachment by inviting the Jesuits to manage its system of education.

The Lucerne challenge evoked some response from both the Swiss and the Powers. Because the canton, at that time directing federal affairs, had not been exercising its federal duties with the requisite impartiality, the reaction of liberal Switzerland against this move was particularly strong. By early 1845 the Aargau government, through a liberal *Catholic* delegate, asked the Diet to forbid the Jesuits in any part of Switzerland. The proposal was defeated then, but the Jesuit issue was increasingly discussed throughout Switzerland. It eventually caused the replacement of at least three cautious cantonal governments by firmly Radical régimes. Indeed, even the Continental Powers were not entirely pleased about the Lucerne decision, as they realized the probable effect on Swiss tranquillity, as well as its possible European repercussions. France tried to persuade the Pope to discourage the Jesuits from accepting the invi-

[14] In addition to the works already cited, see Paul Schweizer, *Geschichte der schweizerischen Neutralität* (Frauenfeld, 1895) or Edgar Bonjour, *Geschichte der Schweizerischen Neutralität* (Basle, 1946) for general accounts of Swiss foreign relations. Carl Eckinger's *Lord Palmerston und der Sonderbundskrieg* (Berlin, 1938) gives a detailed account of the events of the *Sonderbund* crisis

tation. Metternich later claimed to have done the same, but at the end of 1844, in Morier's opinion, the Austrian Minister in Switzerland had done nothing to discourage the Lucerne government from patronizing the Jesuits.[15]

Despite widespread disapproval of the Lucerne decision, the Radical position in Switzerland suffered some setbacks in 1844-45. First, in the spring of 1844, a counter-revolution in the Valais returned a Conservative government to power. A second development was more serious: in December volunteer bands of extreme Radicals from Berne, Aargau, and Basle-country[16] attacked Lucerne in the hope of changing its government. From both a legal and a moral point of view, the episode was humiliating for the liberal cause. In early 1845 a special session of the Diet voted measures which were intended to prevent such an outbreak in the future.

All the Powers took strong stands against the obviously illegal attack. They all wanted to encourage Swiss moderation, but since they did not agree about the extent to which it was necessary to threaten Switzerland, their messages to the Diet were sent separately. The French message, ironically, was the most criticized by the Swiss, although it was accompanied by assurances of respect for Swiss independence. French policy-makers, while wanting to cooperate with Austria to some extent, were restrained by domestic opinion, which tended to favour a limitation of Jesuit power. For this reason the French note was actually milder than the British message. The Foreign Office also affirmed respect for Swiss independence, but went on to emphasize the possible consequences of the dissensions which threatened 'dissolution of the Federal Bond'. The British Foreign Secretary, the Earl of Aberdeen, claimed that destruction of the Federal Pact by any means would require the consent of the Powers, in view of their 1815 guarantee of Swiss neutrality.[17] Even Metternich had already admitted, in 1841, that the Powers had not guaranteed the Pact, but now he was quick to let the Swiss know that he endorsed the British message. The Swiss apparently accepted Aberdeen's message with no ill feeling, and Morier reported that it did have the effect of toning down some of the more extreme Radicals.

Why was the British note so strong, when in fact Britain was much less

[15] Morier to Aberdeen, 30 December 1844 (FO 100/41)
[16] In the early 1830s disagreement between the city of Basle and the rest of the canton brought about its division into two parts, which have since shared the cantonal vote in national affairs. The division still exists, although negotiations are now taking place with a view to reuniting the two halves
[17] Aberdeen to Morier, 11 February 1845 (BPP 1847/48 [897] LXV, pp 36-7)

15

able or willing than France to enforce it with further intervention? The line Aberdeen took was not very different from that taken by Palmerston in 1832, although the latter had made a clear distinction between the establishment of a unitary government and the mere revision of detail. Aberdeen's usual inclination was to maintain the *status quo*, and the recent Tahiti incident, which had caused some Anglo-French irritation, combined with Morier's reports that the Radicals were relying on French support, probably encouraged him to cooperate with Austria in order to isolate France.

Still another important factor in the formation of this British policy may be found in the character and reports of David Morier, Her Majesty's Minister Plenipotentiary to Switzerland. He was not a very talented representative of Britain and was quite unable to understand the fundamental peaceful tendencies in Switzerland. Always measuring political success by moral standards, he saw only the selfishness and materialism of this period, now described by historians as the Swiss 'Regeneration'.[18] In June 1845, after a second and more humiliating defeat for more volunteer bands in early April, he wrote to Aberdeen of the decomposition of Swiss society, of the '*Société poussière*, where there is no Cement of authority, or moral principle, or religious feeling to make the unit grains of dust cohere'.[19] His suggestion of urging the Pope to order the withdrawal of the Jesuits was quite to the point, but his analysis of the situation was often confused. In one dispatch, he wrote that 'the Swiss people in general are too practical in their notions & habits to engage in a contest for mere Chimeras';[20] yet he also reported a general spirit of lawlessness, the 'feverish state' of men's minds, and described the Radicals as 'itinerant demagogues'.[21] He was friendly with the representatives of the Continental Powers and was probably very much influenced by their opinions. Indeed, his accounts of the plans of the Radical party contain the same error as the reports of his colleagues in Berne, namely that the Radicals would establish a unitary government. Hence, to some extent, Aberdeen was the victim of poor reporting.

In May, a month and a half after the second attack on Lucerne by volunteer bands, Metternich made an attempt to rally the Powers to

---

[18] Rudolf H. Vogeli, *Die schweizerische Regeneration von 1830-1840 in der Beleuchtung englischer Gesandtschaftsberichte* (Diss. U. Zurich) (Weida i. Thur., 1924), p21
[19] Morier to Aberdeen, 6 June 1845 (BM 43151)
[20] Morier to Aberdeen, 13 January 1845 (FO 100/44)
[21] Morier to Aberdeen, 6 March 1846 (BM 43151)

action on the Swiss question by proposing a joint announcement of opposition to the Radical plan for Pact revision. As he expected, on the basis of the British message of February, Aberdeen agreed. But Guizot of France did not, considering it an unwarranted interference in Swiss internal affairs which could produce serious disturbances. A few weeks later Guizot conferred with representatives of Austria and Britain in Paris and managed to convince them not to press for joint action, because the Swiss were still being moderate enough. Notes to the Diet were drawn up by both Britain and France, in protest against the volunteer bands. The French urged maintenance and stabilization of the *status quo*, but they did not deliver their note. The British note was delivered; it stressed the importance of calming Swiss tempers and the danger to Swiss neutrality from changing the nature of the confederation. Aberdeen did, however, admit that 'the power of the Cantonal Governments to revise that Compact by Legal and Constitutional Means is questioned by no one ...'.[22] Thus, joint action by the Powers in this situation was prevented not by Britain but by French reluctance to stir up trouble on her south-eastern frontier.

The second half of 1845 and much of 1846 were relatively quiet, while the two parties inside Switzerland consolidated and the attentions of the Powers were drawn to other issues. Although the Swiss Radicals were somewhat weakened and sobered by the two attacks on Lucerne, their position improved continually from then on. As early as February 1845 the government of Zurich had taken an unexpectedly aggressive position in voting for the expulsion of the Jesuits from Switzerland. Some days later the Vaud government fell because of popular dissatisfaction with its excessive caution on the Jesuit question. Berne (canton), in February 1846, elected a decisive Radical majority and approved Radical plans for liberalization of the cantonal constitution. Yet the Powers had reason to hope for maintenance of the *status quo* since the Diet, meeting in the summer of 1845, still refused to expel the Jesuits, would take no further action on the Aargau monasteries, and approved more measures against volunteer bands.

The Conservative cantons also consolidated to improve their resistance to Radicalism. The informal discussions of 1843 had not been effective enough, for the Radicals since then had threatened the Conservatives with force in Lucerne and verbally in the Diet. In December 1845 the Conservatives decided to formalize their association with a special league, or *Sonderbund*. It was both an offensive and defensive alliance whose aims were restoration of the Aargau monasteries, pro-

[22] Aberdeen to Morier, 24 June 1845 (BPP 1847/48, pp 94-5)

tection of the Jesuits, and prevention of any revision of the Federal Pact. Because the Federal Pact prohibited the formation of alliances within the Confederation, *Sonderbund* members kept its existence secret for as long as they could. However, news of the alliance did leak out, in June 1846, and the other cantons were highly displeased. The *Sonderbund* was discussed heatedly by the 1846 Diet, but a resolution calling for its dissolution was defeated. The illegally organized Conservative opposition further strengthened the Radicals' position. In early October a revolution in Geneva put one more canton in the Radical camp. Yet the seven cantons of the *Sonderbund* were undaunted by the disapproval of their league in the rest of the Confederation.

In the summer of 1846 Palmerston replaced Aberdeen in the British Foreign Office, and some revision of British policy was to follow. The continental governments were generally uneasy about his return to power, but in fact his basic aim in policy toward Switzerland was the same as Aberdeen's, namely, to preserve peace there. His first step was to re-examine the ingredients of the Swiss question. The Foreign Office prepared and printed a long confidential memorandum on Swiss affairs, at about the same time as the October revolution in Geneva. Its conclusion, couched in cautious language, seems to be that the trend toward Radicalism was irreversible and that a Radical majority would soon be obtained in the Diet.[23] As a result of this memorandum, Palmerston's approach to the Swiss problem became more realistic than Aberdeen's.

Palmerston's second step was to improve British communication with Switzerland. Morier's reports had become increasingly emotional about Swiss Radicalism, and Palmerston left most of them unanswered. When, in November, Morier complained bitterly about the lack of respect shown to him by the Berne government, Palmerston granted him a leave of absence which later became a recall. Robert Peel, the more liberal 25-year-old-son of the former Prime Minister, was left in charge of the British Legation. This change in personnel made the other Powers jittery, because their representatives in Berne had been on good terms with Morier and did not trust Peel, whom they considered irresponsible.

Another mark of British realism and independence added to the Powers' nervousness. Before leaving Berne, Morier reported that Ulrich Ochsenbein, a former leader of the volunteer bands, had been elected President of the new Berne government, and thus of the confederation for 1847, and that the other Powers were showing their disapproval of the choice by keeping their legations in Zurich. Morier suggested that

[23] There is no trace of it in the Foreign Office archives for Switzerland but a copy is found among the Canning papers (FO 352/30)

18

Britain should do the same. Palmerston disagreed. He instructed Peel to stay in Berne and to follow the usual practice of paying a courtesy visit to the new President on New Year's Day. The October memorandum was put into effect, with this show of support for the legal order chosen by the Swiss, and the Radicals, incidentally, were delighted. Thereby Palmerston abandoned Aberdeen's close cooperation with Austria and Russia, both of whom sent notes to the Berne government to urge restraint. Britain was moving closer to the line taken by Guizot in 1845.

1847: THE CRISIS APPROACHES

Transfer of the federal government to Berne did not bring on the immediate explosion which most of the Continental Powers had feared. During the winter the main concern of governmental authorities in Switzerland, and indeed in all European countries, was to find an adequate food supply, because the last harvest had been poor. Food shortages and financial crisis rendered the uncoordinated cantonal Customs and commercial systems even more obviously a liability for Swiss national life, so that the Radical programme gained more support. By late spring the Powers had reason to fear an explosion in Switzerland, because in May the Radicals obtained a slight majority in St Gall, which at last gave them a majority in the Diet.

The European context for developments in Switzerland had changed since 1845. The Great Powers had been faced with many international problems besides Switzerland, such as the suppression of the Cracow Republic, the Spanish marriages, Greek affairs, and discontent in Italy, as well as the general economic crisis. The Anglo-French entente had suffered considerably since 1841, most recently because of French policy toward the Spanish marriages, and Austria and France were perhaps on better terms. Consequently, the Great Powers were in no position to give full and united attention to Switzerland. After the St Gall election, Britain, France, and Austria indicated their increasing concern about the prospects for peace in Switzerland, but they were unable to cooperate on a joint policy toward it. Metternich proposed an intervention to France, but the French government, still restrained by a strong liberal public opinion, was unable to agree without assurance of British cooperation, which was not forthcoming. The Austrian representative in Switzerland had by this time made several visits to the eastern Swiss cantons to encourage the *Sonderbund* to resist any infringements on their sovereignty and to threaten the Ticino and the Grisons (not members of the *Sonderbund*) with blockade if they cooperated with the

19

Radicals. The French representative, Bois-le-Comte, was not instructed on this point by Guizot, but none the less he busied himself similarly.

Palmerston used different methods to try to cultivate a spirit of moderation. After the opening of the Diet in July, he complimented Ochsenbein on his efforts to 'maintain the informal tranquillity', remarking that 'the known energy of his character affords a guarantee that those means of influence will be used to the utmost to calm conflicting Passions, and to prevent differences of opinion from leading to inter-cantonal contests'.[24] Unfortunately, the message seems to have had anything but a moderating effect, for only a few days after it was delivered the Diet voted the first of its measures against the *Sonderbund*, and less than a week later it approved the formation of a commission to revise the Federal Pact.

The British Foreign Secretary then tried another approach. He wrote to both Metternich and Guizot to ask them, first, to exert their 'powerful influence' with the *Sonderbund* cantons to 'induce [them] to replace themselves within the legal boundaries of the Helvetic Constitution' and, second, to persuade the Pope to recall the Jesuits.[25] But, as might have been expected, this attempt was fruitless. The two Catholic Powers had already urged the Pope to recall the Jesuits, without success. Metternich reported the *Sonderbund*'s refusal to cooperate and Guizot did not even reply, although Bois-le-Comte expressed his satisfaction with the Austrian report.

The situation in Switzerland became increasingly tense. At the end of August, the Diet voted to expel the Jesuits and to prohibit the service of any federal soldier in the *Sonderbund* army. Yet the Powers still hoped that a conflict would be avoided. The Austrian and French reports dwelt entirely on *Sonderbund* strength, and Peel, too, wrote that the Radical majority was probably not strong enough to enforce its decisions. For the first two weeks of September, the Diet adjourned to try again to persuade the *Sonderbund* cantons to comply. It was during this interval that Palmerston made his next effort to preserve the peace.

Palmerston's third attempt to encourage moderation in Switzerland shows clearly that he connected the situation there with other European questions. He was worried about increasing Italian discontent which could threaten the position of the Austrian empire and tempt France to intervene. To try to avert this, the British Cabinet agreed, in mid-September, to send one of its members, the Earl of Minto, on a special

[24] Palmerston to Peel, 3 August 1847 (BPP 1847/48, p158)
[25] Palmerston to Normanby and Palmerston to Ponsonby, 17 August 1847 (*ibid*, pp 161-2)

mission to Italy to offer advice, when requested, about constitutional reform. On his way to Italy, Minto stopped in Switzerland. Palmerston instructed him to urge moderation on both parties and to warn them again that the use of federal force against the *Sonderbund* would probably have serious international implications. Regarding Pact revision, the British government still considered that the 1815 guarantee included the principle of cantonal sovereignty as the basis of Swiss political organization. Unfortunately, these instructions reached Minto only after he had gone to Italy, but he did follow them in essence.

Minto was surprised by what he learned in conversation with Swiss leaders and by the Swiss response to his counsel of restraint. Ochsenbein was well aware that any use of force might bring Austrian intervention, but he appeared to Minto to be 'strangely possessed with the notion' that domestic unrest in both France and Austria might prevent their intervention.[26] Ochsenbein pointed out that the defensive position of the *Sonderbund* was weak and claimed that if any Power sent an army against Switzerland, it was not unlikely that the *Sonderbund* cantons would join the federal forces to defend the country. On the more fundamental issue of Pact revision, he assured Minto that a large majority of the Radicals were in favour of maintaining cantonal independence. Minto attempted to make clear the limits of British good offices in the event of a serious conflict between Switzerland and the Powers. In subsequent talks with Ochsenbein, Peel also tried to engender more caution on the part of the Diet, emphasizing British freedom of action in case of foreign intervention. But the Diet would not heed the repeated warnings from Britain and, much to British annoyance, the Swiss press continued to report or imply British support for an aggressive Radical policy.

Palmerston then made a fourth attempt to reconcile the Diet and the *Sonderbund*. Ochsenbein had admitted to Minto that a papal decision to withdraw the Jesuits from Lucerne would be a most favourable solution of the situation. On the basis of this, Palmerston instructed Minto to press the Pope for the recall of the Jesuits, stressing 'the particular interest of an Ecclesiastical Power in preserving peace'.[27] His efforts in this quarter also proved useless, because they were undertaken too late in the game and because the Pope relied on reports which were both inaccurate and reactionary.

In mid-October the Diet reassembled to consider the *Sonderbund*'s persistent refusal to dissolve itself. It decided to use force and appointed

[26] Minto to Palmerston, 4 October 1847 (*ibid*, pp 184–5)
[27] Palmerston to Minto, 22 October 1847 (*ibid*, pp 188–9)

General Dufour to command army operations. It also appointed two commissioners to visit the recalcitrant cantons to make yet another effort to work out a peaceful settlement. As a further conciliatory move, it issued a proclamation disavowing any federal attack on cantonal, religious, or political rights. Compromises were suggested on both sides, but each was convinced of its moral, political, and military strength and neither would concede enough.

At the end of October Palmerston made his last attempt to restrain the Radicals. He sent a note to Ochsenbein in which he recognized the illegality of the *Sonderbund,* but questioned the extent to which it was a threat, in actual fact. He elaborated on the 'evils of great magnitude' which could be produced by an armed conflict, the devastation and bitterness of war, and the possibility of 'the permanent Establishment of Foreign Influence ... essentially impairing the Political Independence of the Country'. He begged the Directory to consider these 'Reflections' and to 'abstain from a course so replete with hazard, and so pregnant with danger ...'.[28] Peel was to tell Ochsenbein of Minto's efforts in Rome, and to ask the Diet to wait for results from this before taking action. Ochsenbein replied that the challenge was one of political principle, not of religion, that it had been made by the *Sonderbund,* and that Swiss national honour required settlement of the question. He found no reason to believe that the British effort in Rome would be more successful than the Austrian, French, or Sardinian efforts had been. This last message from Palmerston was apparently interpreted by Ochsenbein in the same way as his first note in August: Peel delivered it on 4 November and later in the same day the Diet declared war on the *Sonderbund.*

CONCLUSIONS ABOUT THIS PHASE OF ANGLO-SWISS RELATIONS

Throughout the development of the *Sonderbund* crisis, British policy aimed at restraining the Swiss Radicals from aggression. Aberdeen was inclined to agree with either Austria or France, or both, in policy toward Switzerland, but Palmerston followed a more independent course. Although Palmerston's comprehension of the fundamental strength of Swiss liberalism brought a change of approach to British policy, the Foreign Office was working throughout to prevent an armed conflict in Switzerland.

The Swiss were fully aware of the possibility of foreign intervention and of the sympathy of the Austrian and French governments for the

[28] Palmerston to Peel, 29 October 1847 (*ibid,* pp 195-6)

Sonderbund. They accurately sensed popular discontent with these governments as well as some disagreements among the Powers, but they overestimated British support, as shown by the documents now available. British advice, while sympathetic, was non-committal and always urged moderation; the Swiss listened attentively to the sympathy and turned a deaf ear to the advice. When the Diet declared war on the seven stubborn cantons early in November 1847, it was ready to trust the issue of national unity to the hazards of war. It had plenty of warning that two important and adjacent Powers might aid the insurgents, but apparently did not fully realize that its one possible ally, Britain, was in no position to offer any material help.

CHAPTER THREE

Civil War and National Consolidation

AFTER THE DIET'S declaration of war, it was clear to the British Government that it could do nothing to prevent an armed conflict within Switzerland. Britain could only hope that the use of force would be as limited as possible. However, much room did remain for manœuvring with the Continental Powers, and it was to this that Palmerston next turned his attention.

At first glance, the balance of power seemed to depend on France, yet for several reasons French policy was itself wavering and dependent on British policy. The Marquis of Normanby, British Ambassador in Paris, reported in July that the stability of the French government had suffered several shocks in domestic and foreign affairs. Louis-Philippe's position was not sure, and consequently both he and Guizot were wary of intervention in Switzerland.[1] However, French discussion of the Swiss question does not seem to have been very well-informed. Bois-le-Comte reported almost exclusively about the *Sonderbund*, so that the French Foreign Ministry could not estimate the Diet's actual strength. Apparently Bois-le-Comte's activity on behalf of the *Sonderbund* was well known in France since Guizot was criticized in the Chamber of Deputies for his failure to disavow it. France was jealous of any Austrian influence in Switzerland (just as the two Powers were to some extent rivals in the Italian states), but the French disagreed among themselves about methods for counteracting or competing with Austrian influence. One faction in France wanted to interfere more effectively than Austria in Swiss affairs, while French business interests favoured a peaceful policy, in order to foster economic development. The latter group considered

[1] Normanby to Palmerston, 5 July 1847 (FO 27/781); and Guizot to Bois-le-Comte, 2 July 1847 (AAE: Suisse: 556)

24

that any intervention move, especially if made without the cooperation of Britain, would produce very disturbing effects. The French were aware of Swiss confidence in Britain, in contrast to growing Swiss distrust of France. In fact, Louis-Philippe had intimated privately, as much as a year before, that it was impossible for French policy in Switzerland to be successful without British support. In the early summer of 1847, when the Powers considered an Austrian proposal for a conference on Swiss affairs, Guizot made French dependence on British support quite clear to Palmerston. Yet, in spite of France's need for British help, her communication with Britain was incomplete, clouded perhaps by Anglo-French disagreement on other questions. The French were apparently unaware of Palmerston's more realistic approach; Bois-le-Comte attributed departures from his own interpretations of the British dispatches of 1832 and 1845 to Peel's irresponsibility, and Guizot did not correct him. Guizot hesitated to join Austria in a move against Switzerland because he did not know the aim of British policy there.

The other foreign antagonist, Austria, was also beset with problems which limited activity in Switzerland. Metternich was most concerned lest France profit from Swiss centralization; he objected to the Swiss Radicals' plans for a more effective government on the ground that, whether a monarchy or a republic, it would be liable to French influence. Austria and France were still rivals for influence in central Europe. Metternich realized that if Austria alone were to intervene in Switzerland, France would react to the threat to her own frontier, in spite of general Austro-French agreement to oppose the Radicals. Prussia, too, because of Neuchâtel and because of rivalry with Austria in the German states, might raise difficulties. Austrian financial resources were limited and her troops were sorely needed in Italy, so that she was not free to intervene in Switzerland to counteract any French initiative there. Austria, therefore, as well as France, was in need of British cooperation in order to keep a vulnerable sphere of influence as clear as possible. Thanks to the ambivalent attitude of France and, to a lesser degree, Austria's need for support, British policy was of crucial importance in the situation.

DIPLOMATIC ACTIVITY DURING THE WAR

A few days before the Diet's declaration of war, the Prussian Ambassador in London, worried about the Radical threat to Neuchâtel, discussed the problem with his French counterpart. The two agreed that British policy, 'uncertain and vacillating', was blocking a definite European policy; the Prussian suggested that France might do something to prevent war, by proposing a collective note.[2] Guizot took up the idea. This might be his chance to regain some prestige at home and in Europe, with the ostensible aim of preserving the peace, which all the Powers agreed to be necessary. He expected Britain to cooperate, in preference to isolation by the other Powers. His proposal called first for joint mediation between the Diet and the *Sonderbund* by the five signatories of the 1815 agreement, on the basis of approval and support of the idea of papal arbitration of religious questions, and second, for an offer of their combined mediation of the political questions between the two sides. If this offer were not accepted, and the civil war stopped immediately, Guizot proposed that the Powers should consider the Confederation defunct.[3]

Reactions to Guizot's proposal were different in east and west. Metternich thought that a joint note to Switzerland should include specific stipulations about Pact revision, but he was willing to agree to the French proposal as better than nothing. Palmerston, on the other hand, was not agreeable to a proposal which recognized the legality of the *Sonderbund* and placed it on an equal footing with the Diet. The Foreign Office analysis of Radical strength the year before had been borne out by subsequent events; the Radicals were clearly the more powerful party in Switzerland and no peaceful advantage was to be gained from undermining their programme.

On 10 November, the day after he received Guizot's final proposal, Palmerston called in Sir Stratford Canning for consultation. As part of his extensive diplomatic experience, Canning had represented Britain in Switzerland from 1814 to 1819, had played an important part in the formulation of the 1815 settlement for Switzerland, and had kept in touch with developments there through his friendship with David Morier. In the Foreign Office records, we find a memorandum from Canning to Palmerston, dated 12 November, which must reflect a development of the conversation of the 10th. Canning recognized the fundamental issue to be neither the existence of the *Sonderbund* nor the expulsion of the Jesuits, but the revision of the Federal Pact. He considered the 1815 Pact to be 'in principle part and parcel of the general arrangements made in 1815', but his agile mind found other important elements in the situation. He discussed the probable consequences of victory for either the Diet or the *Sonderbund*, or of prolonged strife:

[2] De Broglie to Guizot, 1 November 1847 (AAE: Suisse: 558)
[3] Guizot to De Broglie, 9 November 1847 (BPP 1847/48, pp 214-15)

26

Switzerland could not be 'enfeebled, convulsed, or mutilated without a shock to the present system of peace,—without suggesting dangerous fears or guilty hopes to the great military monarchies which nearly surround it'. To withdraw the guarantee of Swiss neutrality would be '... in effect to nullify their usefulness in the system of European policy ...'. In any mediation proposal, the Powers should follow a 'strictly European principle', which might include support for Pact revision if unanimously accepted by the Swiss cantons; the Powers should call upon the *Sonderbund* cantons to submit to a papal decision to recall the Jesuits, which would bring about a natural dissolution of the *Sonderbund*. The Powers should also pledge themselves, in case the proposal were refused by the Swiss, not to intervene without the consent of all.[4] Canning was not concerned with the ideological aspects of the situation; this was hard political realism.

The next British move came soon. On 15 November Palmerston received a message from the Swiss Consul in London saying that his country would 'decidedly and most positively refuse any Foreign intervention'.[5] Meanwhile, the French Ambassador did his best to conceal his government's eagerness for a favourable British reply and took pains to say friendly things in public about the Anglo-French entente. By the 16th Palmerston had received Peel's more favourable estimates of the Diet's military operations against Fribourg, which the *Sonderbund* was not expected to defend. Palmerston had also had time to consult the Prime Minister, the Cabinet, and the Queen, so that he was ready to send a counter-proposal to Guizot. His note reflects many of the ideas in Canning's memorandum: Her Majesty's Government could not consider the present situation to be of such magnitude as to release the guaranteeing Powers from the 1815 agreement on Swiss neutrality; in fact, the general interest of Europe required its preservation. However, Britain would consider a request for papal mediation if the Powers would agree that the Jesuits should be recalled, and then, the Jesuit question being settled, the Diet should renounce any aggressive intentions against the *Sonderbund* and declare its respect for the 'Principle of Separate Sovereignty', which, in turn, would allow the *Sonderbund* to dissolve itself. If both sides accepted the Powers' mediation under these conditions, there should be an immediate armistice until an agreement could be reached. Refusal of the proposal by either side would not entitle any of the Powers to intervene with force. The proposed conference

[4] Canning to Palmerston, 12 November 1847 (FO 100/54), see Appendix I.
[5] Prévost to Palmerston, 15 November 1847 (BPP 1847/48, p227)

was to be concerned only with 'present difficulties', not with Pact revision.[6]

Palmerston's boldness in preparing a new proposal took the French by surprise. Guizot agreed with it in principle, but suggested some changes: The Powers should recommend recall of the Jesuits to the Pope, not direct it, and the Diet should renounce any revision of the Pact without the consent of all the cantons. He was reluctant to renounce armed intervention, but consented to postpone discussion of that until later.

Palmerston held his ground in urging the French to agree to a new proposal. By the time Guizot's reply reached London, he had learned of the capitulation of Fribourg. His next note to Normanby emphasized that the two fundamental conditions of a joint note must be the withdrawal of the Jesuits and a renunciation of armed intervention. He knew of the liberal pressures in France and used the fact to persuade Russia, Prussia, and Austria to accept his proposal, arguing that the Powers should recognize the important restraining influences of British and French public opinions and that his proposal was 'in spirit and substance' much the same as Guizot's.[7] Discussions of detail continued for a few more days. By 25 November Louis-Philippe and the French Cabinet agreed to the British proposal, with only minor qualifications.

Meanwhile, the Foreign Office received more reports from Peel. The young diplomat found it impossible to maintain contact with the representatives of the other Powers, because nearly all of them had left Berne in protest against Radical policy. On the 17th he wrote of the French government's fear of liberalism, its intrigues with Conservatives in Switzerland, the popular sympathy beyond Switzerland for the Radical cause, in Italy, in Alsace, and in Baden, and the impossibility of a positive French or Austrian intervention without British cooperation. This last point in Peel's dispatch was underlined by Palmerston.

On the 22nd Peel received Palmerston's report of the proposed joint note, and he was instructed to sound out the Swiss government informally as to its acceptability. Here, the historian is tempted to inject an unwarranted element of drama. The British records show that, by the 22nd, Peel expected outright victory for the Diet; he immediately sent Palmerston a message, in cipher, to say that by the time the offer could be made, the war would be over and the *Sonderbund* dissolved. The following day, presumably after talking with a member of the Directory,

[6] Palmerston to Normanby, 16 November 1847 (BPP 1847/48, pp 227-30)
[7] Palmerston to Ponsonby, Bloomfield, and Howard, 20 November 1847 (*ibid*, pp 239-40)

he sent another cipher urging Palmerston 'to hesitate adoption of the proposed mediation' because the Swiss would be hostile to it. 'Agreeing to it, we shall lose the influence at our disposal to discountenance whatever endeavours His [sic] Majesty's Government may think fit.'[8] Some writers, however, have gone so far as to claim underhand British influence on the Diet. Their assertions are based on reports from Bois-le-Comte, which he himself had received secondhand. According to them, the news that Britain would cooperate in a joint note upset Peel so much that he immediately sent word to General Dufour to 'finir vite'.[9] This story finds no substantiation in the British archives, and the source of Bois-le-Comte's report proved in later instances to be unreliable. A British clergyman and a reporter from *The Times* did apparently visit Dufour at this crucial time, but in his own account of the war, the General states that no diplomatic influence, either direct or from a distance, affected his army's strategy. The same writers also suggest that Peel was under secret instructions from Palmerston, but again no evidence is to be found. Indeed, the evidence indicates the opposite: Peel was hardly an experienced agent; and, as he was appointed by Aberdeen, he had had no official conversations with Palmerston before leaving England. Furthermore, would Palmerston have used an official dispatch to warn him about Bois-le-Comte, the 'most artful and cunning & intriguing of the French Diplomatists',[10] if they were also communicating secretly?

Palmerston was sincerely hopeful that the Swiss would accept the proposals of the joint note. Since dispatches from Switzerland took four or five days to reach London, Peel's messages in cipher would not have reached London before Britain and France agreed on the form of the note. Palmerston, therefore, had relatively little information about the strength of the Diet or about the progress of the war, so that he had no way of knowing that the civil war might be settled quickly without help from the Great Powers. In his dispatch telling Peel confidentially of his proposal, he added a postscript suggesting that if the Diet took Fribourg, bad weather and need of money might make both sides more interested in accepting the Powers' proposals. Minto's most recent report was pessimistic about any papal initiative to find a solution, so that all other chances of settlement were dim. The British conditions for a joint note were designed to respect Swiss independence, and France had at last

[8] Peel to Palmerston, 22 and 23 November 1847 (FO 100/53)
[9] Eckinger, p115; Donald Greer, *L'Angleterre, La France et la révolution de 1848* (Paris, 1925), p153
[10] Palmerston to Peel, 17 November 1847 (FO 100/51)

agreed to them in substance as well as in principle. Hence, it was prudent to proceed to the next step in the negotiations.

THE END OF THE WAR AND CANNING'S MISSION

The situation at the end of November was fluid, and Palmerston could anticipate various reactions from both the Continental Powers and the Swiss in the next few weeks. If the Swiss refused the mediation offer, the other Powers, more dissatisfied than ever, might find a pretext to intervene. If the Radicals were victorious, they might punish the defeated *Sonderbund* excessively and implement their programme for constitutional reform too quickly. Whether or not the Swiss accepted the offer, it was important to strengthen the British mediatorial role. Unfortunately, British influence had declined with the Diplomatic Corps in Berne, which was an important point of contact. Although Peel's reports probably seemed reasonable to the Foreign Office, he was still very young and, in the eyes of the other Powers, too favourable toward the Radicals. Clearly, a more experienced diplomat was needed to act as an informal mediator, one familiar with the Foreign Office point of view and trusted by both the Swiss and the other Powers. Palmerston appointed Canning for the special mission.

Canning's instructions contain the continuing theme of British policy in this question, namely, restraint of both the Radicals and the Continental Powers from immoderate policies. On his way to Switzerland, he was to stop in Paris for consultation with Guizot and the representatives of Austria, Prussia, and Russia. If the *Sonderbund* had been dissolved when he reached Berne, he was not to present the note, but was to keep an eye on things and to use his 'utmost endeavours to inculcate moderation ...'.[11]

By 2 December, when Canning reached Paris, the representatives of all the Powers had agreed to the joint note. More important was the news that Lucerne had fallen to the Diet forces and that the *Sonderbund* was at last dissolved.

During his discussions in Paris, Canning communicated fully with his counterparts, in an attempt to reassure them about British intentions in Switzerland. He gave them copies of his instructions and, in turn, gathered impressions about their reactions to developments in Switzerland. Their governments' readiness for more action against Switzerland particularly impressed him, as did their conviction that the Radical programme posed a serious threat to cantonal sovereignty. Austria and

[11] Palmerston to Canning, 27 November 1847 (BPP 1847/48, pp 259-60)

Prussia were especially concerned about cantonal independence, Austria in fear of extended French influence, and Prussia because of her king's nominal sovereignty in Neuchâtel. Canning assured them that Britain also would continue to press the importance of cantonal sovereignty on Switzerland. With Louis-Philippe, he talked about the Spanish situation as well as about Switzerland, and came away with the impression that France was 'anxious to recover lost ground in English estimation'.[12] France was uneasy in isolation after her victory in the affair of the Spanish marriages, and, indirectly, Switzerland benefited from it through the French government's need for British cooperation.

When Canning arrived in Berne he found that France, Austria, and Prussia had presented their notes; the Russian message was presented later. In contrast, Canning followed his instructions to withhold the British copy. However, in talks with Swiss leaders, he did emphasize that Britain had helped to formulate the mediation offer, thus implying that, regardless of what might happen in Switzerland, the Swiss should not count on British support. The Swiss replied quickly and firmly to the other three Powers that, as the war was over, their offer was no longer applicable. Because no international quarrel was involved and Switzerland was not threatening her neighbours, the Swiss asserted that acceptance would be contrary to international law. As for the Radical programme of reforms, cantonal sovereignty had never been absolute and unlimited, and the minority had always had to cede to the majority.

The conduct of the war itself was quite remarkable for its speed, thanks to popular support for the Diet and to the intelligence of General Dufour. Within three weeks, the army was mobilized and the recalcitrant cantons vanquished, with losses of 104 dead and 374 wounded.[13] Funds were quickly obtained from foreign sources – not British – to finance the war. The Radical parties in all seven cantons of the former *Sonderbund* came into power immediately, though admittedly with the help of the occupying federal troops.

The efficiency of the Radical victory augured well for the future, if moderation could be assured. However, as Palmerston had anticipated, this was a real problem. Canning found his mission more protracted than expected, until it was clear that the more moderate elements of the Radical majority would prevail. His attention was required for a whole series of more or less related matters: regulation of the status of Neuchâtel, Swiss relations with the other Powers, federal policy toward the

[12] Canning to Palmerston, 3 December 1847 (FO 352/30)
[13] Edgar Bonjour, 'Der Sonderbundskrieg' (*Schweizer Monatshefte*, November 1947, Heft 8), p498. Dufour gives somewhat lower figures

defeated cantons, the religious issue in the canton of Vaud, demobilization, and Pact revision. Each of these requires some of our attention.

Because Neuchâtel was a principality of the King of Prussia, its growing Republican party (similar in philosophy to the Radical party) was a source of irritation to the Prussian monarchy. At the outbreak of *Sonderbund* hostilities, the canton was in an equivocal position; it did not join the *Sonderbund*, but neither would the Royalist cantonal government comply with Diet demands for military and financial contributions. The Prussian government itself disliked Jesuit activity, but it more strongly disapproved of what it considered a sort of liberal cancer in Switzerland as a whole. Insistence on cantonal sovereignty was one way of limiting Radical power, so the Neuchâtel government, supported by Prussia, declared its neutrality and refused the Diet's demands. During negotiations with the Powers over the joint note, Prussia asked for Neuchâtel as the site of the conference as a way to assure its neutrality, and the Powers acceded to the request. Frederick William IV wrote to Queen Victoria to ask for British support for Neuchâtel against the '*Gottlos und Rechtlos*' Swiss Radicals and the 'thousands of emigrated malefactors' who, he claimed, were waiting in Switzerland for the opportune moment to invade Germany. The Queen was sympathetic about Neuchâtel, but not about the larger, and exaggerated, issues which Frederick William injected.[14] The Prussians kept up their pressure on Britain by explaining to Palmerston, and to Canning, that Neuchâtel had a right to be neutral and that it was the duty of Prussia and Europe to support its neutrality.

The Diet's stand against Neuchâtel, and thus against Prussia, was firm. Ochsenbein added to the Prussian discomfort about the Radicals by refusing to guarantee the neutrality of Neuchâtel, and the Directory even discussed military occupation of the Royalist canton. The Diet argued that, in joining the Confederation, Neuchâtel had accepted the same rights and duties as other cantons, with no exception. The Diet was further irritated by the fact that the representatives of Austria, Prussia, and Russia, absent from Berne in protest, took refuge in Neuchâtel and, from there, kept up their pressure against the Radicals.

Prussia was pleased that Britain took an interest in the question, but Prussian gratitude to Britain did not diminish the danger of the situation. During his conversations in Paris, Canning found that the position of Neuchâtel 'wants only a spark of indiscretion in the Diet to make it thoroughly explosive. It will perhaps be [considered] a godsend by those

[14] Victoria, *The Letters of Queen Victoria, 1837-1861* (London, 1908), ii, 137

who lament the cooler policy of England.'[15] Canning's first task, therefore, was to work out a settlement between the Diet and the Royalist
government in Neuchâtel. After a brief stop in the canton, during which
he could talk with some of its leaders, he was hopeful that the canton
would make monetary payment which would be acceptable to the Diet.
By 13 December he had persuaded the Diet to be satisfied with a payment of 300,000 francs by Neuchâtel. This settled a delicate and dangerous phase of the problem arising from the special status of the King
of Prussia in the canton.

In urging the Diet to be moderate, Canning's main argument was the
continued threatening attitude of the other Powers. The Continental
Powers still claimed the right of armed intervention if circumstances became bad enough, and Austria, Prussia, and France actually had troops
very near the Swiss border. Short of armed intervention, a commercial
blockade could be a very powerful weapon against the Radicals. If the
Swiss could put their house in reasonable order quickly, their existence
would be much less precarious. All of Canning's persuasive abilities
were needed to goad them on.

After the Neuchâtel question, another obvious pretext for foreign
intervention might have been the Diet's abuse of its victory over the
Sonderbund cantons. The first tendency toward such abuse appeared in
early December, when the new Radical government in Fribourg voted
considerable financial penalties against individuals who had voted
against the Diet. Within a week Lucerne and the Valais did the same.
Many members of the Diet disagreed with this policy, but since the
country was still governed under the 1815 Federal Pact, the Diet was
powerless to reverse such cantonal government decisions. Ochsenbein
agreed with Canning's expostulations against such severe cantonal
policy, but he could promise very little action. More positively, Canning
strongly urged the Diet to pass a political amnesty for most of the individuals who had supported the *Sonderbund*, but again, although
Ochsenbein and many of his colleagues agreed with the idea, the Diet
postponed discussion of the proposal, primarily because of hesitation
about the limitations of its competence. Individual cantonal governments may have relaxed their decrees to some extent, but in spite of
Canning's continued pressure, the Diet never passed the general
amnesty.

Canning also recommended a change in the federal policy of
penalizing certain institutions which had supported the *Sonderbund*.
The Federal Pact made no provision for payment of war expenses, and

[15] Canning to Palmerston, 3 December 1847 (FO 352/30)

an obvious expedient was to levy a charge on the defeated *Sonderbund* cantons and on certain institutions. Because most of the penalized institutions were Catholic, they appealed to the Pope for help, and he, in turn, asked Lord Minto for British pressure on the Swiss to alleviate such injustices. Palmerston responded with little sympathy for the Pope and reminded him that earlier action on his part would have avoided such difficulty. One can imagine with what pleasure the Foreign Secretary must have written that dispatch! None the less, Canning did try to improve the situation. As early as 15 December Ochsenbein expected that the charges would be diminished, and in the end all the cantons made some contribution toward payment of the war debt.

Canning also felt called upon to intervene to mitigate suspicion of Catholic activity in the non-*Sonderbund* canton of Vaud which, for some months, had been taking action against all dissenters, Catholic or Protestant, from the official cantonal Church. Unfortunately this action had occasionally included a few British missionaries. On this question, Canning wrote unofficially to the cantonal government instead of addressing an official note to the Directory. Because the Vaud authorities disliked Canning's informal approach, they would give no indication that they might change their policy. However, Canning's private correspondence with at least one friend in Vaud tended to reassure him that the measures were temporary and that there was no intent to use the cantonal Church for political ends.

Another subject of concern for Canning was the status of the federal army. Victory had placed it in occupation of the *Sonderbund* cantons, and the Continental Powers claimed that this was a flagrant violation of cantonal sovereignty. With Canning's encouragement, demobilization of the army began as early as mid-December and continued gradually but steadily for the next two months. By mid-February Dufour was able to resign his command and by the end of the same month all occupying troops had been disbanded.

On the larger question of constitutional reform, Canning was reassured by his conversations with Ochsenbein. New proposals were still being discussed and would not be taken up by the Diet until the following year (1848). The Powers might be sure that, whatever the new constitution provided, cantonal sovereignty would be respected and that a revised Pact would be imposed on the country only by reason and persuasion. Canning had some doubts about the degree of credence to be given to these assurances, but his tendency was to accept them, because there is 'so much sterling worth in the character of the Swiss' that they would be less prone to unwise decisions than many other nations.[16]

Although the success of Canning's mission was not entirely evident when he left Switzerland at the end of January, from the historian's perspective it does seem to have done much good. Up to the end of his stay, the British diplomat felt that he was being 'kept in hot water' by the 'very uncompromising elements' he found among the Swiss. He had not even ventured to advise that the Swiss government should not answer a second joint note from the Continental Powers, for fear of his advice being shunned.[17] However, the Neuchâtel question had not exploded, some cantonal sovereignty was assured, the army was quickly demobilized, and settlement of the war debt did not seem grossly unfair. He did not have as much success with the amnesty, but he may have prevented more excessive measures. The most important result of his mission was probably its effect on the other Powers: they all admitted that it was a good thing. The Prussian Foreign Minister went so far as to suggest that the peace was perhaps being more rapidly and effectively organized by Canning than it might have been by a Great Power conference. The mission probably had the effect of diminishing the urgency felt by the Continental Powers about the Swiss situation, thereby slowing down their preparations for an intervention until it was too late.

CONTINUED THREATS FROM THE CONTINENTAL POWERS

Despite Canning's conciliatory efforts, the Swiss continued to harbour suspicions about the activities of the Continental Powers. The Radicals remembered that Austria had sent Prince Schwarzenberg to give military advice to the *Sonderbund*,[18] and that France had tried to smuggle arms to the *Sonderbund* and had diverted a federal battalion to Geneva by keeping troops near the border during the war. More recently, the joint note reminded them of their neighbours' hostility, and Palmerston, through Canning, warned them about the continuing threat from the Continental Powers.

Unfortunately, the Continental Powers were not yet convinced that Switzerland could be trusted. True, Prussia was slightly mollified by the Diet's settlement with Neuchâtel, and all the Powers were relieved by the relative success of Canning's mission, but their distrust of the Radicals was so strong that they did not expect that the promises made to Canning would be kept. Their prestige had suffered as a result of their

[16] Canning to Palmerston, 27 December 1847 (FO 100/55)
[17] Canning to Palmerston, 3 February 1848 (FO 352/30)
[18] The Prince barely escaped capture by the federal forces

gross overestimate of *Sonderbund* resources and their almost comic presentation of a mediation offer followed by the Swiss rejection. In contrast, British prestige in Switzerland was distinctly unharmed. Consequently, the Continental Powers were glad to have Britain use her influence for moderation, but they continued to discuss among themselves what to do next.

Armed intervention by one or all of the Continental Powers was still a possibility. Even before the war was over, Austrian and Prussian representatives had been sent to Paris for further talks about such a step. The course of these negotiations reflected the same national hesitations as the earlier discussions about the *Sonderbund*. The French were unable to evince much enthusiasm, so action was delayed. Prussia, in conversations with Britain in early December, again insisted on Neuchâtel as the site of a conference on Swiss affairs, but Palmerston maintained that conference arrangements were no longer relevant, although Britain would not have objected to Neuchâtel. Metternich, in a valiant effort to win over Palmerston to a policy of intervention, asserted that the Swiss Radicals would unite with the French Radicals 'whose chief object was the humiliation of England ...'.[19] Palmerston was not convinced.

Unable to agree on an immediate armed intervention, the Powers considered a second joint note. On 20 December Guizot prepared a mediation offer which demanded demobilization and respect for cantonal sovereignty. Palmerston refused the proposal because, with no unneutral tendencies evident in Switzerland, he considered the 1815 guarantee still in force. Since Britain had not presented the first identical note, she could scarcely agree to a second one. Austria and Prussia rejected the proposal because they wanted a stronger stand. France, Austria, and Prussia did agree eventually to a note which was presented to the Swiss in mid-January 1848. Again, Guizot tried hard to claim the role of European mediator for France, but many Frenchmen disapproved of cooperation with Austria and Prussia without Britain. The *Chambre de Pairs* applauded his justification of this policy only when he used part of Palmerston's message of 1832 to the Swiss.[20] Palmerston was distressed by such a misrepresentation of the British position, and Guizot later apologized privately to Normanby. The French government was weak and Guizot desperately needed British support in his foreign relations.

The Powers waited nervously until mid-February for the Swiss reply

[19] Ponsonby to Palmerston, 18 December 1847 (FO 7/337)
[20] See pages 9-10

to their second note. Palmerston tried to persuade the Swiss to answer the second mediation offer in a conciliatory manner by again warning them of French connivance in the plans of Austria, Prussia, and Russia for an armed intervention. Simultaneously, Ochsenbein told Peel that his government had learned of a French-Austrian plan to occupy Switzerland as part of an agreement about Italy. Thus the Swiss knew of the measures being prepared against them. None the less, a large majority of the Diet approved a flat rejection of the second mediation offer. The Swiss note contained a responsible statement of their neutral position. They recognized that neutrality required duties as well as privileges, and argued that they would be able to fulfil their obligations much better when their independence from all foreign influence was recognized. The note was symptomatic of a nation coming of age, and it has become an important document in Swiss foreign relations.

The immediate effect of the Swiss message was lost in the European upheavals of 1848. It was such an impressive document as to inspire Bois-le-Comte to advise his conservative colleagues to declare their satisfaction with it and resume their posts at Berne. In his last dispatch to Guizot, Bois-le-Comte even recommended acceptance and publication of the Swiss reply.[21] Unfortunately, this dispatch reached Paris the day Louis-Philippe's government was overthrown. Guizot's fall from power was due to many causes, mostly domestic, but it must be admitted that his opposition to Swiss liberalism and the failure of his policy, in contrast to Palmerston's success, helped to contribute to his overthrow.

BRITISH POLICY TOWARD THE *SONDERBUND* RECONSIDERED

Several theories have been suggested to explain Palmerston's strategy and motives in dealing with the *Sonderbund* crisis. The Morier family believed that Palmerston's humiliation in the Spanish marriages question made him determined to get revenge on Guizot and, given the French confusion about Swiss affairs, here was his chance. According to them, all Morier's attempts to mediate were repudiated by Palmerston, and Peel was sent to precipitate the war which, by its example, eventually caused the fall of Guizot himself.[22] A writer with less personal interest in the matter asserts that French and British interests all over the world were coming into conflict, in the Orient as well as in Europe, and that in Switzerland Palmerston at last had an opportunity to be on

---

[21] Bois-le-Comte to Guizot, 22 February 1848 (AAE: Suisse: 560)
[22] Wemyss, i, 38-9

the winning side.[23] That Palmerston was angered by French policy toward the Spanish marriages cannot be overlooked, but the theory that the prime British motive was revenge ignores many more important considerations. Strong internal and external factors were at work against the governments of Austria and France, and Palmerston was not alone in doubting the stability of the French régime.[24]

British public opinion with respect to Switzerland was influenced by several writers at this time. Some favoured the *Sonderbund* position; their arguments may be attributed to reaction against the (Radical) Vaud religious policies, since the British missionaries affected had good publicists in their ranks.[25] More notable, however, was a series of seven articles in the *Spectator* by the historian George Grote, published in the early autumn of 1847.[26] He emphasized the strength and responsibility of the Radicals, and his reports engendered increasing British sympathy for the Diet. Palmerston may well have read Grote's articles, but whether it affected a profound change in his thinking, as Hall suggests,[27] is doubtful. The Foreign Office memorandum of the year before[28] had, after all, analysed the situation along similar lines, although the Grote analysis is a more thorough one.

Palmerston has been the beneficiary of a good deal of misdirected credit in the *Sonderbund* question. His prime concern, as we have seen, was to maintain peace in Europe. In this respect, his course was wholly consistent with the accepted aims of British policy, and it represented the attitudes of the British commercial and industrial interests.[29] Seton-Watson has overemphasized an idealistic strain in Palmerston's thinking by ascribing his *Sonderbund policy*, 'One of his most successful enterprises,' to an interest in promoting constitutional government, which would, *ipso facto*, avert revolution.[30] In the dispatches of both Palmer-

---

[23] Else Gutknecht, *Die Diplomatie des Auslandes in der Schweiz während des Sonderbundes* (Zurich-Selnau, 1917), p7; also Frank Eyck, *The Prince Consort, A Political Biography* (London, 1959), p47 (on Cracow)

[24] For example, doubts were expressed by leaders of the British opposition party, in the correspondence between Aberdeen and Sir Robert Peel (BM 40455)

[25] For example, see Rev. Michel J. Mayers, *The Jesuit & the Sonderbund Contest in Switzerland* (London, 1847)

[26] George Grote, *Seven Letters on the Recent Politics in Switzerland* (London, 1847)

[27] John Hall, *England and the Orleans Monarchy* (London, 1912), p424

[28] See page 18

[29] Incidentally, the pro-British influence of the expanding industrial interests in France probably exerted some restraining effect on Guizot also

[30] R. W. Seton-Watson, *Britain in Europe, 1789-1914: A Survey of Foreign Policy* (Cambridge, 1937), pp 248-51

ston and Canning, the recurrent aim is the preservation of peace in Europe, not support of constitutionalism. That the Radical party ultimately had the strength to make Switzerland a tranquil nation was a happy coincidence for idealistic admirers of Palmerston, the *Realpolitiker*. His instructions to Peel and to Canning are invariably of a conservative nature, directed towards restraining the Radicals from extreme and precipitate Pact revision which would provoke intervention and war. As late as 10 October he considered the Radical plans objectionable as he understood them. He was not against some Pact revision, but he was anxious lest it go too far. He may have under-estimated Radical support in Switzerland, but his unwavering advice of caution was as much based on his knowledge of external threats as on reports of the domestic situation.

Again, Palmerston is often given credit for aiding the Diet against the *Sonderbund* by using delaying tactics with the Great Powers. Several authors assert, with varying degrees of emphasis, that he dragged out the negotiations over the joint mediation offer as long as possible in order to give the Radicals time to win, and thus to show up the false position of the other Powers.[31] This puts the episode in a more dramatic light than it deserves. Palmerston had continually warned the Diet of the dangers to Switzerland of any internal violence, and he was probably taken by surprise with the outbreak of hostilities in early November. Consequently, it was only after the receipt of the French proposal, close on the heels of the Diet declaration of war, that the British government was forced to formulate its position, and this took a few days. The French, in their desire to appear to be the principal peacemakers, did not want to give the impression of impatience, and after 17 November they contributed as much to the delay as the British. It was fortunate for Switzerland, and for Europe, that the telegraph was not yet in use.

As the French themselves recognized at the time, Palmerston's attitude toward the negotiations was a perfectly sincere one. If he had been preparing to play a trick on Guizot, would he have suggested to Peel that bad weather and need of money might make the Diet more amenable to the offer? His insistence on conditions of mediation more favourable to the Radicals was more than a play for time; it was based on a recognition of the strength of the Radical party as described in the October 1846 memorandum. The British government had no way of foreseeing an early Radical victory, and thus made an honest and

---

[31] For example: Hans Bessler, *La France et la Suisse de 1848-1852* (Paris, 1930), pp 7-10; Antonin Debidour, *Histoire diplomatique de l'Europe* ... (Paris, 1891), i, 447; and Greer, pp 144-53

realistic effort to anticipate other eventualities. Canning's mission was a positive one, aimed at stabilizing the situation in the European interest, rather than merely a negative one calculated to emphasize the failure and unrealistic policy of the other Powers.

CONSOLIDATION OF THE NEW SWISS GOVERNMENT AND ITS INTERNATIONAL POSITION

Whatever the explanation of the diplomacy of the *Sonderbund* question may be, the Radicals did win and they were able to put Swiss government on a firmer basis in a very short time. In the summer of 1848 the new constitution, giving much more authority to the federal government, was adopted by a large majority. It provides for legislation to be handled in two assemblies, similar to the American system, one, the Council of States, composed of two uninstructed delegates from each canton, to give equal representation to cantonal interests; and the other, the National Council, composed of representatives elected according to population. The administering body is a Federal Council which is separate from cantonal governments, selected from the Federal Assembly (the name given to the combined houses of the legislature), and permanently established in Berne. The new federal government is financially independent from the cantonal governments, and has greater authority than the old government in both foreign and domestic affairs. Even so, the cantons retain much of their authority, particularly in education and law enforcement.[32] Within a few years, the money and Customs systems were unified, and the army was organized more effectively. All the Powers except Russia recognized the new government soon after it came into existence in September 1848.

Unfortunately, this important step toward national consolidation did not bring immediate security for Switzerland's international position. The revolutionary wave of 1848 was not as successful elsewhere as in Switzerland and conservative governments soon controlled most of Europe again. A large number of political refugees, many of them expelled from their own countries by alarmed conservative régimes, sought asylum in Switzerland, as some of the conservatives themselves had done when revolution was rampant earlier in the year. Their presence put the Swiss government in an increasingly awkward position. Canning had noted as early as December 1847 that 'the sympathy which exists between the partizans of popular power in Switzerland, and those in

[32] See Edouard His, *Geschichte des neuern Schweizerischen Staatsrechts* (Basle, 1929), ii, 180-86

Germany, France and Italy cannot be doubted'.[33] The Bavarian government did not want to 'meddle' in Swiss affairs, but it also considered that its policy would be different if Switzerland became the centre of revolutionary projects.[34] Ochsenbein had confidently assured Canning that the cantons would not allow the use of Switzerland as a centre for revolutionary activity, but whether the Swiss would be able in fact to carry out this duty of neutrality was still a real question.

We have seen that, for the King of Prussia, the Neuchâtel question was something of an obsession, and the situation there was to become worse for him. The Neuchâtel Republican party was encouraged by the events in Paris at the end of February to overthrow the Royalist government on March first. The federal government did not challenge the change of government and the new cantonal constitution ignored any relationship to the king, so that the Prussian government's attitude to the new régime in Switzerland was even less indulgent than in 1847. The king's pride was wounded by the loss of Neuchâtel and he determined to press the Powers for the restoration of his treaty rights over the principality.

The refugee and Neuchâtel questions were two issues which were to plague the independence and neutrality of the Swiss as they put their new constitution into practice.

[33] Canning to Palmerston, 20 December 1847 (FO 352/31)
[34] Milbanke to Palmerston, 18 December 1847 (BPP 1847/48, p305)

CHAPTER FOUR

The Neuchâtel Question: Part I

THE PROBLEMS OF LIBERAL AND NEUTRAL SWITZERLAND AFTER 1848

THE DECADE following the suppression of the *Sonderbund* was critical for Swiss independence. Enthusiasm for economic growth and a strong desire for stability augured well, but the traditional right of asylum and cantonal disagreements about the obligations of neutrality contributed to misunderstandings with neighbouring Powers. The fears of the continental conservatives were nourished by one faction of the Radical party which, encouraged by the easy defeat of the *Sonderbund*, advocated a policy for Switzerland as an aggressive liberal state, the 'high altar of freedom in Europe'.[1]

Questions about the nature of Swiss neutrality were in open debate early in 1848. The first major discussion was occasioned by a Sardinian proposal for an offensive and defensive alliance. Several leading Radicals warmly supported the proposal, arguing that it would help to strengthen Italian liberalism and that it might provide Switzerland with an outlet to the sea.[2] Peel's report of the proposed alliance alerted Palmerston to a potential crisis, and he quickly warned the Swiss government against any embroilment in Italian politics, because France might not like the prospect of an increase in Swiss territory and 'the result would probably be that the Swiss would have forfeited all the future and permanent security which their neutral condition affords them ...'.[3] The Diet debated the proposal heatedly, and fortunately a majority of the Radicals understood the realism of the British argument. Switzerland declined the Sardinian offer, but, through the public discussion of

[1] Jacob Baumgartner, *Schweizerspiegel: Drei Jahre unter den Bundesverfassung von 1848* (Zurich, 1851), p207

[2] Edgar Bonjour, *Geschichte* ..., p208

[3] Palmerston to Peel, 20 April 1848 (FO 100/57)

42

it, the Powers became acutely aware of the temptations facing Swiss foreign policy as a result of the 1848 unrest and the liberal victory of the previous year.

In the years after 1848 the Continental Powers were represented in Switzerland by men more conservative than their governments.[4] These diplomats were quickly alarmed by any 'democratic' tendencies in Switzerland and their reports often dwelt exclusively on dangerous developments – mostly imaginary – in Switzerland, so that the information on which the European Powers based their policy was frequently inaccurate. For example, the Prussian representative, von Sydow, gave his king the impression that, at least until 1852, the Republicans controlled Neuchâtel only with the help of the bayonets of the neighbouring cantons of Berne and Vaud, when in fact both the latter cantons kept carefully out of the situation. Diplomatic reports from Switzerland tended to overlook the important elements of stability in Swiss political life. At times, even the British were uncertain about the reliability and sobriety of the Radical party. Hence it was small wonder that the Powers continued to worry about the 'liberal cancer' of Switzerland and that they persisted in attempts to restrict Swiss independence.

The pretexts for considering intervention were the refugee issue and the status of Neuchâtel. Since the latter was sometimes an excuse for dealing with the former, it is difficult to separate the two. Switzerland had discussions about refugees with France, Austria, and the German states. Because the German refugee issue was at one time very closely connected with the Neuchâtel question, we shall consider both in this chapter, reserving examination of the refugee problem as a whole for the next.

1848 DIPLOMACY OVER NEUCHÂTEL

The Neuchâtel Republicans chose a favourable time in both domestic and international politics to overthrow the Royalists. In recent years the Swiss adherents of the Prussian king had become increasingly disliked, and popular support for the new cantonal régime was evident immediately. The new republican constitution, which omitted any reference to the king, was accepted by an overwhelming majority. On the international political scene the German states were in ferment and the new French régime, sympathetic toward the Swiss, would countenance no active intervention by Prussia, so that Switzerland was

[4] There were two exceptions: France had a liberal representative for part of 1848 and Russia had no representative at all until 1856

temporarily insured against further Prussian moves to restore the Royalists to power.

The British government again advocated a policy of restraint for all parties concerned. To the Swiss, Palmerston gave no indication of any support. On several occasions, he endeavoured to persuade the King of Prussia to accept his loss. Indeed, even before the Royalists were overthrown on 1 March, Palmerston made it known that his government would recognize the special position of the King of Prussia in Switzerland only as long as the Royalists governed with popular consent, and he warned Frederick William IV against any interference in matters related to the Confederation: '... it is manifest that the Sovereign of Prussia would practically exercise a veto upon the resolutions of the Swiss Confederation, and thus in regard to all measures of internal improvement in Switzerland a direct and controuling foreign influence would be established in contradiction with the deliberate opinion of the 8 powers ... It would not be surprising if the Swiss ... were to determine to expel Neuchâtel ... if no other means could be resorted to for freeing themselves from such foreign controul.'[5] Prussia was very much annoyed by the events of 1 March, and sent a sharp protest to the Swiss. However, according to the British Minister in Berlin, Lord Westmorland, the Prussian government was not planning to restore the Royalists to power in Neuchâtel, and was inclined to end its commitments there. Palmerston quickly indicated his agreement with these intentions since Prussia was losing 'no real advantage' in Neuchâtel and was indeed 'relieved from an embarrassment.'[6]

However, Frederick William was not so easily persuaded as most of his ministers. His mind did not always respond to arguments of political realism, no matter from what quarter they came. He was a deeply religious and romantic person, believing in a mystical, divinely-sanctioned relationship between himself, as sovereign, and his people. The concept of popular sovereignty was beyond his understanding. The Neuchâtel question was, for him, a matter of principle in the defence of Europe against the wave of liberalism which seemed to be sweeping away the whole social order. Despite the fact that his official ministers tended to represent a more realistic outlook, he was probably more influenced by a group of unofficial advisers whose approach was not exactly dispassionate. It was sometimes difficult for the (official) Minister of Foreign Affairs even to communicate with the king, let alone to execute a realistic foreign policy. This situation was to hamper and prolong negotiations about the Neuchâtel question for some years.

[5] Palmerston to Westmorland, 11 January 1848 (FO 64/282)
[6] Palmerston to Westmorland, 14 March 1848 (*ibid*)

Palmerston must have realized that, because of the strange character of the king, it was not sufficient for the Prussian ministers to wish to end their commitments in Neuchâtel. At the end of March, he sent Sir Stratford Canning on a special mission to the German states, and one of the questions to be discussed with Frederick William was Neuchâtel. Canning appealed to the king's 'good sense and sound judgment' in the hope that he would be reconciled to the new situation, and pointed out that restoration of the Royalists could be achieved only by a successful war against France.[7] Canning's evaluation of the king's intentions was fairly optimistic, but the stubborn and distraught monarch promised nothing.

This might have been an opportune moment for the Swiss to persuade the King of Prussia to renounce his claims, but they were too busy with internal reorganization to press their advantage. Soon a growing number of more urgent internal questions, such as the revolutionary movement in Germany and the fate of Schleswig-Holstein, pushed Neuchâtel off the diplomatic scene.

THE PRUSSIAN THREAT IN 1848–49

The neutrality of the German-speaking cantons was put to a severe test by the 1848 uprisings in the Germanies. The Directory tried to control the situation by prohibiting the departure of any groups of armed men from Switzerland (bound for either Germany or Lombardy) and by increasing the frontier guard. Consequently, the Baden uprising in April did not receive much support from Swiss soil. When it failed, many of the unsuccessful revolutionaries sought refuge in Switzerland very near the Baden border. Baden demanded their internment, but without success, since the Swiss Directory would not act without proof of violation of their privileges of exile.

Instigators of a second Baden revolution in September did receive help from volunteer bands based in Switzerland. They too failed, and once more a flood of unsuccessful revolutionaries sought Swiss asylum. Again the government of Baden protested, and on this occasion its protest was, for several reasons, handled more sympathetically by the Swiss. First, violations of Swiss neutrality were obvious. Second, the Swiss had adopted their new constitution and the new federal government was in a firmer position to act, legally and politically. Encouragement from Britain may also have helped to change Swiss policy; Palmerston sent a strong note about the importance of preventing Swiss

[7] Palmerston to Canning, 18 March 1848 (FO 30/117)

territory from being an 'arsenal where the hostile expeditions are prepared against the internal tranquillity of other countries'.[8] The Germans were reassured by Palmerston's interest in the situation and, subsequently, by Swiss promises to use more care in the future (reported by Peel). Thus, gentle pressure from Britain helped to diminish tension. In January 1849 the Federal Council deported some refugee leaders and decreed that all other refugees should reside at least six hours travel time away from the border; this too reassured the German governments, but only temporarily.

As 1849 wore on, mutual distrust increased between the German states and Switzerland. Sydow continued to encourage the Neuchâtel Royalists, which annoyed the Swiss, and secret revolutionary societies of refugees in Switzerland planned changes for their homelands, which made the European Powers more nervous. In May a third uprising in Baden sent thousands more refugees to Switzerland, and the German states protested again. The Swiss responded by expelling more refugee leaders and by moving the internees farther from the border, but the Germans were still unsatisfied. At the end of July another incident added to German-Swiss tension. A battalion of Hessian troops, whose mission was to quell domestic unrest, crossed the Swiss frontier at Büsingen. The Swiss disarmed them immediately and sent them back across the border within a few days. The German Confederation was momentarily alarmed about Swiss aggressiveness in forcing the Hessians to disarm, and the Swiss, fearing more to come, had partly mobilized before the episode was over. Palmerston quickly sent assurances to the Germans that the Swiss action was a reasonable practice for a neutral state to follow.

The Swiss were especially nervous during the summer because of persistent rumours that the Prussian army, which had helped to suppress the Baden insurrection, would march into Switzerland to restore the Royalist régime in Neuchâtel. The rumours had some foundation. It was well known that the Prussian government wanted to curb the 'Plots against the tranquillity of Germany & the neighbouring Countries [which] were hatched & directed' in Switzerland.[9] In July Frederick William received a memorandum which argued that Prussian sovereignty in Neuchâtel should be enforced in order to stop the abuses of Swiss asylum by the refugees. The British representative in Baden reported rumours of Prussian plans to reoccupy Neuchâtel and of Franco-German agreement to partition Switzerland, to destroy 'that

[8] Palmerston to Peel, 11 October 1848 (FO 100/57)
[9] Howard to Palmerston, 20 September 1849 (FO 64/302)

46

hotbed of communism'.[10] The swift Swiss reaction to the Büsingen incident, indicating readiness to resist intervention, may have had a sobering
effect on Prussian policy makers. Even so, in early September, the
Prince of Prussia, commanding the Prussian army in South Germany,
asked Britain to advise Switzerland to cease 'assisting the views of the
democratic Party in Germany'. The Prince hinted that continued provocation might bring on more action by Prussia.[11] On this occasion
Palmerston refused the Prussian request for still more pressure on the
Swiss government.

Peel later asserted, in defence of Swiss policy, that the Prussian
allegations of plotting in Switzerland were merely a cover for the plots
in Berlin against Switzerland. He may have been somewhat confused
about cause and effect in this situation, but it is true that Prussia had
unsuccessfully approached France for common action against Switzerland. Similarly, Russia showed no interest in organizing a conference to
discuss plans for dealing with the Swiss question. Austria and Prussia
were divided over plans for the composition of the German Confederation (an aftermath of the Frankfurt Parliament) and, although a tentative
agreement was reached, this disagreement ruled out serious Austro-
Prussian measures against Switzerland. Thus Prussia was forced by the
other Powers to abandon any thoughts of collective military or economic
action in 1849.

1849–50 ATTEMPTS TO NEGOTIATE

In early November 1849 both Prussia and Switzerland made diplomatic
attempts to negotiate a settlement of the Neuchâtel question. In London
the Prussian Ambassador, Chevalier Bunsen, asked for British support
to settle the matter peacefully; he included with his request an account
of the sufferings of the Royalists and he emphasized Prussian abstinence,
hitherto, from military intervention. The Foreign Office was prompted
by this to prepare a memorandum on the Neuchâtel question; it argued
that Prussia had already, in 1848, appeared to agree to the new state of
things in Switzerland. Palmerston's reply to Bunsen was less forthright
than the memorandum; he noted Prussian rights to Neuchâtel 'in virtue
of existing Treaties' and offered assistance 'to bring about an amicable
arrangement', but he only implied that the treaties were not the sole
factors to be considered.[12] Bunsen responded with a slightly more specific

[10] Loftus to Cowley, 3 July 1849 (FO 519/161)
[11] Cowley to Palmerston, 2 September 1849 (FO 30/129)
[12] Palmerston to Bunsen, 26 November 1849 (FO 64/308)

request for British support for the Prussian position in talks with the Swiss government, interpreting recent Swiss overtures as a desire to end the 'illegal state of affairs' in Neuchâtel.[13] Palmerston was apparently marking time: he vaguely agreed to instruct the British representative in Berne 'to be useful in any way he can properly be so'.[14] The Prussians were grateful for the British attitude which seemed, to them, to uphold their honour, in the form of the king's claims on Switzerland. They also assured the British representative in Berlin that they were contemplating no further steps in Switzerland. Even though these British and Prussian messages were based on entirely different assumptions, the discussion did serve for a month or so to allay the king's worries about Switzerland.

The Swiss did not know of the Anglo-Prussian exchange. For more than a year they had been inconvenienced by the Prussian refusal to recognize passports issued by the Republican Neuchâtel government. Recently the military scare of the Büsingen incident had caused uneasiness. Therefore, in early November, they informed Prussia of their wish to settle the question. Their opening was doomed from the start. The Prussian reply ambiguously expressed a desire for settlement 'only as the real interests of Neuchâtel demand' and asked for specific proposals. Their representative in Berne assured Peel that 'no pecuniary considerations would induce' Frederick William to renounce his principality. Peel suspected that Prussia really wanted to 'get the Swiss into a scrape' which could provide a new pretext for intervention.[15] The Prussian representative told the Swiss President that the newly appointed British Minister to Switzerland had been instructed to 'support the demands of the Prussian government for the unconditional renewal of relations ...' between Prussia and Neuchâtel, an obvious distortion of the Bunsen-Palmerston correspondence.[16] When Peel learned this, he immediately advised the Swiss to disregard the story, even though the Foreign Office had sent him no instructions on the matter. The Swiss apparently took Peel's advice. Their note to Prussia suggested, as the bases for further negotiation, that the king renounce his claims to Neuchâtel and that Prussia accept legal documents issued by the new cantonal government. The Swiss did, however, delay the delivery of this message until early February. Then the Prussian Chargé d'Affaires merely acknowledged it and was immediately recalled, so that Prussia was without a ranking representative in Berne. Such a sign of disapproval

13 Bunsen to Palmerston, 27 November 1849 (*ibid*)
14 Palmerston to Bunsen, 4 December 1849 (*ibid*)
15 Peel to Palmerston, 7 December 1849 (FO 100/62)
16 Peel to Palmerston, 28 December 1849 (*ibid*)

alarmed both the Swiss and the British. A week later the British Minister in Berlin reported negotiations between Prussia, France, and Austria about the refugee problem and more rumours of a Prussian army build-up because of the Swiss question reached England.

With this news of renewed danger to Switzerland, Palmerston was stirred to more positive action than his earlier delaying tactics. He drafted a note to Prussia stating that the 1815 treaties did not guarantee Prussian rights in Neuchâtel and that an attempt to re-establish the Royalists would expose Prussia to strong opposition not only from Switzerland but from France also. He suggested bases for mediation which he hoped would be acceptable to Prussia: 'while on the one hand the existing state of things in Neuchâtel or some modification of it should be acknowledged by Prussia, on the other hand full Security & sufficient compensations should be provided for those adherents of the King in Neuchâtel who are represented to have been grievous sufferers ...'.[17] The Foreign Office records do not indicate that this proposal was actually made to Prussia. Whether it was presented or not, subsequent developments made it less urgent. In March Prussia assured Britain that her relations with Switzerland were not suspended; the Prussian Legation was still officially open. The Swiss, too, showed some restraint. In March and April British reports from Berne told of more efforts to control the German workmen's societies, and generally of increased national support for a careful federal policy toward refugees. The British government also learned that France had made a strong protest about the increase of the Prussian Rhine army and that Prussia had, in turn, assured the French government of its desire to cooperate on policy toward Switzerland and the refugee question. In these circumstances, with other forces favouring security for Switzerland, it was not necessary for Palmerston to forward his dispatch. None the less, he did urge the French to object to Prussian military intervention in Switzerland, and his representative in Berne continued to encourage the Swiss to follow a moderate course in dealing with the refugees.

Although the Swiss were irritated to learn of some French diplomatic moves in Berlin to protect Swiss interests,[18] they could have wished that Britain might have been more active on their behalf. As long as Prusso-Swiss relations were relatively calm, Britain was unwilling to jeopardize her relations with Prussia. Stronger activity by Britain on behalf of the Swiss was impossible at this time because other negotiations were more

[17] Palmerston to Westmorland, 25 February 1850 (FO 64/310)
[18] For a description of these moves, see Paul Matter, 'Les missions de M. de Persigny à Berlin' (*Revue d'histoire diplomatique*, 1898, Paris)

urgent: the necessity of obtaining Prussian concessions on Schleswig-Holstein precluded any discussions about Neuchâtel. Furthermore, neither France nor England wanted to push Prussia into an entente with Russia or Austria.

REVIVAL OF THE QUESTION IN 1851

For the next year the Powers continued to worry about the refugee problem, but they devoted very little diplomatic attention to the Neuchâtel question. The only two developments in the situation took place in Switzerland. In June 1850 the Neuchâtel government sold some of the former Crown and Church holdings. Naturally, Prussia protested, but the sale was not stopped. This brief exchange gave the Swiss another chance to assure Britain of their continuing desire to settle the matter and of their disposition even to make certain concessions. In November, however, the Federal Council suffered a setback, when the Federal Assembly criticized its initiation of correspondence with Prussia the previous year. The Council was explicitly instructed not to open negotiations unless it could 'predict a satisfactory result with certitude'.[19] This decision gave the Swiss executive much less scope for manoeuvring. In the latter half of 1850 the Prussian concern with the refugee problem also diminished, largely because the number of German refugees in Switzerland had decreased considerably and because the French government of President Bonaparte, as it became more conservative, was increasing its own pressure on Switzerland.

In 1851, however, Frederick William's interest in Neuchâtel was revived. Although at least one of his advisers argued that the idea of restoring the Royalists to power was illusory and that expediency demanded renunciation, Sydow, the Prussian diplomat in Switzerland who was so firmly convinced of Royalist strength, pleaded the importance of Prussian honour, an argument which particularly appealed to the king. The matter was to be raised again, starting with a series of attacks on Switzerland by the Prussian press. In April, calculating that Britain needed to strengthen her position in Europe, Frederick William asked Palmerston to call a conference of the other three Powers to arrange the restoration of Prussian rights in Neuchâtel. Palmerston disappointed the king; he refused to agree and reminded Prussia that intervention in Switzerland would probably precipitate war in Europe. The king drew an obvious – but wrong – conclusion from this exchange,

[19] *Feuille Fédérale de la Confédération Suisse* (Berne, 1850), iii, 199

namely, that Britain would not cooperate on this issue as long as Palmerston was Foreign Secretary.

Frederick William IV did not give up hope. During the summer he renewed his promises to the Royalists, who might otherwise have been reconciled to their fate. Indeed, the general European situation showed signs of becoming more favourable for Prussia. For one thing, political developments in France were causing some uncertainty. Also, the summer saw a growing tariff dispute between Switzerland and the Zollverein over respective duties on iron and corn; while Prussia had no desire to be involved in this or even to perpetuate it, an impatience with Switzerland among the south German governments was a point which favoured Prussian manœuvring. Britain was worried enough about this source of irritation to offer her good offices.[20]

During the autumn the Neuchâtel question was raised again, but Prussia turned to other Powers than Britain for help. Ostensibly, Frederick William's aim was only to put an end to the oppression of his subjects; in fact, this was another way of asking for restoration, since 'oppression', for the Royalists, meant simply the necessity of living under a Republican régime. The Prussian king's Foreign Minister asked Austria, Russia, and France to consider a way to 'repair the breach' in the 1815 treaty arrangements.[21] When the British learned of the renewed discussion, they pointed out that the unstable political situation in France was not favourable for such an action; Palmerston did not expect the Prussian move to succeed. The Swiss Federal Council also learned of the Prussian move, and it confidently expected both French and British support, reasoning that Prussia would soon be discouraged by the strong likelihood of diplomatic defeat. The Swiss did not reckon on the need of the other Powers to conciliate Prussia, because of her central position in Europe, nor did they realize the intimate connection, assumed by the Continental Powers, between the Neuchâtel and refugee questions. In fact, Prussia did obtain confidential expressions of support from Austria and Russia for her proposal for Neuchâtel, and France also was much nearer to agreement than the Swiss thought.

---

[20] Switzerland was grateful for the offer, but little seems to have come of it, except that the British representative in Baden and Württemberg wrote that he was continuing to urge 'the inexpediency of retaliatory measures' against Switzerland. Christie to Palmerston, 2 August 1851 (FO 100/69) and Malet to Palmerston, 26 July 1851 (FO 192/11)

[21] Howard to Palmerston, 16 October 1851 (FO 64/333)

Louis Napoleon's *coup d'état* in December influenced the Neuchâtel question in several ways. The French government became more nervous about the refugees in Switzerland; hence France pressed Switzerland with a severe ultimatum in January[22] and showed an interest in co-operating with the other Continental Powers. Britain wanted to prevent a continental entente, and was therefore more willing to make some concessions. Second, the Powers were alerted to any French tendency to rebuild the empire of Napoleon I. Although Russia, Austria, and Prussia supported the French charges about refugees in the January ultimatum, they also realized the possible necessity of closing their ranks against French expansionism. Third, Palmerston's quick recognition of the *coup d'état* precipitated his own 'retirement'. Also, the Prussians calculated that because Queen Victoria seemed to disapprove of Napoleon's *coup d'état*, Britain would no longer encourage France to oppose Prussia in Neuchâtel. The prospect of cantonal elections at the end of March was another factor which influenced Frederick William to take more action.

Within a month of the removal of Lord Palmerston, the supposed antagonist, from the Foreign Office, Prussia made her next conference proposal in January 1852. The offer made no concessions on Neuchâtel; not only were recognition and re-establishment of Prussia in Neuchâtel to be the bases of a settlement, but also the canton was to be separated from Switzerland. The initial British reaction to this was mixed. Lord Russell and his new, inexperienced Foreign Secretary, Lord Granville, had not had much chance to study the question. While they recognized that, from the technical and legal points of view, the king's sovereignty should be restored, they doubted that such a settlement would promote European peace, and they suspected that Prussia was trying to get Britain to take the initiative in making a break in the treaty system. In early February a frustrated Prussian government pressed Britain to acquiesce in continental policy toward Switzerland, since Britain had no vital interest there; objection to its proposal should come 'from that quarter to which it belongs'. Here is a hint that Prussia was envious of the favoured position of Britain *vis-à-vis* the Swiss. The irrational king threatened 'to act for himself ... in order to ... vindicate rights sanctioned by solemn European treaties as soon as He can'.[23] Such emotional arguments impressed Granville no more than Palmerston.

[22] See Chapter Five
[23] Bunsen to Granville, 12 February 1852 (FO 64/348)

The fall of the Russell ministry, in late February, might have given Prussia more reason for optimism, but Lord Derby and his Foreign Secretary, the Earl of Malmesbury, continued a policy of steadfast opposition to continuing Prussian calls for restoration in Neuchâtel. In mid-March the British government again turned down the proposal, even though it had been revised precisely to meet some of the British objections. Malmesbury wrote privately to Lord Cowley, now Ambassador in Paris, that however much Britain might acknowledge Prussian treaty rights in Neuchâtel 'there would be no advantage in repeating such an undisputed fact by a new protocol, unless collateral objects recommend it'. One 'collateral object' might be an explicit recognition of Swiss independence and neutrality, but Malmesbury doubted that France would agree to that. He himself did not consider the present moment to be appropriate; 'we ought at this moment to appear to the Swiss as the independent and real friend, offering honourable and reasonable advice in their present difficulties. I think that if, simultaneously with our present representations in this sense, we urged the acknowledgment of the King of Prussia's claims in conjunction with two nations who are in the act of bullying them, the Swiss would no longer follow our advice with the same confidence which they have apparently shown.'[24] Malmesbury's concern with the effect of British policy on the Swiss was an interesting point. The acceptability of British advice was important if Britain was to continue in her role of informal mediator between the Swiss and their neighbours.

In Switzerland, the Neuchâtel elections at the end of March resulted in a decisive defeat for the Royalists, and it was obvious that they could regain power only through a Great Power diplomatic or military intervention. None the less, the undaunted king again sent encouragement to his supporters. His government tried to persuade the Foreign Office, on the basis of alleged election irregularities and many abstentions, that a Royalist majority did in fact exist, but Malmesbury was still highly sceptical. In mid-April an election in the canton of Berne rejected a Radical proposal to unseat the Conservative government. To the Powers, so wary of socialist tendencies in Switzerland, this was enough assurance to diminish whatever enthusiasm they might have had for intervention, despite the earlier Royalist defeat.

The international questions facing the Powers in April also helped to modify their thinking about Neuchâtel. Prussia had seen in the French ultimatum to Switzerland a threat of an extension of the French

[24] James E. Harris (Earl of Malmesbury), *Memoirs of an ex-Minister* (London, 1884), i, 315

influence. For the same reason all the Powers were alarmed by a continuing Franco-Belgian dispute. Thus Prussia and the three Powers (Britain, Austria, and Russia) saw a French challenge to the 1815 settlement in both Belgium and Switzerland, while in Neuchâtel France and the same three Powers feared a Prussian threat to the same settlement. During the winter rumours had circulated about plans for military intervention in Switzerland by Austria and Baden, and, although this was not taken as seriously as the French and Prussian threats, any breach of the 1815 settlement was an eventuality to be prevented. Another important factor in the general situation was the negotiation of an agreement regarding Schleswig-Holstein which was nearing a conclusion, but whose success depended on Prussian concurrence; the Powers were prepared to concede some other matter to Prussia in order to obtain her signature for the convention on Danish succession.

In early May the official Prussian proposal for a conference on Neuchâtel was made to France. The French Foreign Minister was not pleased, because he suspected its basic aim to be a change of the Swiss constitution; he gave Cowley his opinion that because Switzerland was at that moment fulfilling her international obligations, it would be best to leave her alone. Cowley encouraged the French to make their objections directly to Prussia, but this did not work either. Because the French could not refuse to discuss the matter, but could make a modified counter-proposal, they accepted the idea of calling a conference of the four Powers, at an unspecified time, to mediate between Prussia and Switzerland. The French proposal recognized both the Prussian and the Swiss treaty rights but included a renunciation of the use of force for Prussian restoration. Thus the French aimed first to tie the Prussian hand and second to 'rivit the connexion [sic]' between Neuchâtel and Switzerland.[25]

Britain also had extracted concessions from Prussia about the conditions of any agreement. In mid-April Bunsen wrote that it was understood and expected that if the protocol were discussed soon it would not necessarily require enforcement. A few weeks later the British Minister in Berlin, Lord Bloomfield, was assured that, in spite of Prussian eagerness for a Great Power agreement on Neuchâtel, the matter was not pressing and the proposed mediation aimed at restoration could be postponed if the moment were inopportune. Here Britain could detect a loophole to avoid the application of the proposed protocol, if it were agreed to.

[25] Cowley to Malmesbury, 9 May 1852 (FO 192/12)

54

The Powers readily accepted the French proposal, and the protocol was signed by representatives of the five Great Powers in London on 24 May. Agreement was reached this quickly for various reasons. Prussia considered some agreement, weak though it was, to be better than none, and Russia unexpectedly urged the Prussian government to sign the protocol immediately because of the importance of getting, as soon as possible, the 'assent of France to a Document in which She declared her recognition of Treaties and the Territorial Arrangements of 1815'.[26] Britain agreed to sign only because Prussia renounced the use of force for the re-establishment of her sovereignty in Neuchâtel. The protocol was clearly intended, by all the Powers, much less to recognize the King of Prussia's rights than for the 'collateral object' of reaffirming the 1815 treaty system, restraining both Prussia and France from any expansionism. In other words, it was a dead letter from the start, in so far as it might permit a Prussian breach in the 1815 settlement for Switzerland. The protocol only conceded some unrealistic flattery to Frederick William.

AFTERMATH OF THE LONDON PROTOCOL OF 1852

The Swiss were not pleased with the news of the protocol, especially since they had not known of the negotiations. Cowley managed to persuade Joseph Barman, the Swiss representative in Paris, that the agreement contained nothing hostile to Switzerland: it was, indeed, advantageous for the Swiss to have both Prussian renunciation of the use of force and French reaffirmation of the 1815 treaties. But Barman was not able to convince his superiors in Berne of these advantages. The Swiss government had been counting on the unqualified support of Britain and France, so that it was surprised and disillusioned by the agreement of these two Powers to the protocol. Fortunately for Anglo-Swiss relations, the Powers had adopted the French draft, and hence it was the French who incurred Swiss displeasure by notifying them officially of the agreement. None the less, the Swiss President spoke at great length to Buchanan, the British Minister, about the unquestionable predominance of the Republicans in Neuchâtel, about Swiss determination, even among Conservatives, to resist any attempt to turn Neuchâtel over to Prussia, and about his country's resentment of any French tendency to assume the role of protector of Switzerland. Buchanan, acting without instructions, emphasized as Cowley had done the value of reaffirmation of the 1815 settlement. Malmesbury was

[26] Bloomfield to Malmesbury, 17 and 21 May 1852 (FO 64/342)

obviously somewhat embarrassed by the situation. On 21 May he had written to Buchanan about the negotiations, but not until 10 June did he send him official notification of the protocol, and then he simply echoed Cowley's reassurances for the Swiss. After the initial surprise had worn off, the Federal Council would have been amenable to further negotiations, had Prussia or Britain pursued the matter, but it would not initiate more discussions with Prussia because of the Federal Assembly's censure of the 1849-50 exchange. The Federal Council did inform Buchanan that it might accept a Prussian proposal for a plebiscite in Neuchâtel but the Foreign Office did not take up the idea.

The Prussian ministry appeared to be content with the protocol, although the king still wavered. When Malmesbury learned of rumours about a Royalist counter-revolution, he urged Prussia to realize the importance of preventing it. Twice the Prussian government professed ignorance of such plans and appeared to agree that any counter-revolution should be discouraged. But Bloomfield remarked that the Prussian Foreign Minister was 'evidently desirous not to be pressed to do more in this matter which ... is left so entirely to the management of the King that the Instructions concerning Neufchâtel generally emanate from H.M.'s Private Chancellerie'.[27] The Prussian ministry was embarrassed by the inconsistent Neuchâtel policy. The king was obsessed by his Evangelical Church responsibilities and he felt that his inability to retain Neuchâtel was both a religious and a political failure. While many Prussian statesmen agreed with Britain that renunciation of sovereignty in Neuchâtel would be the most advantageous and realistic policy, they were unable to convince their royal master.

It was almost as difficult to guide the Swiss into a consistently conciliatory course. In early July the Royalists planned a demonstration near Valengin, a Royalist stronghold, and the Republicans countered by arranging a rival one. The cantonal government tried to reduce whatever sympathy the Royalists had by legislating against treasonable activity and by dissolving an old association, the 'Bourgeoisie of Valengin', which had become a Royalist political society. Throughout these developments Buchanan urged the Federal Council to advise the cantonal authorities to be more cautious, to avoid inciting Frederick William. The Federal Council agreed, but the cantonal government would not comply with such a passive policy because it had to give some satisfaction to factions which wanted a showdown; a few of these were even hoping for a Great Power attack because 'Switzerland would

[27] Bloomfield to Malmesbury, 10 July 1852 (FO 64/343)

56

never enjoy real independence until Europe has been convinced that she possesses the power to defend herself.'[28] Proponents of this point of view were counting on indirect support, in case of war, from a renewal of the revolutionary struggle in Europe. Their arguments surely must have given support to European reactionaries who feared subversion of their own governments as a result of the Swiss political system. However, the majority of both the Radicals (which included a majority of the Neuchâtel Republicans) and the Royalists wanted to settle the matter peacefully, by negotiation.

As Buchanan and the Federal Council had feared, the Prussian government was roused again by the anti-Royalist policies in Neuchâtel. In mid-August it requested Britain to call the conference for mediation stipulated in the protocol. The Foreign Office disagreed fundamentally with the Prussian arguments about the Royalists' impatience and the subversive Swiss influence, but officially its position was simply that the time was not ripe for the conference. France and Russia agreed. Nevertheless, Prussia was not satisfied. Finally, an impatient Malmesbury reminded Prussia that she had already promised, before the protocol was signed, that the recognition of her rights would be 'not so much because [she] considered them as useful, but ... as ... a point of honour ...' and that 'all [she] required was a document ...'. Britain had agreed to the protocol only on the condition that Prussia relinquish the authority to call the conference, and Britain now thought it best to wait until 'after a further abatement of the Political fever of 1848 shall have prepared the Swiss Nation to meet this subject with calmness and a reasonable desire for settlement'.[29] Perhaps Britain was also waiting for calmness and reasonableness in Frederick William.

The question simmered in both camps during the autumn of 1852. For a few months at the end of the year, in order to stop the 'flood of subversive ideas',[30] Prussia prohibited Prussian subjects either to travel to or reside in Switzerland. The British did little about that temporary restriction, but, in Switzerland, Buchanan did try to make the Royalists understand the improbability of any Great Power support for their cause if they tried to re-establish themselves by force. Malmesbury made two other attempts to improve the situation: first, he asked for specific information from the Royalists about their 'humiliations', but their answers were very evasive, and could give the British no basis for future conciliatory moves. Then he instructed Buchanan to work with

[28] Buchanan to Malmesbury, 3 August 1852 (FO 100/73)
[29] Malmesbury to Bloomfield, 14 September 1852 (FO 64/339)
[30] Manteuffel to Bunsen, 16 August 1852 (FO 64/348)

the French representative toward an informal mediation between Switzerland and Prussia. Buchanan had several conversations with the Swiss President to explore possibilities for a solution; his resulting reports on the whole question clearly supported the Swiss position that Prussian renunciation was a necessary condition for negotiation.

After the fall of Derby ministry in 1853, and when the Swiss were in trouble with Austria over refugees, Prussia again asked Britain to call the conference. Lord Clarendon, the new British Foreign Secretary, wanted to arrange a settlement of the situation, so 'mortifying' to the king, in order to 'promote a close alliance between England and Prussia, but I would not on that account press any arrangement that might be obnoxious to Switzerland'.[31] Clarendon was soon to learn that it would be very difficult to satisfy both the Swiss and the King of Prussia. Christie, British Chargé d'Affaires in Berne, made many unofficial inquiries about the Swiss position and reported – privately – at great length. Sydow had been hard at work with the Royalists to prevent railroad development in Neuchâtel, because such improved communication would tighten the cantonal bonds with the Confederation. For this reason, the Swiss were more adamant than ever in rejecting any concession to Prussia. Christie concluded that the only solution possible would be through British mediation 'on the basis of *no essential alteration of the present state of Neuchâtel and satisfaction of the King's honour*' [sic]; he emphasized the inconsistent and unreasonable nature of Prussian policy by finding a letter from the king to the Royalists in which Frederick William released his subjects from their obligations to him, just before the vote on the new cantonal constitution.[32] Here Clarendon's explorations had to stop, in midsummer 1853, because the Powers' attentions had become fully absorbed by the Eastern Question.

REVIEW OF THE NEUCHÂTEL DISCUSSIONS TO 1852

The 1852 protocol was far from being a return to the pre-1848 status of Neuchâtel; in several respects it marked progress toward settlement of the question. It necessitated a clarification of the issues by Britain which could only redound to Switzerland's favour. The Foreign Office rejected Prussian restoration, and Prince Albert, who carefully reviewed the volumes of documents on Neuchâtel in 1853, wrote that he could see no solution except Prussian renunciation; the Swiss government, after all, was 'not likely to pave the way for its own destruction' by allowing

[31] Clarendon to Christie, 29 April 1853 (Clar. ms. c. 125)
[32] Christie to Clarendon, 30 May 1853 (Clar. ms. c. 9)

58

restoration.[33] In the British view the overall geographical and political facts of Neuchâtel's position, the relations and rivalries between the Great Powers, and the consolidated internal Swiss political organization all argued for Prussian renunciation. As another result of the protocol, the Swiss were forced to have a better realization of the complexities of the question as it affected both themselves and the Powers. A by-product of the discussion within the country was more popular support for the central government's foreign policy.

The circumstances surrounding the signing of the protocol itself were in many ways typical of all the post-*Sonderbund* discussions about Neuchâtel. The question was more or less related to Frederick William's fears of liberalism in central Europe, depending both on his moods and on the exigencies of European politics. The Swiss were eager for a settlement, but were neither willing nor capable of negotiating without the active support of one of the Powers, and the only Power to whom she would trust this mission was Britain. The British favoured the *de facto* cantonal government and opposed restoration of Prussian sovereignty, but they did not consider the matter serious enough to risk a deterioration of relations with the other Powers on its account. Although Palmerston later wrote that the 1852 protocol was a mistake, his own policy in earlier years was not more decisive; in other words, British policy on Neuchâtel was bipartisan. The protocol was an uneasy compromise which, perhaps because of the 'collateral objects' underlying its existence, did not endure the test of time. The final settlement was made in 1857 but, before examining those negotiations, we shall look at some other issues in Anglo-Swiss relations in the 1850s.

[33] Prince Albert to Clarendon, 19 September 1853 (Clar. ms. c. 9)

CHAPTER FIVE

The Refugee Problem

THE NUB OF THE PROBLEM

THROUGHOUT their history, the Swiss have experienced considerable pressure from the Continental Powers because of their willingness to receive political refugees seeking asylum. This pressure was particularly strong after 1848. Extradition treaties which the Swiss had made with their neighbours applied only to criminals; the Swiss would not agree to expel the political offender on the demand of his national government when he was not breaking the law of his new country of residence. On the other hand, the continental governments were very nervous about political opposition from the left after the upheavals of 1848, and their uneasiness about the refugees who took up residence near their frontiers is understandable. This was the nub of the problem. While the pressures on Switzerland came now from one neighbour, now another, and were sometimes concerted, the Swiss manœuvred within the framework of domestic exigencies and a constantly shifting balance of power.

The issue was essentially political and ideological. The Powers made many allegations of illegal activity within Switzerland, but their charges were seldom based on sufficient information for the Swiss to take police action. Just as the Neuchâtel question was a cloak for protest by Prussia against Swiss liberalism (and refugees in Switzerland), so the refugee question was used by Austria, France, and the German states as the means to try to force changes in Swiss politics. When the new Swiss government appeared to gain in strength and support at home, the challenge to it from neighbouring governments became more covert until at last they were forced to recognize the stability of the Swiss political system established in 1848 and to drop the matter.

The Italian canton of the Ticino, cut off from the rest of Switzerland by the Alps, was a particularly vulnerable spot for Swiss neutrality. A large part of its trade went to Austrian Lombardy and many of its citizens resided in Lombardy; in short, its economic and cultural ties to the south were very strong. Since 1815 the anomalous position of this canton had contributed to conflict between Austria and Switzerland. The tension increased in the 1840s when, in strong contrast to the Austrian régime in Lombardy, Ticino politics moved leftward. In March 1848 the Lombards made an abortive attempt to throw out the Austrians. One of the organizers of the insurrection was Mazzini, and one base of his operations was the Ticino.[1] Strict Swiss neutrality would have prohibited any help for the revolutionaries, but because the Radical Ticino government was sympathetic to the Lombards, it did little to prevent Lombard recruitment of its citizens to fight against Austria. Thus, when the Diet was tempted to ally with Sardinia in April, the Ticino had already made a breach in Swiss neutrality.

It is not surprising that Austria, already hostile after the *Sonderbund*'s defeat, was exasperated by these links between Switzerland and the revolt of her Lombard subjects. The Diet could do nothing to placate Austria, because it had authority neither to guard the southern frontier effectively nor to force the cantonal government to prevent participation in a foreign struggle. Although there were rumours of Austrian plans to invade part of Switzerland, throughout the spring the Austrians were too busy in Italy and at home to take action against the Swiss. By mid-summer, Austrian forces turned against the Lombards, so that more refugees flooded into Switzerland from Italy. Then, with a stabilized situation in Vienna, Austria was in a position to put pressure on the Swiss. At the end of August the Austrian military commander in Lombardy, Marshal Radetzky, demanded that the Ticino government should control the refugees more carefully. The Ticino government complied by merely evacuating refugees from the immediate border area, and the matter was referred to the Berne government, which asked Britain to assure Austria of Switzerland's good intentions.[2]

---

[1] See E. Weinmann, 'Der Anteil des Tessins am italienischen Risorgimento und die schweizerische Neutralität 1848' (*Zeitschrift für Schweizerische Geschichte*, 1932, Zurich), p434

[2] Berne was still the directing canton under the 1815 Pact. The Swiss turned to Britain because Austria had withdrawn her representative from Berne in protest against the dissolution of the *Sonderbund*. The British transmitted the Swiss assurance to the legation in Vienna, but there is no record of any action on it

None the less, Austrian suspicions of Swiss complicity persisted. Garibaldi and many of his supporters asked for asylum in Switzerland, and it was granted. Fortunately, they were interned some distance from the border and soon left the country altogether, but large numbers of other refugees did remain near Lombardy. For this reason, in mid-September Austria blockaded the Ticino to prevent further interference from Switzerland. The Swiss did not ask for British help on this occasion, perhaps because they realized that Britain could do little. Peel reported that the Diet had set up a commission of inquiry, but that its 'good intentions' were neutralized by 'want of energy' in the Ticino.[3] The Foreign Office sent a report about the Swiss action to Vienna, but since it went in the same bag with a dispatch expressing British disappointment at Austrian insistence on retaining absolute government in Lombardy, it probably had little effect. In the view of the new Austrian government, Britain was so clearly on the side of the Lombards that pleading the Swiss cause with Austria would have been of no avail. Fortunately, the stalemate did not last long. The federal government took stronger action on both northern and southern borders when it assumed power in the autumn, so that Austria, seeing better evidence of Swiss control, reopened communications within a few months. With the threat of more violence in Lombardy in March 1849, both the Ticino and the federal governments were quicker to take preventive action: both called out troops to be sure that a neutral and independent position would be maintained.

The relationship between the Ticino and the rest of the Confederation was particularly delicate at this time because of their divergent views about the obligations of a neutral toward its neighbours. The Ticino was not pleased to be virtually occupied by federal troops, and rumours reached Berne that it contemplated leaving Switzerland to join Lombardy if the latter were freed from Austrian rule. The canton was caught between two fires in 1848. Since Austria managed to stay in Lombardy for another decade, the Ticinese bonds with Switzerland were sufficiently strengthened in the interval to avoid a separation. As the new Swiss constitution was put into effect, federal policy towards refugees was stronger and more effective, but nevertheless Austria remained highly distrustful of the liberal Swiss régime, making little distinction between federal and cantonal policy. Many Ticinese remained sympathetic with moves for liberating Lombardy, and Mazzini, despite police efforts to keep him out, continued to use the canton as one of his various bases.

[3] Peel to Palmerston, 21 September 1848 (FO 100/59)

Hence, during the decade following 1848, Austria was ready to seize any opportunity to benefit from developments in the European scene which would enable more pressure to be exerted on Switzerland.

DISCUSSIONS WITH GERMANY IN 1848–49

In 1849 the refugee issue became more pressing in the north, in relation to south Germany and to France. Toward Germany, the federal government eventually found less difficulty in fulfilling its obligations as a neutral.[4] Some alarm was caused by rumours of the organization of a 'German-Helvetic Legion', to be used to liberate Germany, but pressure on the cantonal governments from the Federal Council for the expulsion of leaders of such groups was effective, except in Geneva. When the third Baden uprising in May was followed by another flood of refugees into Switzerland, the Federal Council again reminded the cantonal governments of the necessity of expelling refugee leaders. Thus the central government tackled the problem, but cautiously, because it was still unsure of the extent of its constitutional power.

Because Prussia was dissatisfied with the Swiss, she initiated moves in July for concerted German action against them, proposing joint military action along the Swiss frontier to back up a demand for the expulsion of all revolutionary leaders. Surprisingly, Austria thought this too severe. Both Austria and Prussia were restrained from stringent anti-Swiss action by the threat of strong objections at home and by their involvement in more urgent issues facing the German Confederation. Furthermore, in this case it was only Baden which had a specific complaint against Switzerland, and by the end of the summer the Federal Council negotiated an agreement with Baden for the restitution of captured arms and an amnesty for most of the refugees.

Apparently the Swiss had little diplomatic help in these discussions with Baden. Peel wrote only of urging the Baden representative to make such an agreement, and the Foreign Office appears not to have bestirred itself in the matter. It is to the credit of the Swiss that they carried on so responsibly and successfully by themselves in the first year of life of the new government. The success of the Federal Council in this question probably encouraged it to initiate the negotiations in November with Prussia about Neuchâtel, which did not turn out as favourably.[5]

[4] See Chapter Four
[5] See pages 47-50

From 1849 to 1852 France was the principal source of complaints about refugees in Switzerland. The initial liberal ardour of the 1848 French government was fast disappearing by the time of Louis Napoleon's election to the presidency, and with it went much French sympathy for Switzerland. The Swiss were sadly disappointed in their hope that Louis Napoleon would gratefully remember that he had once been a refugee in Switzerland himself. Following an abortive uprising organized by Ledru-Rollin in the spring of 1849, the number of French refugees in Switzerland increased; they naturally tended to settle in the French-speaking cantons, close to France – and particularly in Geneva. The French government directed many protests to the Federal Council, demanding either internment or expulsion of these refugees.

Expulsion of refugees entailed a significant tactical problem for land-locked Switzerland. The Swiss considered that it would be unfair to force any refugee to leave his asylum only to face certain arrest, and they discussed this problem with the French on several occasions. By August 1849 the French were persuaded, 'after some demur', to allow transit through their country for expelled refugees bound for Britain or the United States.[6] French cooperation in this respect, although not very graciously given, made it much easier for Switzerland to deal with complaints from any country about refractory foreign residents. While no official Foreign Office instructions urged France to take this line, the closeness with which the British followed and reported on these Franco-Swiss discussions does suggest some unofficial encouragement.

The French government kept up pressure on Switzerland in 1849 for several reasons. In the first place, it considered the Swiss attitude toward refugees, and toward alleged plotting in Geneva, to be too lax. A more covert motive was the hope of a change to a more conservative Swiss government, a hope which the French shared – in principle – with Austria, Prussia, and Russia. A third stimulus, in the autumn of 1849, was not related to French refugees but to the Italian Mazzini, who was reported to be busy in the canton of Vaud trying to influence Sardinian elections. French protests drew responses from both the Swiss and the British. The Federal Council appointed a special commissioner to investigate the situation in Geneva, and Peel attempted, vainly, to assure the French representative in Berne that there was little to be feared from French or Italian refugees in Switzerland.

[6] Cowley to Palmerston, 1 August 1849 (FO 30/129)

Early in 1850 Prussia was encouraged by the ambiguous British promise about Neuchâtel to propose joint action with Austria and France to settle the Swiss question.[7] Because France was alarmed by the prospect of Prussian and Austrian action against Switzerland, she defended the Swiss position and insisted that the matter be treated by a Great Power conference. Palmerston agreed with the French view and noted that the Austrian and Prussian intent was 'not to obtain a Remedy for any specific and existing Evil but to exact from Switzerland some general engagement applicable to future as well as to present cases ...'. Because of the probable 'embarrassing discussions' concerning enforcement, Britain considered the proposal 'liable to serious objections'.[8] Although the Foreign Office was thus aware of the issues involved, its role was negligible. British participation in the discussions would have alienated the confidence of the conservative Powers unnecessarily, while they were not yet seriously threatening the Swiss, and it might have prevented settlement of more outstanding international questions. It was simpler to encourage the French to restrain Prussia and Austria, a device similar to that used in the *Sonderbund* negotiations.

Although the Swiss did adopt a more positive policy at this time, their attitude toward France became no more sympathetic. News of the conference proposal alarmed them, as did the presence of Austrian and Prussian troops near their borders. A second report from the Federal Council's commissioner in Geneva suggested a few more expulsions, but in general the report showed the French allegations of the previous year to be much exaggerated. While the Swiss treated French demands with respect, they resented an increasing note of protectiveness in the French attitude. They had not forgotten their humiliation under Napoleonic conquest fifty years earlier, and when, in early March, the French Foreign Minister spoke publicly of French protection of Switzerland, their fears were renewed. The French further wounded Swiss pride by omitting the tactful gesture of consultation before beginning discussions in Berlin about Neuchâtel and the refugees, subjects so vital to Swiss interests.[9]

Britain's role at this time was little more than that of a sympathetic listener. In Paris, Barman told Lord Normanby, the British Ambassador, about the sincere efforts of his government to satisfy French demands and about Swiss worries over the attitudes of all the Continental Powers. Barman appealed for help because Britain was 'certainly

[7] See pages 49-50
[8] Palmerston to Normanby, 8 February 1850 (FO 192/9)
[9] See page 49

interested in maintaining the independence of Switzerland, and having no partial interest on this subject would be better able to estimate whether Switzerland really executed faithfully the duties of good neighbourhood'.[10] In response, Normanby promised nothing and emphasized Swiss responsibilities as a neutral. Two weeks later, Barman reported yet another French demand for expulsions and claimed that the French complaints were unjust. Normanby merely listened. Napoleon later offered reasons (to Normanby) for his policy toward Switzerland: he wanted to prevent Prussia from having a pretext for taking any kind of military action on Neuchâtel which would bring Prussian troops to the French border.[11] This explained the increase in French troops near Switzerland, which the Swiss considered as a warning only to themselves. The Foreign Office did nothing to reassure the Swiss about this, probably with the idea that it was better to let them be warned by threats from neighbours, thus ensuring that they would control the refugees. Again, it was evident that Switzerland's neighbours were for the moment jealous enough of each other to prevent any actions ultimately prejudicial to Swiss independence.

A few minor incidents in 1850 served to perpetuate Franco-Swiss distrust, in spite of increasing Swiss activity to prevent violations of neutrality. In August the Federal Council decided against sending a delegation to Strasbourg to compliment Napoleon (on the theory that such etiquette was not necessary between two republics), and this displeased the French. Some weeks later, the Geneva police arrested a French *agent provocateur* named Schnepp, which occasioned another French protest. The incident was played down by both governments, but it did publicize the biased way in which the French were getting the information on which their demands were based. It also mobilized anti-French feeling and support for the federal government throughout Switzerland so that in December the Geneva government was more cooperative about a federal decree which required that the refugees should be kept farther from the border.

Perhaps the most remarkable feature of Anglo-Swiss relations in 1850 was the contrast of British inactivity with Swiss faith in Britain as a sort of guardian angel. The Federal Council report on foreign relations for 1850 is critical of all the Powers except Britain, who, it said, had 'not ceased to show a great kindness toward the Confederation, and ... has not failed to represent to the other Cabinets that there was no ground

[10] Normanby to Palmerston, 5 February 1850 (FO 27/868)
[11] Normanby to Palmerston, 1 March 1850 (FO 27/869)

for measures against Switzerland'.[12] Official records of such representations by Britain are few and far between. 1851 brought somewhat more British activity on behalf of the Swiss, but scarcely as much as the Swiss believed.

THE FRENCH ULTIMATUM OF 1852

In early 1851 the Federal Council was the recipient of still another French protest and, this time, a demand for assurance that the refugees, once interned eight leagues from the border, would stay there. The Swiss were 'driven almost to despair by the importunities' of France, whose information was still based on the exaggerated reports of spies.[13] Although the total number of refugees in Switzerland had been reduced to fewer than 500, the Swiss responded to the latest French demand with more investigations, expulsions, and internments. Within a month the number was reduced by another 100.

At this juncture, Britain also raised her voice in protest. Because France and Austria had also been complaining about refugee activity on British soil, these last expulsions from Switzerland provoked Foreign Office protests both to France and to Switzerland: the French, after all, were not justified in complaining to Britain as long as they helped Switzerland to send refugees there; and the Swiss would ease the British problem by preventing 'the further congregation of men of this kind in England'.[14] Because Britain had so often aided Switzerland, the Swiss were willing to cooperate. Christie, now British Chargé d'Affaires in Berne, could report in mid-April that Switzerland would send no more refugees to Britain.[15] The Federal Council questioned neither the justice of the British request nor the desirability of Swiss compliance. Its response is explained both by a general policy of cooperating with foreign demands of this sort in so far as they did not damage the national honour, and by a strong desire to keep British goodwill.

On occasion the Swiss had reason to reverse roles with France with respect to refugees, requesting French internment of certain *Sonderbund* refugees. The outstanding case was that of Marilley, Bishop of Fribourg, who, after the *Sonderbund* defeat, had fled to a small town in France

[12] Christie to Palmerston, 1 August 1851 (FO 100/69)
[13] Herries to Palmerston, 19 February 1851 (FO 100/68)
[14] Palmerston to Normanby, 18 March 1851 (FO 27/983) and Palmerston to Christie, 8 April 1851 (FO 100/67)
[15] Christie to Palmerston, 15 April 1851 (FO 100/68). After this all refugees would be sent to America

67

near the Swiss border, whence he easily continued to direct the political activities of the Conservative (and clerical) party in Fribourg. The unstable politics of Fribourg had worried the Federal Council, since the Radical party was still in power there only by grace of the *Sonderbund* defeat and it was afraid to allow much Conservative political activity for fear of the Jesuits' return. The French were suspected of intriguing to put the Radicals out of power, and the central government was sensitive to any suggestions of foreign interference. Twice in 1849, the Swiss asked for the Bishop's removal to another part of France, with no success, and the pattern was repeated at the end of 1850. In 1851 the British took some interest in the question. After a short outbreak of violence there in March, Christie wrote that the Bishop's internment farther from Fribourg would probably help to alleviate tension in the canton. Palmerston immediately instructed Normanby to suggest to the French government that 'as the Swiss Gov't have shewn great Readiness to comply with the wishes of the Gov't of France in regard to French Refugees in Switzerland, it would be but a fair Return of good offices if the French Gov't were to cause the Bishop of Fribourg to remove further from the Frontiers of Switzerland'.[16] Two weeks later, however, the Federal Council had second thoughts about Marilley: the Fribourg Conservatives might be aroused to acts of desperation if he were removed. Furthermore, Christie surmised that the Fribourg Catholics were eager to have France intervene actively in their cantonal politics. In view of these considerations, Palmerston dropped the matter. By July the situation in Fribourg had calmed down sufficiently so that the Federal Council decided not to renew its request for Marilley's internment.

Toward the end of 1851 French displeasure with Switzerland increased for several reasons. The first was alleged discrimination against French Jews in the city of Basle. The city had passed an ordinance against certain business practices,[17] and this led to the expulsion of a few French traders. By an exchange of notes in 1827, France had explicitly recognized that Jews in Switzerland did not have the same privileges as Christians, so that the Swiss were on firm ground legally if not morally. France used the 1851 Basle ordinance to press the Swiss government for a revision of the 1827 agreement and, more important, for a change in the federal constitution, which guaranteed rights of establishment only for Christians. Swiss explanations would not satisfy

[16] Palmerston to Normanby, 3 April 1851 (Fo 192/11)
[17] The system of 'prête-noms' was prohibited. It had been used by some Christians as well as Jews, and by Swiss, French, or other nationals

the French. A second reason for French displeasure resulted from the *coup d'état* in early December, which caused more French refugees to flee to Switzerland.[18] An additional factor was the attitude of a new and reactionary French Minister in Berne, Count Salignac-Fénelon. Within a month of his arrival, this gentleman concluded that the federal government was weak and Swiss public opinion predominantly anti-French.

Fénelon wanted a firmer and more effective policy toward Switzerland, and his government, already irritated by the questions of refugees and Jews, was ready to take his advice. Early in January 1852 the French tightened their visa requirements for holders of Geneva passports, an unexpected move causing much inconvenience for the Swiss. Then, on 24 January, the French government sent an ultimatum to the Federal Council requiring a promise for immediate expulsion of any French refugee from Switzerland whenever the government of France might issue such a demand.[19]

Other Continental Powers also made brief appearances on the Swiss diplomatic horizon at the turn of the year. In December, perhaps annoyed by the tariff dispute with Switzerland, Baden had suggested to Prussia, Austria, Württemburg, and Bavaria that the time was favourable for military occupation of part of Switzerland, in order to force a more stringent Swiss policy toward refugees. Prussia opposed military occupation at that moment, possibly because she was jealous of an increase of Austrian or south German influence in Switzerland. Austria was willing to assist in the scheme and had approached France about it.

This threat to Switzerland from the east was reported to Granville by the French Ambassador in London, Count Walewski, in discussing the French ultimatum of 24 January. He made clear that an important reason for French pressure on Switzerland was the German menace, which was discomforting to France. The French action, Walewski said, was designed to protect the Swiss against German attacks and against the calling of a general conference on Swiss affairs. He later defended the ultimatum as self-defence because Austria had moved first.[20] Such concern for preserving Switzerland from unfriendly influence had been an ingredient of the *Sonderbund* diplomacy and of French pressures on Switzerland since 1848. Austria, in turn, was eager to be on good terms with France and to restrain the south German states from severe measures, and so she also complained about Swiss treatment of French refugees (while omitting to mention *any* Austrian refugees).

[18] See page 52
[19] Turgot to Salignac-Fénelon, 24 January 1852 (AAE: Suisse: 569)
[20] Granville to Christie, 6 February 1852 (No. 6) (FO 100/70) and Malmesbury to Cowley, 4 March 1852 (FO 519/196)

Although the Swiss did not ask for their help, the British did react to this sudden pressure on Switzerland. To Walewski, Granville expressed his hope that the Swiss would 'by moderation avoid giving just grounds for complaint ... but I must reserve my opinion as to whether the demands of France did not go far beyong [sic] what the French had a right to expect from a friendly neighbour ...'. Because France wanted Britain to persuade Switzerland to agree to the demands, Christie was instructed to point out that Swiss independence would be respected only as long as neutral duties were fulfilled, to inquire 'whether it might not be possible to find means consistent with the Swiss Laws of satisfying the reasonable demands of France', and to 'counsel them above all things to abstain from language or measures irritating the French Govt ...'.[21] The Federal Council promised to do everything legally possible to meet the French requirements. It appointed two commissioners to supervise the enforcement of decrees against refugees, but it could not agree to pledge expulsion on demand, without conducting its own investigation of each case. Fénelon disliked this British move, noting that the Swiss waited for the British message before refusing the French demands. Eager to assert French predominance in Berne, he considered that Britain was acting to save the Radicals from 'certain defeat'.[22] The French Foreign Minister, the Marquis de Turgot, also expressed the hope that Britain would not support Swiss opposition to French demands. Here was a tinge of French envy of Britain's good relations with Switzerland.

In addition to encouraging Switzerland to be as conciliatory as possible, Britain made some effort to discover the precise French aims and limits of action. Through Barman and the Federal Council, Britain heard that Napoleon did not wish to humiliate Switzerland, that 'all he wanted was the certainty that the Swiss Government would send away dangerous persons'.[23] On the other hand, Turgot threatened that France might eventually permit Austrian occupation. This was a bluff and in fact the last thing that France would tolerate in Switzerland. Short of that, France could use commercial and police restrictions to force Swiss compliance. Cowley assured Turgot that Britain would never countenance Swiss neutrality as a 'mask for proceedings hostile to the Peace'; but he pointed out that the French complaints were entirely matters of Swiss internal administration and could not really be considered grievances. In a subsequent conversation Turgot admitted the underlying motive of French policy. He compared Belgian cooperation with

[21] Granville to Christie, 6 February 1852 (No. 6 and No. 7) (FO 100/70)
[22] Salignac-Fénelon to Turgot, 17 February 1852 (AAE: Suisse: 569)
[23] Christie to Granville, 15 February 1852 (FO 100/71)

70

Swiss obstinacy, which he explained by the fact that Belgium had a 'regular' (i.e. monarchical) government and Switzerland had no government at all. He had already mentioned his dislike of the Radicals in Berne, where a cantonal election was planned for April, and he was also displeased because the Conservatives had recently been defeated in the Ticino.[24] By making demands of the Federal Council which would so strain its relations with the cantonal governments, and then by exerting economic pressure, the French hoped to make chaos of the presumedly feeble government machinery and ensure reversion to a more conservative régime. Turgot was encouraged on this line by recommendations from Fénelon that the Powers should insist on the political reorganization of Switzerland and that France might do well to risk diplomatic isolation in order to achieve it.[25] Toward the end of February Turgot seems to have realized the dangerous implications of such a policy; in another conversation with Cowley, he vehemently rejected any British right to interfere and lashed out at an allegation of Swiss determination to insult France, but in conclusion he disavowed any desire to back up the French demands with force.[26] Perhaps he had been sobered by Fénelon's discussions of possible French isolation.

Britain now began to urge a more conciliatory approach upon the French. Before leaving office, Granville instructed Cowley to point out to Turgot that the demand for a promise of arbitrary expulsion at any time in the future 'does not appear to be in accordance with the respect hitherto paid by France to the Guaranteed Independence of Switzerland' or with Napoleon's earlier statements of pacific intentions. France might be reassured that the British, 'without in the least degree taking upon themselves the character of Mediation', were advising Switzerland to be moderate.[27] Malmesbury realized that as long as Austria supported the French demands and Russia took no stand, Britain could not prevent the French from taking action, but he recommended direct discussion with Napoleon, who was thought to have some personal sympathy for the Swiss. 'He will if it suits him throw over Turgot.' Swiss neutrality and independence were 'valuable to the welfare of all Europe', and the government of France, 'so great a nation', would scarcely increase its popularity by a harsh policy against Switzerland, 'the smallest in Europe'.[28]

[24] Cowley to Granville, 21 and 22 February 1852 (FO 27/929)
[25] Salignac-Fénelon to Turgot, 21 February 1852 (AAE: Suisse: 569)
[26] Cowley to Granville, 25 February 1852 (FO 27/929)
[27] Granville to Cowley, 20 February 1852 (FO 27/924)
[28] Malmesbury to Cowley, 2 March 1852 (FO 519/196) and 5 March 1852 (FO 27/924)

British pressure had some effect. At the end of February Turgot assured Cowley that his next note to the Federal Council would be milder and would take care to show that French complaints were only against a 'false interpretation of the duties of international law'.[29] Because Fénelon was still pressing for harsh terms,[30] the new French note was greeted with some relief: Turgot did not follow his representative's advice and, furthermore, he admitted to Cowley that France could not demand a change in Swiss government without the agreement of all of the 1815 signatories. Thus the French government began its retreat from the January ultimatum.

The Swiss government also judged the second French note to be conciliatory. In turn, it answered the tangible complaints in a friendly manner, and more French refugees were expelled from Geneva.

The main question was still unsettled in mid-March, however, as Turgot had not yet dropped his demand for a promise of future expulsions from Switzerland. Fénelon's dispatches about the relations between Swiss 'socialism' and increased socialist activity in Paris continued to worry him, and he was also concerned that Swiss instability might reopen the problem of Piedmont. He threatened to refer the dispute to a five-Power conference in order to limit action by other Continental Powers.[31] Cowley reminded him that such a course would allow Prussia to raise the Neuchâtel question, which would displease France. Indeed, in view of the international situation, settlement now seemed the best course for France, and Turgot confessed to Cowley that British good offices might be 'of essential use', although France, naturally, would not retreat from her demands.[32] Walewski, in London, went further; he agreed with Malmesbury's proposal that France should ignore the part of the ultimatum alluding to future claims if the Swiss would expel certain refugees and intern others. While France was worried about restraining an Austrian intervention in Swiss affairs, the Austrian Ambassador in Paris agreed with Cowley that the French demands on Switzerland for the future were 'preposterous', but he nevertheless predicted that 'the day of explosion would come when the neighbouring states would be forced to interfere', in favour of a change

[29] Cowley to Malmesbury, 27 February 1852 (FO 27/929)
[30] He argued, among other points, that Swiss Conservatives had found moral support in the first French note. Salignac-Fénelon to Turgot, 1 March 1852 (AAE: Suisse: 570)
[31] Prussia as well as Austria had been pressing him on the Swiss question. Cowley to Malmesbury, 14 and 18 March 1852 (FO 519/209)
[32] Cowley to Malmesbury, 18 March 1852 (FO 27/930)

of Swiss government.[33] Cowley wondered whether Britain might be forced to agree to a conference in order to restrain both Austria and France. Then, to his great surprise, Turgot expressed pleasure with the British suggestions for a settlement.

The Swiss reaction to the British proposal was cool. They did not object to the internment idea, but they were uneasy about expulsions. Malmesbury urged them to accept the compromise in order to avoid any kind of Austro-Prussian interference,[34] and the British Minister in Berne, Mr Magenis, emphasized that they must remember the importance of detaching France from Austria and Prussia. The Swiss did not seem alarmed lest the Neuchâtel question be involved too. In conversation with Magenis, they claimed to prefer direct negotiations with France, and their reply to a third French note had already been prepared. However, in Paris Barman's report was somewhat different: he believed that the latest Swiss note to France was modified to eliminate anything bitter as a result of Malmesbury's proposal.

The French reaction to the last Swiss note was one of disgruntled acquiescence. To Barman, Turgot appeared very irritable and indicated that France would still try to keep the Swiss in suspense. To Cowley, Turgot volunteered that his government, 'although far from satisfied with the Swiss note ... [had decided] to refrain from answering it ...'. He even said that he found the note boring, which prompted Cowley to venture that perhaps his intentions were 'equally soporific'.[35] In the end, Turgot did not designate any individuals for expulsion, which made the whole French case seem more trumped up than ever.

THE BRITISH ROLE IN FRANCO-SWISS RELATIONS

The role of Britain in settling the dispute was important. As a nation removed geographically from Switzerland she did not arouse the same kind of jealousy in France which Austria, Sardinia, or the German states could, and she had the confidence of the Swiss. Cowley's activity in Paris was crucial. He was able to allay some of the unjustified fears of both France and Switzerland and to foster moderating considerations which might have been overlooked. The French were blind to the

[33] Cowley to Malmesbury, 21 March 1852 (FO 519/209)
[34] In conclusion, Malmesbury promised that, although Britain could offer Switzerland no physical assistance, she would continue to use her 'moral influences ... to save Switzerland from those abuses of despotic Power which are so odious to all parties in this country ...'. Malmesbury to Magenis, 22 March 1852 (FO 100/70)
[35] Cowley to Malmesbury, 11 April 1852 (FO 27/931) and 8 April 1852 (FO 519/209)

essentially conservative nature of the Swiss government which, by 1852, had established considerable control over the refugees and had long since declared itself firmly against an aggressive policy. The Swiss, for their part, were not fully aware of the precariousness of their position, and were extremely sensitive about their national honour. Early in 1853 some Swiss politicians even asserted that the French threats were backed by the British and that the Swiss government alone had saved the country. Those who knew better were unwilling to publicize a defence of Britain's role in the face of strong nationalistic feeling. Both French and Swiss governments appeared to need reminding of the more important aspects of the general European situation. Cowley had nudged the unbalancing forces back into equilibrium.

One may suppose that, with the settlement of their Swiss dispute of 1852, the French gave up their active attempts to get a change of government in Switzerland. In any case, from this point on relations between the two countries improved a great deal. The immediate problem of the Neuchâtel protocol, which was signed at the end of May, and, within the next year, the increasingly difficult Eastern Question forced France to appear to cooperate with Britain on crucial matters and kept French attention effectively diverted from serious schemes for Switzerland.

THE AUSTRO-SWISS DISPUTE, 1853–55

While France had put her extreme demands upon Switzerland to the test before the rest of Europe and had lost, the Schwarzenberg government of Austria had yet to find the right occasion. It still took a disapproving view of Swiss affairs and expected that an issue would yet arise on which Switzerland could be challenged with a more favourable result than had been achieved by France.

As we have seen, Austria was dissatisfied with the Swiss during the period of the Franco-Swiss dispute. She was particularly jealous of Prussian influence in Germany and Switzerland – and France was jealous of her in Switzerland and Italy. All three countries wanted a change of Swiss government, but none was willing to let another effect it, lest unfriendly influence predominate there. While France threatened Switzerland, Britain encouraged an Austro-Prussian concert to counteract French pressure; this combination lasted only as long as the French threat but the fact of its existence helped to persuade the French to stop threatening. In late March of 1852 Austria approached Prussia again about measures to be taken against Switzerland, but the Prussians would consider no more than a commercial blockade and passport restrictions, probably because of the importance of keeping things relatively quiet in order to court British and French support for a conference on Neuchâtel.

As before, the arena for an Austrian challenge was the Ticino, where some oversight or imprudent action could easily furnish a grievance. During the Franco-Swiss dispute, the Austrians expressed their displeasure with the election defeat of the Ticinese Conservative party, but the Swiss quickly disproved allegations of voting irregularities. In June the liberal Ticino government acted against the Federal Council's advice by suppressing several monasteries which were believed to be reactionary clerical strongholds, thus opening a long smouldering dispute with the Bishop of Como. In the autumn the Ticino government pushed matters further, seizing, first, the property of a seminary which had been particularly active politically, and then, several weeks later, a monastery, for the same reason. The latter institution had several foreign members, mostly Austrian, and these were summarily expelled from the canton. Here was a clear opening for the Austrian government. In late December the protest came; it included a demand for immediate revocation of the Ticinese decree, and a threat that if this were not done within fourteen days, Austria would expel all Ticinese – about 6,000 – residing in Lombardy.

The Federal Council was caught in a dilemma. While it regretted the imprudence of the Ticino, it had little choice but to defend an accomplished fact: it, too, claimed the right to expel any foreigner whose conduct was suspected of being hostile to Swiss institutions. In its reply to Austria, the Council offered to delay the expulsion until the nationality of the monks in question had been ascertained; it criticized the time limit as too short to allow an investigation; and it expressed the hope that any expulsions of Ticinese from Lombardy would be for individual reasons. The Swiss President was optimistic about the outcome, counting on the goodwill of Austrian officials in Lombardy towards Switzerland. A second Austrian note tended to confirm his optimism, since, although Austria regretted the Swiss attitude, she no longer insisted on the return of the Capuchin monks to the monastery, and would settle for a money indemnity. In their second reply, the Federal Council rejected the Austrian claim for an indemnity as unreasonable, since the monks owned no personal property anyway, but it did suggest annual allowances for three years.

Before the second Swiss note could reach Austria, the situation was complicated by an uprising in Milan. At the first news of this, the Federal Council sent a commissioner to supervise the preservation of Ticinese neutrality, but he was unable to prevent a fast deterioration of Austro-

Swiss relations. As Lombard unrest grew, the Austrians cut off all communications with Switzerland, setting up a blockade. The Swiss were further alarmed, first, by an Austrian order for the expulsion of all Ticinese from Lombardy in mid-February because of the Capuchins and, second, by another Austrian note protesting against Ticinese help to the Lombard insurgents and the evident inability of the Swiss government to guarantee its frontier. The Swiss answered quickly. They, too, deplored the Milan insurrection, but could not answer the charges completely without more information. The federal commissioner in the Ticino had already found that Austrian accusations were greatly exaggerated.[36]

Both Austria and Switzerland hastened to inform the other Powers of the situation, each eager to have support against the other. The Austrian representative in Berne claimed that his government was seeking the support of France and Britain; however, the British records yield little evidence of Austrian persuasive efforts. In mid-January Lord Westmorland, then British Minister in Vienna, reported strong Austrian feeling against the 'most harsh and unjustifiable' expulsion of the Capuchins; in his opinion, Austria would never be satisfied with the Swiss attitude.[37] Since, concurrently with pressure on Switzerland, Austria was protesting to Britain about treatment of foreign refugees, she was scarcely in a position to enlist British support against the Swiss.

In the express hope of getting the British to agree that the Ticino had been unjustly accused about the Milan outbreak, the Swiss took care to keep the British government fully informed, but they did not immediately strike a responsive chord with the Foreign Office. Because of the Austrian position in the growing Eastern question, Britain wanted to avoid a Great Power discussion of either the Neuchâtel or the refugee question. Also, because of the recent Austrian protests about refugees, Britain was not in a favourable position to help the Swiss vis-à-vis Austria. For these reasons, Clarendon sent no dispatches to Switzerland until mid-March, and then he was very restrained, emphasizing the obligations of neutrality and expressing only qualified satisfaction with reports on Ticinese activities. Barman and Cowley discussed the prob-

[36] The Ticino government had seized arms destined to help the Lombards, and, of the twelve Lombard refugees then residing in the Ticino, only one was implicated in the Milan insurrection – and he had already been expelled. However, the Federal Council was dismayed to learn that the Ticino government had known about insurgent preparations for two months, and had done little about it. The Council could do no more than send the Ticinese a message criticizing such negligence of national obligations
[37] Westmorland to Clarendon, 18 January 1853 (FO 7/416)

76

lem, but Barman could glean no encouragement about British support from Cowley. The Federal Council was warned that Britain might not be as interested in Swiss affairs as she had been the previous year.

While the British may have encouraged Swiss sobriety by withholding any expression of support, they none the less disapproved of Austrian policy toward Switzerland, and they did make their disapproval clearly understood to the French government. As on previous occasions when Swiss security was endangered, the Foreign Office would try to influence continental politics through France. Recent Austrian policy to Switzerland annoyed the French and, despite their own similar policy of only a year before, the French government was initially unsympathetic toward the Austrian measures. The French Foreign Minister, now Drouyn de Lhuys, criticized Austria for 'drawing the cord too tight' in Lombardy, because he feared it might even force an alliance between Switzerland and Piedmont, a formidable coalition which could pose a threat to France.[38] French jealousy of Austrian influence in Switzerland persisted, and it was Britain's business to encourage it. When Cowley asked what France would do if Austria occupied the Ticino, Drouyn de Lhuys was vague about the limits of French action to preserve Swiss independence; after all, if Austria could enter Switzerland, there was no reason why France could not enter Belgium. Thus, the fear of French expansionism which had been uppermost in the thinking of the other Powers in 1852 was raised again. Although probably not taken very seriously, this fear must have been one reason for the British decision to suggest Franco-British cooperation to work out a settlement of the Austro-Swiss question.

At the same time, Austrian pressure on Sardinia about refugee policy led to some disagreement between Switzerland and Sardinia. The Swiss were indignant because Sardinia was furnishing passports for Switzerland to Italian refugees, whom the Swiss were trying to keep out. They complained vigorously and threatened to refuse visas to all Sardinians if the Turin government were not more circumspect. The two countries soon settled the matter, and the settlement served to strengthen the Swiss case before Europe, since Britain, in discussions with France and Austria, could cite the quick resolution as 'strong testimony to the general strictness of the Federal Government on the subject of Refugees ...'.[39]

The Austro-Swiss correspondence continued, while Europe looked on. In early March the Federal Council protested to Austria about the

[38] Cowley to Clarendon, 7 March 1853 (FO 27/964)
[39] Christie to Clarendon, 17 March 1853 (FO 100/79)

77

mass expulsions from Lombardy, and it refused to assume any responsibility for prejudicial complications from the measure. While the Swiss had proved that Mazzini was not in the Ticino as Austria had alleged, the governments of the Ticino and the Grisons had arrested some Swiss who were implicated in the uprising, and planned to try them for their activity in Lombardy. The Federal Council decided against expelling all Austrians from the Ticino, as a retaliatory move, and it also rejected mobilization, in the belief that Austria would be forced to consult the 1815 signatories before venturing to occupy the Ticino. Thus the Swiss responded to Austria in a fairly conciliatory way at this stage in the dispute. The Swiss President optimistically attributed to pride the Austrian evasion of the Swiss request for specific information, but his hopes were dashed when the blockade was strengthened some days later. On 21 March the Swiss repeated their protest against the Austrian blockade, and they suggested negotiation to settle both the refugee and the Capuchin questions.

By the end of March several facts pointed to an underlying Austrian aim of changing the Swiss government, similar to the French aim early in 1852. Clerical instigation was evident in a brief outbreak which occurred in the Ticino, and plans for a second were discovered. Concurrently the Milan press printed several articles which supported Austrian policy toward Switzerland and recommended a change of Swiss government. Refugees from the Ticino were known to be plotting with Austrian authorities for their kind of (very conservative) Ticinese government. Indeed, knowledge of similar schemes had led the cantonal government to expel the Capuchins in the first place. A month or so before the dispute began, the British Minister had written of some groups in Switzerland which were working against the 1848 constitution with the undoubted encouragement of Austria.[40] In the light of these developments, it is not surprising that the Swiss attitude toward Austria soon became less conciliatory.

Although the French government had retreated from its strong stand against the liberal Swiss government in 1852, it was still under some reactionary pressure to cooperate with Austria. Indications of French support for Switzerland were seen in the negotiation of the Neuchâtel protocol and in the dismissal of Turgot as Foreign Minister, but the British realized that some factions in France still wanted to advance Swiss Catholicism and to encourage the Swiss Conservative party. Fribourg was the sore point where such French policy was manifested.

[40] Buchanan to Malmesbury, 6 October 1852 (FO 100/74)

It so happened that in March 1853, when the Austrian question had clearly become serious, Fribourg politics were also in a particularly unsettled state. In spite of French criticism of Austrian policy in Switzerland and declarations of friendship for liberal opinions, Britain could not be sure that France was averse in principle to Austrian policy.

Thus the British realized the necessity for more diplomatic activity, and the Swiss, by early April, also felt a greater need for diplomatic help. When the Swiss Chargé d'Affaires in Vienna had asked for Westmorland's good offices, they were gladly promised, and British discussions about Switzerland were renewed, particularly in Paris. Cowley again suggested that Bishop Marilley's removal might help, but Drouyn de Lhuys responded merely that his government would consider it. Clarendon complimented Drouyn de Lhuys because France was 'favourable to the maintenance and development of liberal Institutions' in Switzerland and noted the dangerous possibility that Austria might be able to get a 'hermetic blockade' from Basle to Austria. If France considered the Swiss explanations to be satisfactory, would she cooperate with Britain on the matter?[41] The first French response was favourable, but two days later Drouyn de Lhuys backtracked, saying that France had already made her objections known to Austria and would continue to do so. The French did send another message to the Austrian government, but their over-all defence of the Swiss case was very weak. Cowley later noticed that Drouyn de Lhuys spoke about the Swiss question in a different vein with representatives of Prussia, Russia, and Austria. Without strong cooperation from France, the British note to Austria made little impression on the Austrian Foreign Minister, Count Buol. None the less, despite the dubious results of his diplomacy so far, Clarendon at last let the Swiss know of his satisfaction with their 'exertions ... to fulfill the duties of good neighbourhood ...'.[42]

The attitudes of both Austria and Switzerland now began to stiffen. Another Austrian note to the Swiss made even more unreasonable demands, one of which was an engagement for the future, reminiscent of the French ultimatum of 1852. The Swiss were still willing to negotiate, but, as this note was soon followed by a small insurrection in Fribourg, they were even less willing to make concessions. The Austrian position was also hardening. While their Minister in Berne complained about Swiss obstinacy, his government persuaded some of the south German states to put pressure on Switzerland in favour of Austria. Britain

[41] Clarendon to Cowley, 5 April 1853 (FO 27/956)
[42] Clarendon to Christie, 19 April 1853 (FO 100/77)

countered in Germany with a defence of Swiss policy, but only after German notes of protest had been presented to the Federal Council.[43]

British diplomatic efforts on behalf of the Swiss were frustrated by the French at this stage. Cowley hoped that the French would not demand more for Austria than had satisfied themselves in 1852, but he could not be sure. In Vienna Westmorland heard that France was urging Switzerland to conform to the Austrian demands and had even approved the Austrian enlistment of south German support against Switzerland. France would tolerate measures which were intended to further the conservative cause in Switzerland only as long as she was persuaded that Austria was not planning a military occupation and, in order to gain French support, Austria surely could forego making the threat of a military occupation. The French were perhaps more tolerant of the Austrian proposals because of their interest in Fribourg affairs, and because of recent complaints of their own about refugees, in both Basle and Geneva.

The Foreign Office kept up its attempts to steer the French toward opposition to Austria, both directly and through continued pressure on Switzerland. Clarendon urged the French 'not to support Austria in requiring from the Swiss Gov't conditions which they will not be able to fulfil. The Swiss Gov't offered what France required, and have kept their word ... [thus] Austria would not be justified in attempting to impose ... conditions of a more stringent nature.'[44] Although the federal government was acting on both the Fribourg situation and the French complaints about refugees, Cowley continued to press on Barman the necessity for Switzerland to do her utmost to 'keep well' with France, even, if necessary, by making some assurance for the future, because in this question France could be more helpful than Britain for Switzerland.[45]

Finally, after the next Swiss note to Austria was available in France, in early May, Cowley reported another switch in French policy. Austria then made another bid for French support, only to be advised by Drouyn de Lhuys to accept the Swiss assurances. Still, because 'the future good behaviour of the Swiss may much depend on their not being now driven into offensive acts or language', Clarendon continued to send pro-Swiss arguments to the French.[46] As one manifestation of Austrian ill will to

---

[43] Fortunately, the German messages were much milder than Austria might have wished, with qualifications distinctly in favour of the Swiss
[44] Clarendon to Cowley, 3 May 1853 (FO 27/957)
[45] Cowley to Clarendon, 9 May 1853 (FO 27/967)
[46] Clarendon to Cowley, 13 May 1853 (FO 519/169)

Switzerland, he cited the inflexible attitude of their representative in Berne. If Austria had no regard for the good disposition of the Federal Council, made no allowance for Swiss internal difficulties, and instigated complaints from other neighbours, there would be no end to the question. Thanks to Cowley's constant but tactful prodding, France moved closer to the British line. In response to another British query about the Fribourg question and the removal of Bishop Marilley, Drouyn de Lhuys towards the end of May seemed more cooperative, and he criticized any Austrian policy which might drive the Swiss to extremes, saying that Austria should try to make the best of things as France had done. Cowley realistically speculated that the changed approach of the French was due to a suspicion of an agreement between Austria, Russia, and Prussia against Switzerland which would be disadvantageous to France.

This French shift contributed to an important turning point in the dispute. Soon after another Swiss note was delivered to Austria, Buol recalled his Minister from Berne. The Swiss responded immediately by breaking off diplomatic relations with Austria, a move which took Buol by surprise. By then, the Austrian government had been urged on several occasions by Westmorland to conciliate the Swiss. More significant from the Austrian point of view were the attitudes of the other Powers. Despite anxiety over Neuchâtel Prussia was cool towards the Austrian position;[47] the other German states had not provided the enthusiastic support for which Austria had hoped; and France had again voiced some hesitations. Consequently, Buol quickly explained that Austria did not intend to break diplomatically with Switzerland. With this assurance, the Swiss Chargé d'Affaires withdrew his 'note of rupture'[48] and the Federal Council again rejected a mobilization proposal. Thus both sides contributed to a slight relaxation of tension, and the problem of negotiating a settlement could be tackled.

Despite professions of good intentions by both the Swiss and the Austrians, they could not agree on even the preliminaries to a settlement. Because the Federal Council was restricted by the 1850 Federal Assembly decision against initiation of any negotiations, it was willing to send its commissioner to Vienna to negotiate only if Austria would empower a representative to conduct preliminary discussions in Lombardy. Britain strongly urged Austria to accept this plan but Buol again dodged, pleading that any proposal should come directly from the Swiss and insisting that all the negotiations should be in Vienna. A memo-

[47] See page 58
[48] Westmorland to Clarendon, 31 May 1853 (FO 7/419)

randum on the question, drawn up by Christie, also included the Swiss suggestion of preliminary discussions in Lombardy. It was approved by the Federal Council, and by the Foreign Office for use in Vienna, but Austria would agree only to certain parts of it. In Paris Cowley tried vainly to persuade the Swiss to drop their insistence on preliminary discussions in Lombardy; the Swiss were too proud to be willing to take the risk of failure. This was to be a big stumbling block in the negotiations. Clearly, if Austria really wanted a settlement, she could afford to agree to some preliminary discussions. On the other hand, if the Swiss knew how much of their position was negotiable, they could concede their request for discussion in Lombardy.

The Swiss position was unclear for two reasons. First, although the Federal Council had been forced to defend the Ticino action towards the Capuchins, little serious discussion had taken place between the federal and cantonal governments to decide specifically what the terms for negotiation should be. Questions of the size of the indemnity and who was to pay were referred and postponed for months, while Austria and the other Powers became alternately exasperated and forgetful of the whole business. Swiss national feeling, which would brook no defeat at the hand of a Power of whatever size, ran strong at this time, and it contributed to the other main problem – leadership. Unfortunately, the Swiss President for 1853 was not as far-sighted as his predecessor; he was easily influenced by those around him and his vagueness and inability to persuade his colleagues to a positive course of action contributed to the delays. Austria demanded more from Switzerland than might have been consonant with a sincere desire for settlement but, on the other hand, the federal government would have been in a firmer position had it worried less about its dignity and survival as an institution.

Although the more important delaying factors were probably Austrian and Swiss unwillingness to make any more concessions, the lack of coordination of Anglo-French policy at this stage undoubtedly contributed also to the postponement of a settlement. Even if the French were unalterably persuaded to support the Swiss position – and that is doubtful[49] – they did not consider themselves bound to cooperate with Britain. In early June they made their own offer of help to the Swiss in negotiations with Austria. At the end of the month the Austrian representative told Cowley that France had all but completed the arrange-

---

[49] Fénelon still wrote about his attempts to urge the Swiss to accept the Austrian demands. One example is Salignac-Fénelon's letter to Drouyn de Lhuys on 3 June 1853 (AAE: Suisse: 574)

ments for a settlement. The Foreign Office was apparently not disconcerted by this story since the Eastern Question was by then absorbing an increasing amount of attention and other signs of French cooperation were more evident. Furthermore, the Austrian boast was premature, for the French effort failed. Although France and Britain urged both Austria and Switzerland repeatedly to take advantage of the favourable moment to settle their dispute, British advice was probable as suspect in Austria as French advice was in Switzerland, with the result that the two could not work effectively together.

After the failures of France and England to promote a settlement, the two Great Powers refrained from offering more help. During the summer a few more conciliatory moves were made by the Swiss, but none came from Austria. The Swiss approached Sardinia, unofficially, about the possibility of transferring the monks to a Sardinian monastery, but, as Austria did not appreciate the idea, it was eventually dropped. The Federal Council also suggested that if the blockade were withdrawn, it would favour sending a negotiator directly to Vienna. In spite of warm British support for this overture, Buol brushed it aside. Public opinion in Switzerland was further aroused against Austria by the discovery of plans for another uprising in the Ticino. The official Austrian report on the Milan insurrection was completed in July and, because the Swiss were not given a copy, they concluded that Austria had found little evidence against them but would not admit it. In effect, the Austrians forced the discussions to a standstill at this point.

Austria's uncompromising attitude was based on an expectation that other international disputes, particularly the Eastern Question, would soon be settled, so that she could force the Swiss to accept her terms. Between 1 June and 30 September 1853 the Foreign Office sent at least seventeen messages to Austria urging settlement with Switzerland, but their frequency diminished after that, as the Eastern Question took up an increasing amount of attention. One British argument used a growing number of examples of good Swiss intentions and strong action; another said that it would be good strategy in the east for Austria to have Switzerland 'beholden to her for a generous policy'.[50]

Indeed, for many Powers the Eastern Question had become an over-riding consideration. The French feared that the Swiss were delaying settlement in order to improve their negotiating advantage if Austria became tied down in the east. In mid-August, Cowley heard that Austria had been trying to influence leading Swiss citizens to persuade their government to settle, by threatening that as soon as the Eastern Question

[50] Clarendon to Westmorland, 15 June 1853 (FO 7/413)

83

was over, Austria would deal with the Swiss 'in a very summary manner' which would bring about the destruction of Swiss institutions.[51] In this view, Austria was restrained in her Swiss policy by developments in the east and, expecting that dispute to be settled soon, delayed serious negotiations with the Swiss on issues of the refugees and the Capuchins in the hope of later being able to obtain a change in Swiss government. The Eastern Question, however, was not quickly settled, so that the Swiss were saved from more drastic Austrian action. In their relations with Austria after the summer of 1854, the western Powers were primarily concerned to enlist her cooperation to check Russia. No room remained for manœuvring about the Swiss question, now a decidedly minor international issue.

Consequently, in the course of the next year the dispute received relatively little attention outside Switzerland,[52] and within that country the stalemate continued. In December the reputation of Austria was blackened still more in the Ticino by a spy trial which brought to light more evidence of the false information with which the Austrian government was supplied, much as in the case of the Franco-Swiss dispute. In January Christie suggested that the appointment of a conciliatory Austrian representative in Berne would do a great deal to remove Swiss suspicions; he remarked that 'a great country can better afford to make concessions than a small one. Where the former will get credit for magnanimity, the latter will be only suspected of fear; and the honour of a small nation is all the more precious to her on account of the inferiority of her physical resources.'[53] In other words, Switzerland would not easily be able to take the first step to break the stalemate.

In the late spring of 1854 the Austrian attitude became more flexible. Several considerations may have contributed to this. In correspondence with Vienna, Clarendon placed his government even more firmly on the Swiss side, telling Austria of 'the sincere regret of H.M. Govt that Switzerland should be pressed to make concessions which are inconsistent with her dignity and independence and which appear unnecessary for the objects sought by Austria'.[54] A new factor for Austria to consider, in the face of the recent formal alliance between France and Britain, was a threat of western support for liberalism in Italy; Austria would be willing to settle with Switzerland if she had assurance from France which

[51] Cowley to Clarendon, 19 August 1853 (FO 27/973)
[52] Austria did make another proposal, in March 1854, but, as it was merely a variant on previous demands, the Swiss still could not agree
[53] Christie to Clarendon, 25 January 1854 (FO 100/85)
[54] Clarendon to Westmorland, 5 April 1854 (FO 7/428)

would enable her to reduce the size of her army in Lombardy.[55] Disapproving of Austrian policy in Italy, but very eager for her cooperation in the Crimea, Napoleon then made some vague promissory statements which pleased Austria. It was to the advantage of the western Powers to have the Austrian army free for action in the east and to make Austria indebted to them for effecting a settlement with the Swiss. It was to Austria's advantage also to have western support for her interest in whatever settlement was made in the Crimean war. For these reasons, and after the Swiss provided more evidence of their determination to control their neutrality,[56] the Austrians at last showed some signs of a willingness to compromise by easing the blockade.

In the summer of 1854 both sides removed obstacles to an agreement. The Austrians appointed a new and conciliatory Chargé d'Affaires at their legation in Berne. In Switzerland, a useful conference at last took place between the federal and the cantonal governments to discuss the conditions for a settlement.

Progress towards agreement was interrupted in late August by another protest from the unpredictable French about refugees in Geneva. As on previous occasions, the federal government found the complaints to be based on exaggerated reports of French spies. France failed to get Sardinian cooperation for this move and, under pressure from the Foreign Office, was forced to drop the matter. This brief Franco-Swiss spat gave Austria another opening to propose a joint protest to Switzerland, but France declined, with relieved British approval. Clarendon quickly sent full information about this correspondence, including news of French and British approval of Swiss explanations, to Austria; Buol expressed his satisfaction with the communication and expected that the dispute with Switzerland would soon be over.

The outlook for Switzerland was now more hopeful. The French government was not much influenced by its reactionary representative in Switzerland, and Austria actually showed some desire to settle the matter. During the autumn the new Austrian representative in Berne began informal negotiations on the outstanding issues. In early November Austria officially proposed a conference in Milan, rather than Vienna, to discuss the Capuchins and the blockade. The Swiss found it difficult to believe in the good faith of the Austrians and considered putting them to the test by giving a negative answer. The British strongly urged the Swiss to cooperate, and in early December, with the

[55] Cowley to Clarendon, 25 February 1854 (FO 27/1008)
[56] In early June the Swiss discovered some documents about more Italian intrigues, and immediately gave the information to Austria

reluctant assent of the Ticino government, the Federal Council agreed to the Austrian proposal. Settlement of the dispute was still, however, uncertain: both Britain and Austria were irritated by Swiss criticism of the Austrian plan, which did in fact meet earlier Swiss demands, and by continuing Swiss internal disagreement.

The Milan conference opened at the end of January. In mid-February President Furrer reported that Swiss hopes for a settlement were 'very far from being realized' because of Austrian insistence on linking the Capuchin question with the jurisdictional dispute between the Ticino and the Bishop of Como, and because of the Austrian demand for an excessive indemnity (half a million francs), as contrasted with the absence of any Swiss request for compensation for the 6,000 Ticinese expelled from Lombardy. Furrer leapt to the conclusion that Austria would be satisfied with nothing less than a change of government in the Ticino and threatened to recall the Swiss negotiators from Milan – unless, of course, Britain could persuade Austria to yield. He did suggest a compromise: if Austria would refrain from discussing the ecclesiastical question and agree to a lower indemnity, Switzerland would admit that the expulsion of the Capuchins had been unwise. Clarendon acted quickly. Westmorland was instructed to make Buol aware of British disappointment with Austrian terms, as being 'so exorbitant and utterly unacceptable', and Cowley persuaded Drouyn de Lhuys to press Buol in the same way.[57] Because Buol at that moment needed British and French cooperation in his attempt to settle the Eastern Question at the forthcoming conference in Vienna, he was forced to concede on the Swiss dispute. New Austrian instructions were sent to Milan and an agreement was signed by the end of March, to the satisfaction of all the governments concerned. The Swiss paid an indemnity of only 115,000 francs and the blockade was raised.[58]

With the main points of difference resolved, the others, such as extradition and the boundary, could be discussed later in a more friendly spirit. The jurisdiction of the Bishop of Como was a thornier problem and, moreover, one which in theory did not directly concern Austria. Because the 1855 settlement with Austria made possible a considerable stabilization of local politics in the Ticino, the Swiss position for negotiating with the papal representative was strengthened. The matter took years to settle. In the course of the negotiations, the Swiss called

[57] Clarendon to Westmorland, 26 February 1855 (FO 7/446) and Cowley to Clarendon, 7 March 1855 (FO 27/1064)
[58] 'Convention entre la Suisse et l'Autriche, touchant l'affaire du Tessin ...' (RO, V, 83-5)

on Britain to mediate several times, the first request coming soon after the Austro-Swiss settlement. Clarendon preferred not to interfere, 'particularly in matters connected with Religion ...' and Palmerston agreed that abstention was best, unless Swiss independence was directly threatened.[59] In later instances when the question was raised by the Swiss, the Papal Nuncio, or the Austrian Minister, Britain persisted in staying out of the discussions, except to encourage all to be moderate. The position of Austria in Europe became more and more precarious in the years after the Crimean war, so that she was never able to reassert dangerous pretensions to influence Switzerland.

COMPARISON OF FRENCH AND AUSTRIAN POLICY TOWARD SWITZERLAND

It is interesting to compare the French and Austrian disputes with Switzerland. Both challengers based their demands on reports of unreliable spies who wrote convincingly about Swiss political instability and about an almost rampant Swiss socialism, especially among refugees who often did not exist. Both France and Austria had ultramontanist elements at home. Both hoped to force a change in Swiss government but, in the end, were forced to recognize that it was a vain hope. External power pressures played a large part in preventing the success of any unilateral Great Power manœuvring to change the Swiss government. In both cases solutions were greatly facilitated by British diplomacy.

With so many points of similarity, it is rather surprising that Austria learned nothing from the French experience. Several factors may explain this. First, Austria perhaps sensed a continuing French temptation to intervene and thought that it might be exploited. Second, her officials were predisposed by their political ideology to persist. Third, the French government was more willing than the Austrian to listen to, and to accept, British advice. While the Austrian dispute took over two years to settle, the French demands were silenced in a few months, because of more pressing power interests during the Crimean war and because of the orientation of the alliance system. It has been suggested that because, until 1854, the Powers had been organized primarily to prevent French expansion, the Crimean war involved a fundamental reorientation.[60] Thus, the old system, or the attitudes which preceded it, was still

[59] Clarendon to Gordon, 26 June 1855 (Fo 100/90) and Palmerston's note on Gordon to Clarendon, 15 June 1855 (Fo 100/92)

[60] Gavin B. Henderson, *Crimean War Diplomacy and other Historical Essays* (Glasgow, 1947), p154, ff.

effective in checking French designs on Switzerland in 1852 but was ineffective the following year against Austria. By 1855, enlistment of Austrian support by the western Powers was less urgent and, in her isolation and desire for a voice in the peace settlement, Austria was impelled to give up her demands on Switzerland.

British policy of non-involvement in Swiss affairs except in serious situations, was reaffirmed. Britain stayed out of the immediate post-1848 skirmishes as long as Swiss independence was not seriously menaced, which meant as long as the constellations of power on the Continent prevented a threat. From 1848 to 1851 enough diversions occurred to keep the Continental Powers out of irreparable mischief in Switzerland. When France decided to force the refugee issue in 1852, British diplomacy was equal to the challenge. Similarly the Prussian demands concerning Neuchâtel and the Austrian accusations based on refugee questions some months later were turned aside. By relaying reliable information about Switzerland and by emphasizing fears, threats, and advantages which directed attention away from Switzerland, Britain took crucial steps to redress the balance. The Swiss usually were willing to accept British help, and, indeed, came to rely on it; without it, maintenance of their neutrality would have been more painful for them and for their neighbours. Much as the Swiss would have liked to play the more independent part of a larger Power, they did not spurn British advice, a quality in the Anglo-Swiss relationship which the other Powers at times regarded with some jealousy.

FRANCO-SWISS DISCUSSIONS OF 1856 AND 1858

When questions about refugees in Switzerland were raised in subsequent years, mainly by France, they were treated with less alarm on all sides. The first instance came in early 1856, when France expressed concern over the application of a former refugee, General Klapka, for citizenship in Geneva. The Federal Council respected the French point of view and the French, recognizing the constitutional problem for the Swiss, did not press the matter. Early in the discussions Clarendon advised the Federal Council to be cautious, but that was the extent of British intervention.

The next occasion for complaints against Switzerland was the Orsini incident, in January 1858. After this famous attempt by an Italian refugee to assassinate Napoleon III, France protested very strongly to both Britain and Switzerland. Of the Swiss, the French demanded internment for all refugees in Geneva without exception. The Federal Council reacted calmly to the message; it was eager to show its disapproval of the Orsini incident and it was also glad to have an opportunity to wring more action from the Genevese police. The British defence of their refugee policy naturally helped the Swiss. The situation became less friendly when the French increased pressure on Switzerland for complete compliance to their demands. Their Minister's daily visits to the Swiss President became annoying and the Swiss press grew hostile to France. The French Foreign Minister at first told Cowley that 'nothing [was] ... more satisfactory than the ... intentions of the federal Government ...',[61] but he became irritated when the preliminary federal report on the matter included an admission by the French Vice-Consul in Geneva that the refugees there gave no cause for suspicion. At this point France stiffened her visa requirements and the inconvenience which this caused the Swiss became a more absorbing topic of discussion than the refugee demands. Some refugees were eventually expelled from Geneva and the French made no more demands.

The new French passport and visa regulations required all travellers to France from Switzerland – British as well as Swiss – to pass through Geneva or Berne to obtain a visa. The Swiss were highly indignant about the inconveniences but their initial protests were of no avail. Cowley's attempts to get exemptions for British travellers were also fruitless. The French did propose to appoint two new consular agents for Basle and La Chaud-de-Fonds, to offer more facilities for issuing visas, but this proposal was greeted by another outcry in Switzerland, where it was feared that these would simply be more centres for French spies.[62] The Swiss had not forgotten the function of French agents in previous years. In subsequent negotiations, the French made some procedural concession over the visa question, but when they named a known former secret police agent as one of the consular agents, the Federal Council was more reluctant than ever to give its approval and the French were forced to replace the suspected agent with another nominee.

The British government wanted the Swiss to accept the French offer to open more consular offices, not so much because the arrangement would relieve the inconvenience for the Swiss themselves as because it would help British travellers, whose number in Switzerland was increasing. The Foreign Office warned the Swiss that they might be faced with diplomatic isolation if they continued to resist, but none the less Fénelon wrote repeatedly of British encouragement of Swiss resistance. The British representative at that time, Mr Gordon, had been in Berne for

[61] Cowley to Clarendon, 29 January 1858 (FO 27/1242)
[62] Swiss suspicions were well founded, as the official correspondence of Salignac-Fénelon provides ample evidence of this (AAE: Suisse: 585)

several years, and he was probably oversympathetic when the Swiss protested that France was interfering in their internal affairs by sending more spies. At length, Malmesbury, back at the Foreign Office, became impatient with the number of dispatches from Switzerland in this vein. In keeping with improved Anglo-French relations, he instructed Gordon to 'abstain from encouraging discontent against a necessity'.[63] The Federal Council finally gave in and approved the new consular agencies.

In this series of discussions, the British role was a quiet and acquiescent one *vis-à-vis* France, because France was not seriously threatening Switzerland. Some effort was needed to persuade the Swiss that this was the case, and that French policy had some justification. It is interesting that the discussions between the Pope and the Swiss about the jurisdiction of the Bishop of Como were active in 1858 and that Britain again specifically refused to interfere. The Swiss could expect little help from Britain on these minor issues which did not endanger their independence.

[63] Malmesbury to Gordon, 6 May 1858 (FO 100/114)

CHAPTER SIX

The Swiss Position during the Crimean War

SWISS NEUTRALITY FACED WITH WAR

IN THE YEARS after 1848 the European Powers came to accept the stronger federal status of Switzerland, more independent though it was, because of lack of agreement on the terms or purpose of collective intervention. Unilateral intervention was too great a risk in view of the balance of power factors and interests that prevailed. Swiss independence and liberalism were detested by Austria, Prussia, and Russia, and this was one of the factors in European politics which contributed to the frequent soundings of the balance, using as issues both the Neuchâtel and refugee questions. The passage of time brought some alleviation of the refugee problem. Thus, by default of action, the Continental Powers appeared to accept the new *status quo*, although still hoping for a strengthening of Swiss conservatism.

The outbreak of the Crimean war brought new tests for Swiss and continental policies regarding neutrality. Absolute neutrality, or even what is today called non-alignment, was more difficult to maintain in war than in peace. Indeed, the extent of the neutrality which the Powers might require was uncertain. Britain, a critical party in the European balance, had always favoured the maintenance of Swiss independence, yet her respect for strict Swiss neutrality in time of war was another question.

Official Swiss policy appeared unhesitatingly neutral. After Britain and France declared war on Russia in March 1854, the Swiss government immediately published an affirmation of its neutral position, which the Allies considered satisfactory. The Swiss also agreed to an Anglo-French circular about the rights and duties of neutrals, although some discussion ensued about the difference between sea and land blockades.[1]

[1] The Federal Council to the British Legation, 15 April 1854 (SFA: Missiven des Bundesraths, März-April 1854)

91

However, popular opinion in Switzerland was not as impartial as were the official government pronouncements. Feeling was already strongly directed against the autocratic governments of eastern Europe since, in the spring of 1854, the dispute with Austria had reached a deadlock. Ever since the *Sonderbund* defeat, Russia had appeared to associate herself with the Power challenging Swiss independence. Furthermore, public opinion had always strongly favoured Britain and, by 1854, anti-French feeling had diminished. Thus it is no surprise that a few Swiss extremists even suggested that their country should join France and Britain in the 'last war'.[2] To some extent Britain exploited this favourable Swiss opinion, insisting on the enforcement of 'neutrality' against any activity in Switzerland that was considered prejudicial to the Allied cause, but pursuing distinctly partisan activities there herself when it suited her own interest.

BELLIGERENT PRESSURES ON SWITZERLAND

For Swiss commercial interests the effects of the war were noticeable. In general the war worked to their advantage, since they benefited from the increased demand and prices for their manufactured goods. Although there was one report of Allied seizure of non-contraband Swiss goods on a Russian vessel, this aspect of the war did not pose much of a problem, since most Swiss trade was carried by British, French, or non-belligerent vessels. None the less, in the form of British interference and restrictions on Swiss communications with the outside world, the war did bring some tangible disadvantages. Swiss applications to the British government for export licences were usually granted, but two difficulties arose. The first, relatively minor, was over the port of destination through which certain strategic goods, such as machinery, were to be sent. The second was about the amount of saltpetre imported by the Swiss for making gunpowder. After less than six months of war, the Board of Trade noted a distinct increase in Swiss imports of this commodity. The Swiss countered British enquiries on the subject with various explanations: that railroad projects were using an especially large amount of explosives; that traditional Swiss rifle practice diminished supplies; and that a Zurich stockpile had recently exploded. The government controlled gunpowder manufacture, but not its sale, so that Swiss merchants could have been exporting this contraband. Be-

[2] Georg Hoffman, 'Die grossbritannische Schweizer-Legion im Krimkrieg, Werbung und Schicksal', *Zeitschrift für Schweizerische Geschichte*, Bd. 22, Zurich, 1942, p575

cause the Federal Council would not supply Britain with a satisfactory written assurance that the saltpetre would be used exclusively for Swiss military arsenals, this British export to Switzerland was temporarily stopped in 1854 and it was limited to small amounts for the next two years. Britain's main purpose, in this instance, was clearly to restrict Russian supplies of gunpowder, rather than to enforce disinterestedly a neutral Swiss position.

British policy toward Swiss neutrality in the economic sphere tended to require benevolence in other respects as well. In July 1854 the Federal Council was urged to prevent quotation of the Russian loan in the Swiss money market; since Switzerland had as yet no public stock exchange, compliance with this request was easy. At the end of 1855 Britain succeeded in getting a statement about the Russian loan printed in the semi-official Swiss newspaper. The British government considered its own purchase of army equipment in Switzerland, particularly clothing, as a normal enough procedure. A few Swiss offered British officials inventions for new weapons, but the offers were seldom accepted; in one instance, the British decision was clearly dependent on whether a similar offer had been made to the Russians and whether they had accepted it.

Russia appears neither to have made the same use of Swiss services as Britain, nor to have protested against British activity in the neutral country. During the war the Foreign Office heard rumours about Russian agents stirring up Italian refugees in Geneva, which would embarrass both France and Austria, and about Russian recruitment of Swiss technical personnel, but they were apparently untrue. Not until the summer of 1855 did the Russian government decide to reopen its Berne legation, which had been closed in protest since the defeat of the *Sonderbund*. The Russians at last realized that the neutral country might be useful as a propaganda centre and listening post.

The Russian decision threw the Swiss and Allied governments into some confusion, because the Russian Minister of 1847 was to return. They feared that he might raise problems of credentials and reclaim his senior position as Dean of the Berne diplomatic corps. When Clarendon heard of the renewal of Russian diplomatic relations with the Swiss, he took pains to let the Swiss know his approval of their restrained reaction, although he added that 'Her Majesty's Government ... [does not claim] any right to express an opinion upon the independent Action of the Federal Council'.[3] The Swiss were determined not to allow any procedural irregularities. When new credentials were presented in Russian as well as in the usual diplomatic language, Swiss hesitations about

[3] Clarendon to Gordon, 6 June 1855 (FO 100/90)

93

accepting them were allayed first by a Russian statement of 'complete adhesion to the new order of things established in Switzerland in 1848',[4] and then by assurances from Britain herself about their acceptability.

The question of precedence was discussed in Paris and London, as well as in Berne. Until the Russian Minister returned, the French and British Ministers respectively were senior. For the Allied Powers to yield the deanship to their enemy might be considered humiliating. Clarendon was inclined to insist on French seniority and France initially agreed, supported by Fénelon's argument that, for the sake of Swiss public opinion, the Allies should make no concessions to Russia. After more facts about the Russian position came to light, Britain and France were willing to leave the decision to the Swiss, who decided in Russia's favour. In this relatively minor question, the Swiss were eventually encouraged to make an independent judgment, and Britain accepted the decision. A principle of equal treatment of all belligerents by a neutral was respected, at least in this rather theoretical realm, but the Russians were too late to insist on Swiss neutrality toward Britain.

THE BRITISH SWISS LEGION

The British government had embarked on its most obvious exploitation of Swiss sympathy and 'neutrality' well before the Russian return to Berne. Since Parliament, despite strong public opinion favouring the war, was reluctant to conscript British subjects to fight in the Crimea, it passed the Foreign Enlistment Act in December 1854 to enable the government, as often on past occasions, to recruit nationals of non-belligerent countries for its army. Switzerland was one of the countries where such recruits were to be found.

Although recognized by treaty in 1648, Swiss neutrality had not precluded the participation of Swiss mercenaries in nearly all European wars since then. The mercenary system was far less extensive by the end of the Napoleonic wars, but as late as the 1850s several cantons had agreements to supply soldiers to Naples and Rome. In 1849 the new federal government prohibited recruitment by foreign governments, and a few years later the penal code provided penalties for those found to be recruiting Swiss citizens.[5] However, because the cantons themselves had made the military agreements with foreign governments, the federal

[4] Gordon to Clarendon, 11 September 1855 (FO 100/93). This was an explicit approval which as yet no other Continental government had given
[5] 'Affaires des capitulations militaires: Décret de l'assemblée fédérale', 20 June 1849 (RO, i, 438) and 'Code Pénal Fédéral', 4 February 1853 (RO, iii, 347-355)

government did not feel competent to abrogate them, at least in its early years, and so the system continued.

British policy since 1815 had tended to favour a liquidation of the mercenary system, particularly in the Italian states where Swiss regiments buttressed reactionary governments linked with Austria. In 1851, when Britain was exerting some pressure on Prussia and Austria, Palmerston sent the federal government copies of Gladstone's pamphlets about political abuses in Naples, as a recommendation for recall. When Austria and Switzerland were on bad terms in 1853, the matter was discussed again in Berne, perhaps at Austrian instigation in order to provoke further embarrassment for the Swiss. Britain made no suggestions then because the Allies needed Austrian cooperation in the east and because the uncertain political situation there would have been too easily upset by a convulsion in southern Italy. In its dispatches to Berne, the Foreign Office did not mention again, until the Crimean war was over, the possibility of recalling the Neapolitan regiments.

Inconsistencies of principle in British policy became apparent soon after the western declaration of war in 1854. Britain immediately asked that the federal government should not allow any Swiss to 'take up colours for Russia'.[6] Before the year was out, and as soon as the Foreign Enlistment Act was voted by Parliament, Gordon was directed to find 'one or two intelligent Swiss officers who are likely to raise men for the Foreign Legion ...'.[7] In Paris Cowley discussed the tactics of recruitment in Switzerland with the French government, which had already undertaken such a project; he found that 'altho' it w^d be impossible for the Swiss Gov't to give their consent to such recruiting they shut their eyes to it if their consent is not asked'.[8]

In the next few months Gordon carefully explored the possible arrangements for a British Swiss legion. The two main problems were determination of the legal position and recruitment of prospective officers. It was clear that open enlistment would be illegal and that secret agents would have to be used. 'Would such proceedings be considered unbecoming the dignity of the British Government?'[9] Clarendon replied, 'We do not mean to infringe the law of Switzerland but we conceive that ... [under certain conditions] the Swiss Gov. would not object.' None the less, he raised the possibility of abandoning the project and

[6] Murray to the Federal Council, 4 April 1854 (SFA: EPD: 152)
[7] Clarendon to Gordon, 29 December 1854 (FO 100/84)
[8] Cowley to Clarendon, 3 December 1854 (FO 519/214)
[9] Gordon to Clarendon, 19 January 1855 (FO 100/91)

had written privately that recruitment 'in stealth' would be undignified.[10] From remarks by the Swiss President, and from Barman, the Foreign Office knew that the federal government would do nothing to stop the British scheme as long as the actual enrolment took place outside Switzerland, and that the Federal Council wanted 'to know as little about such proceedings as possible'.[11] The Council knew of British proposals to officers in the Swiss army, yet it did not protest; it would accept no more applications for discharges, but it would grant long leaves of absence.

At this point in their development, an independent Swiss policy of positive neutrality was not possible. For several reasons the government had little choice but to tolerate Allied recruitment efforts. First, the Swiss needed western support since the Austro-Swiss dispute was not settled until early April. In December 1854 the Swiss President had remarked on his country's 'obligations ... to the British Government, for their good offices, on many late occasions ...'.[12] Second, it was during the war that an Anglo-Swiss commercial treaty was negotiated.[13] Third, economic growth had not yet caught up with the increase in population, so that pressing problems of unemployment would be eased by foreign enlistment. Fourth, the mercenary tradition was still stronger than the habit of centralized conduct of all foreign relations. Popular sympathy for the western side and the support for the scheme from the influential press played their part too.

By May the British government had made its firm decision to form a Swiss legion. Information about it was circulated in Switzerland, but the enlistment, in principle, took place in depots set up at various points just beyond the border. Recruitment was slow at first, but it increased in the last six months of the war. The legion grew to more than 3,000 men. A few of them actually reached the Crimea, but not early enough for battle, so that casualties were very few.

It was fortunate for the plans for British recruitment that all the neighbours of Switzerland were either allies or neutrals in the war. Even so, a certain amount of diplomatic discussion about the arrangements took place. Understandably, the eastern neighbours of Switzerland were less cooperative than those on the west.

Austria did not object to the recruitment project itself, but she did

[10] Clarendon to Gordon, 20 January 1855 (FO 100/90) and 12 January 1855 (Clar. ms. c. 131)
[11] Gordon to Clarendon, 8 February 1855 (FO 100/91)
[12] Gordon to Clarendon, 4 December 1854 (FO 100/87)
[13] See Chapter Seven

prevent the British from opening an enlistment depot in Constance. Although for some years the Austrian government had permitted such a Neapolitan depot on her soil, it objected to the British plan which, it inferred, would mean the training of the British Swiss army on Austrian territory. Westmorland attempted to make the limited British request clearer; he was also instructed to point out that such a 'small service' would hardly be a 'breach of neutrality', when Russia was encountering no difficulties in recruiting medical men and artisans from the German states.[14] The British concept of neutrality was evidently quite flexible. Clarification of the British request was of no avail, for Austria refused to allow activity which might be interpreted by Russia as an act of hostility, and perhaps did not want to encourage competition for recruitment for the Neapolitan regiments.

With France the diplomatic tasks posed by the organization of the British Swiss legion were somewhat different. The French could have no objections in principle to the British project because long before this they themselves had decided to form a Swiss legion. But, precisely for this reason, the two governments soon found themselves bidding against each other for recruits, especially for officers. The major instance of this was the French enrolment of Ochsenbein, the former Swiss President, with whom Gordon had also been negotiating. After Cowley complained of this in Paris, Fénelon was immediately instructed to cooperate fully with Gordon. Thus a small point of friction in the Anglo-French alliance was quickly smoothed over. British agents were instructed to use the utmost care not to enrol any soldier recruited by French agents, but still the British legion soon proved much more popular in Switzerland than the French legion, and French recruiting was very slow. This, combined with her interest in ending the war, led France to offer her Swiss legion to Britain in the autumn of 1855. Secret negotiations about the transfer lasted for about two months, but they were unsuccessful, for two reasons. First, administrative problems were difficult to resolve; one of them was the future of Ochsenbein, whom the British now refused to have in their service. A second probable reason is that this was a way in which Britain could press France to continue her responsibilities for the achievement of western war-aims.

Within Switzerland itself, as was expected, Britain encountered relatively few impediments. Some voices were raised for enforcement of the anti-recruitment laws, but these usually came from factions of the Conservative party which favoured Russia and Prussia, rather than from those wanting a more positive neutrality. Gordon was worried about

[14] Clarendon to Westmorland, 5 June 1855 (FO 7/448)

steps toward legal action against British recruitment by some cantons, particularly Basle, but the action was avoided by increased caution on the part of the recruiters. The Federal Council turned a blind public eye and refused to bring the matter before the Assembly; none the less, it did keep a close watch on British and French activities. After the war, the Swiss government pressed British authorities vigorously about discharge arrangements, to be sure that non-Swiss soldiers did not return by mistake. In the 1860s, questions of pension claims even came before Parliament. Despite these points of friction, Britain's reputation does not appear to have suffered very much in Switzerland.

The Swiss mercenary system did not long survive the Crimean war. During the war the Federal Council used some fancy legal logic to rationalize its tolerance of western efforts, although prevailing government opinion, even in 1855, seemed to disapprove of the practice. Within a few years the Swiss economic position had improved sufficiently to provide employment for returning soldiers. The agreements with Naples expired in 1859 and were not renewed. The Swiss Guards now at the Vatican are recruited on a different basis and would certainly not be expected to fight.

REALISM IN THE DEVELOPMENT OF NEUTRALITY

That British policy toward the mercenary practice was one of expediency was evident seven months after the Crimean peace settlement. In October 1856 Switzerland was again in difficulty over Neuchâtel; Britain then suggested that the regiments in Rome and Naples be recalled to help Swiss self-defence, weaken Austria, and increase Prussian isolation. But when the Swiss asked for British ships to transport the soldiers, Britain refused because of the encouragement which the presence of the British navy might give to Italian revolutionaries.

Realistic political considerations motivated the policies of the Swiss also in this period. Although the Austrian threat, between 1853 and 1855, had engendered some national solidarity, the Swiss people had not yet attained a strong sense of national unity. Because they were still somewhat weak politically and because the Allied transgressions were of a much less serious nature than the earlier French and Austrian challenges, the Swiss could muster little disposition to oppose their British friends. Indeed, to have protested against British activity might have robbed them of a protector of their independence. Hence the British gained their legion.

Swiss realism was manifest again after the Paris peace treaty was signed in 1856. While the Congress of Paris made no agreements directly affecting Switzerland,[15] it did invite the Swiss to adhere to the Declarations of Maritime Law and of International Mediation. Switzerland agreed to the Declaration of Maritime Law, but she was unwilling to be bound to submit an international dispute to mediation. The Federal Council was apprehensive that the Neuchâtel question would be raised again by Prussia and, if that happened, it was 'doubtful how far Switzerland would then consider it consistent with her interest or honour to act in conformity with ...' the declaration.[16] Swiss independence and neutrality were not yet established facts in the European system.

[15] Clarendon refused a Prussian request to discuss Neuchâtel. Clarendon to Bloomfield, 14 October 1856 (FO 192/20)
[16] Gordon to Clarendon, 3 June 1856 (FO 100/102)

CHAPTER SEVEN

Anglo-Swiss
Economic Relations

THUS FAR, WE have been concerned with the diplomatic discussions surrounding the *Sonderbund* crisis and the task of reconciling the conservative Continental Powers to the existence of a small but prospering independent liberal state in their midst. In the *Sonderbund* question itself Britain played a decisive role in favour of Switzerland, and in the Neuchâtel and refugee questions her role was at least a mediating one. In these three questions the Swiss tended to place more reliance on British friendship than was justified – and during the Crimean war the British tended to exploit Swiss goodwill for their own benefit. Now it will be useful to add another dimension to this study by taking a brief look at the economic relations between Britain and Switzerland, to discover how and to what extent the Swiss economy was linked with British commerce.

ANGLO-SWISS ECONOMIC RELATIONS BEFORE 1848

Before 1848, British policy-makers had been interested in the workings of the Swiss economy as an example of a country with free trade, showing the salutary effects of foreign competition on domestic industry.[1] Indeed, Swiss industry had been stimulated to modernize by competition from British textiles at home and in the foreign market. Swiss entrepreneurs went to England from time to time to learn new techniques and they frequently employed British technicians in Switzerland. British commerce supplied the Swiss with manufactured goods and with many raw materials for their industry. The Swiss were unable to export very much to Britain at this time because of high British tariffs and their

[1] Their interest was manifested, for example, in the Bowring report: see page 11

own poor competitive position.[2] Although precise statistical information about the volume of trade in this period is very difficult to find, it does seem clear that the Swiss were spending more for imports from Britain than they were able to earn by selling in Britain.[3] Their unfavourable trade balance was probably compensated partly through interest on their private investment in Britain, partly through favourable balances with other countries, and partly through British investment in Switzerland. Even before 1848 Britain was apparently increasing her investment in Switzerland.

The Swiss were very pleased by the gradual dismantling of the British protective system after 1842. British markets were opened to Swiss products and more Swiss exports to distant points could be shipped by way of British ports. The Swiss Consul in London wrote in 1846 that 'It is evident that the reduction of the English tariff can only favour the commerce which already exists ...'. British imports of silk ribbons, embroidered goods, kidskins, watches, and straw-plaiting had increased even then, and the Consul anticipated that new products, such as cheese, might be introduced.[4] The Swiss hoped that the British example would induce the Continental Powers to do likewise, so that their goods could be sold more easily near home. They also considered it beneficial to have British merchants handling an increasing amount of their overseas trade; obviously this would be profitable for Britain also.

SWISS ECONOMIC GROWTH AFTER 1848

The changed internal political climate after 1848 brought many improvements for the Swiss economy, the most important being the political stability so fundamental for industrial growth. The new constitution provided for the right of establishment, so that the labour force became more mobile, with citizens of one canton at last being able to move to another without losing their citizenship. In 1849 the Federal Assembly passed legislation for a centralized postal system. The following year a single monetary standard replaced the thirty-eight different currencies

[2] See Chapter Two
[3] It has been estimated, on the basis of known Geneva imports, that 1835 Swiss imports from Britain were worth 70 million francs, but this figure seems exceptionally high, partly, perhaps, because 1835 was a boom year. Swiss exports to Britain in silk ribbons, embroidered material, and straw hats were reported to be worth two million francs in 1845. William Waldvogel, *Les Relations Economiques entre la Grande-Bretagne et la Suisse dans le passé et le présent* (Neuveville, 1922), pp 70 and 76
[4] Prévost to the Federal Council, 21 April 1846 (SFA: Tagsatzung: 1972)

which had previously been in use. In 1852 legislation for railroad development was approved but, after stormy discussions, the Assembly refused to assume a strong role in planning the new transportation system. Rather, it required merely its own approval for each scheme, giving the primary authority for charters and routes to the cantonal governments. The Federal Assembly thus chose a middle way between the advocates of complete federal control and the protectionists who opposed all railroad development.

One of the most important improvements after 1848 was the inauguration of a unified commercial policy. The first year of the new government brought much debate between the free traders and the protectionists – so much debate, in fact, that the British could not be confident that the Swiss would adopt a policy of free trade. The Federal Assembly appointed a commission to make plans for a new customs system which had to provide revenue for both the federal and the cantonal governments. The protectionists lost this debate also. The Federal Assembly adopted the commission's recommendations for a unified and essentially liberal tariff policy. Under the new system, all internal cantonal tolls were abolished. External duties were for the most part levied for revenue only, but because some items were assessed by weight, some by value, and cattle was assessed by head, its net effect is difficult to appraise with any precision. A few branches of the Swiss economy were protected: for example, wheat was taxed at a rate designed to maintain higher domestic prices than in neighbouring countries. The new fiscal régime was so successful that it could report a financial surplus for 1850, in other words, an increased customs revenue. Abolition of internal tolls and duties led to such an increase in the volume of trade that freight rates quickly dropped by as much as one-third.[5]

In addition to the creation of a larger free trade area within Switzerland and a general lowering of duties on foreign commerce; customs unification conferred another benefit on the Swiss economy. With a single central tariff authority, the Swiss could more easily negotiate commercial treaties with other countries to obtain tariff reductions, and they were in a better position to resist any economic pressure which a neighbouring Power might choose to apply. As early as 1851 the Swiss made a commercial treaty with Sardinia; it included a most-favoured-nation clause and reduced Sardinian duties on cheese and Swiss duties on rice, noodles, and meat. Frequent discussions with the *Zollverein* were also necessary because of Swiss dependence on German foodstuffs.

[5] Peter H. Schmidt, *Die Schweiz und die europäische Handelspolitik* (Zurich, 1941), p75

Thus many obstacles to faster Swiss economic development were removed. The surge of activity that followed was dramatic. One of its symptoms was the formation of a large number of cantonal banks after 1848, following the pattern of banking growth elsewhere on the Continent and continuing a trend which had begun in the 1830s. Of thirty-five banks established in Switzerland between 1830 and 1860, only six were founded before 1848 while at least sixteen came into existence between 1848 and 1856.[6] An increasingly complex economy needed and used their facilities for domestic transactions and their short-term loans to help the export trade, as well as their investment capital. Other signs of growth were the rapid mechanization of Swiss production in the textile, embroidery, and machine industries and the establishment of schools for training apprentices, particularly in the watch industry, as another means of improving the quality of Swiss exports.

SWISS EXPORT INDUSTRIES

Trade relations between Britain and Switzerland in the 1850s present an interesting paradox. While the main Swiss industries competed with some branches of British industry, there seems to have been little animosity between the two. Free trade philosophies held that competition was healthy for industry and this view was accepted by both sides. The relatively small-scale and high-cost Swiss industry represented, of course, little threat to large-scale British industry, but it is notable that the manufacturers of this small but aspiring nation were ready to take competition for granted without resentment. Probably the main reason for the paradox was that the Swiss economy found ample opportunity in developing along lines similar to those in Britain at this time. With increasing incomes everywhere, demand was rapidly expanding and the overseas market seemed insatiable, Switzerland, like Britain, was selling in both North and South America, and in the Near and Far East. It was only in the 1870s that competition with Britain for the overseas market forced the smaller country to specialize almost exclusively in industries which complemented rather than competed with British industry. There were two other important aspects of the paradox: first, that a large proportion of Swiss exports was carried by British shipping and, second, that Swiss commercial agents in search of distant markets were instructed, with Foreign Office approval, to call on British consuls for help when needed.

[6] Auguste Vitu, *Guide Financier; répértoire général des valeurs financières et industrielles* (Paris, 1864), pp 500-23; BPP 1860 [2716] LXVI, p183

The Great Exhibition of 1851 provided an excellent opportunity for the Swiss to show their products to the world. Although the number of Swiss exhibitors seems to have been small compared with the showings of many countries – the *Economist* does not even mention Switzerland among the European exhibitors – they won many prizes. The classes of exhibition goods and the awards won by Swiss are shown in Table II.

Table II. Switzerland at the Great Exhibition of 1851

Class		Council Medal	Prize Medal	Honourable Mention
I	Mining, metallurgical operations, and mineral products	–	2	1
II	Chemical and pharmaceutical processes	–	–	–
III	Food substances	–	1	1
IV	Substances used in manufacturing	–	–	1
V	Machines for direct use (as for railways)	–	–	–
VA	Carriages generally (not railway)	–	–	–
VI	Manufacturing machines and tools	–	1	–
VII	Architecture and 'Building Contrivances'	–	2	1
VIII	Military ordnance and accoutrements	–	1	3
IX	Agricultural implements	–	–	–
X	'Philosophical Instruments ...'	1	4	3
XA	Musical instruments	–	–	1
XB	'Horological Instruments'	1	7	6
XC	Surgical instruments	–	1	–
XI	Cotton manufactures	–	7	2
XII	Woollen manufactures	–	–	–
XIII	Silk and velvet manufactures	–	16	11

Class		Council Medal	Prize Medal	Honourable Mention
XIV	Flax and hemp manufactures	–	–	1
XV	Mixed fabrics including shawls	–	–	–
XVI	Leathers, skins, furs	–	1	1
XVII	Paper, printing	–	–	–
XVIII	'Woven, Spun, Felted & Laid Fabrics when shown as specimens of printing or dying'	–	3	–
XIX	Embroidery, etc.	–	11	3
XX	Ready made articles of clothing (straw plaiting included)	–	3	2
XXI	Cutlery and edge tools	–	1	2
XXII	Iron and general hardware	–	1	–
XXIII	Works in precious metals, jewellery	–	4	2
XXIV	Glass	–	–	–
XXV	Ceramics	–	–	1
XXVI	Decorative furniture	–	–	2
XXVII	Manufactures in mineral substances used for building	–	–	–
XXVIII	Manufactures from animal and vegetable substances not included in other sections	–	4	1
XXIX	Miscellaneous manufactures	–	1	–
XXX	Sculpture	–	–	–
	Total	2	71	46

SOURCE: United Kingdom, Royal Commision on the London Exhibition of 1851, *Reports by the Juries* (London, 1852)

The reports of the Exhibition judges include some interesting comments on Swiss products. They also give some indication of the more important Swiss export industries, although, because the Exhibition was in London, the reports may reflect a slight bias in favour of more specialized Swiss products purchased by the British rather than those in direct competition with British goods in overseas markets.

The Swiss cotton industry, a pioneer among Swiss exports, made an excellent showing at the London Exhibition. As we have seen in Chapter Two, it had its start under Napoleon, and then suffered a set-back in the post-war period because of British competition. By the 1830s and 1840s, as a result of more mechanization, the Swiss had found markets in which they could compete. Between 1844 and 1857, the number of mechanized spindles in Switzerland nearly doubled.[7] As mentioned earlier, the factories were, however, on a much smaller scale than British factories and, correspondingly, total Swiss production was relatively small. The 1851 Exhibition's judges of cotton manufactures wrote that Swiss yarns were 'of very beautiful quality', and their dyed yarns were singled out as especially remarkable.[8] Ten years later Andrew Ure, in his study of the British cotton industry, wrote that Switzerland had 'quite superseded, in the markets of Germany and Austria, the yarns of Great Britain'.[9] It does seem clear that Britain herself was not buying much of the Swiss cottons. In 1849 the Swiss Consul wrote that while this was the case, the transit trade through Britain to the colonies and other overseas countries was 'of some importance'.[10]

Two specialized branches of the cotton industry were the cloth printing and embroidery industries. Of the former, the Exhibition judges said that the Swiss products shown were 'unsurpassed in execution by any in the Exhibition' and that they were competing successfully with French and English products in European markets.[11] The jury on embroidered goods was also impressed with the Swiss displays and awarded eleven prizes; it wrote that the Swiss had 'long-enjoyed celebrity' in the field, citing particularly the variety of Swiss goods and the excellence and beauty of their design. The jurors estimated that England imported

[7] Switzerland, Eidgenössischen Volkwirtschaftdepartement, *La Suisse économique et sociale* (Einsiedeln, 1927), i, 167. The number of spindles in 1857 was 1,152,000 which, considering the size of the country, compares well with Britain's 20,977,000 in 1850

[8] United Kingdom, Royal Commission on the London Exhibition of 1851, *Reports by the Juries* (London, 1852), p347

[9] Andrew Ure, *The Cotton Manufacture of Great Britain* (London, 1861), p477

[10] Prévost to the Federal Council, 24 May 1849 (SFA: EPD: KD: 1)

[11] United Kingdom ..., p458

100,000 pairs of embroidered Swiss curtains annually and that the Swiss were selling even more in Europe and the Americas.[12]

A second important branch of Swiss textile manufacturing was the silk industry, which won sixteen prizes and eleven honourable mentions at the Exhibition. The judges found that the Swiss exhibit 'demands a discriminating notice', and that the Swiss were designing their production specially for the consumers' needs.[13] Swiss silk ribbons sold particularly well in Britain. In fact, their success aroused some envy among the British, whose silk industry was doing poorly. In 1852 the *Economist* noted that British silks had long been heavily protected and were still the least prosperous (of British textiles), being unable to compete with France and Switzerland in the export trade; it suggested that the answer to the Swiss and French challenges should be a lowering of the tariff so that competition would force British improvement.[14]

An important secondary branch of Swiss textiles was the straw-plaiting industry, which also won prizes at the Exhibition. The Swiss articles, mostly hats, were said to have 'great taste in their design and execution'.[15] Swiss straw goods sold well in Europe, and especially in Britain, until faced with competition from the Far East later in the century.

The other major Swiss industry, machinery, was just beginning in this period, so that it had not reached a stage of development in exports comparable to the textile industry. None the less, the exhibits of 1851 did take a few prizes and were reported to be of very good quality. The industry's primary aim in this period was to make domestic needs less dependent on foreign machine-makers. Some firms were exporting, but certainly not to Britain. Indeed, in the 1850s this industry received a great deal of technical help from Britain, and it relied heavily on imported British machinery as it expanded. It was only some decades later that a high level of exports in hydraulic and electrical machinery was attained.

The Swiss watch industry had firmly established its high reputation in the world by 1851 and quite naturally won several Exhibition prizes. The judges' report implied that the excellence of Swiss watches, 'especially the small and cheaper ones', was greater than the number of prizes indicated.[16] In 1855 the value of Swiss clocks and watches

[12] *Ibid*, p467
[13] *Ibid*, p364
[14] *Economist*, Vol. x, 27 November 1852, p1321
[15] United Kingdom ..., p483
[16] *Ibid*, p341

exported to Britain was estimated to be over seven million francs.[17] Even so, the growing British watch industry provided some keen competition for the Swiss, forcing them to adopt a more efficient factory system. British watchmakers considered some of the Swiss trading methods to be unfair and on several occasions they protested to the Board of Trade that watches were arriving from Switzerland with a trademark imitating one of their own. The British government threatened to stop all watch imports from Switzerland, but it took no action because the Swiss promised, several times, to correct the matter.

Other Swiss goods shown in the Exhibition of 1851 can be mentioned very briefly. The class described as 'philosophical instruments' included precision tools such as drawing instruments, a minor branch of the machine industry in this period. It was not destined to much of a future. On the other hand, a few exhibits in leather goods were a good sign for the future. One of the prize-winners in this category was Bally, who soon after established a shoe industry which was to find a good market in Britain and throughout the world.

Thus the Great Exhibition gives a kind of survey of the Swiss export industries in 1851. There is little doubt that it gave British merchants who attended it, or who read the reports, a better idea of the qualities of Swiss goods available. In short, the Exhibition gave the Swiss valuable publicity for more expansion. As shown in Table III later in this chapter, Swiss exports of manufactured goods more than doubled between 1851 and 1860. At the end of the decade, the products exported were much the same. An 1858 account showed that two-thirds of the Swiss working population were engaged, at least part time, in the cotton, silk, or watch industries; all three were clearly making very good progress.[18] Cheese also became increasingly important, as the Swiss Consul had predicted in 1846, and a few secondary commodities, such as liqueurs, were added.

BRITISH PARTICIPATION IN SWISS
ECONOMIC DEVELOPMENT

Although expansion of Swiss export industries naturally required considerable capital investment, railway development probably posed the most difficult problem of finance for the Swiss in the early 1850s. The banking system had not yet developed sufficiently to provide the

[17] BPP 1857/58 [2444] LV, p49. Some of this may have been in transit or destined for re-export
[18] BPP 1859 (Sess. 2) [2570] XXX, p58

enormous amounts of capital needed to construct a system of railroads in difficult terrain, so the Swiss had to rely heavily on foreign capital and technical advice. The investment prospects attracted financiers both from Britain and from continental countries, which had much greater commercial and political interests in the development of Swiss routes than Britain.[19]

Evidence of official British activity to help the development of Swiss railroads is sparse. Although the *Economist* indicates little interest – domestic and other continental schemes were admittedly much vaster – the Foreign Office took pains to inform the Swiss government of its support and readiness to help to overcome any political difficulties, but it declined to 'meddle with any pecuniary Questions connected therewith'.[20] The Swiss asked Britain to encourage the German states to give financial help, but it is doubtful whether the Foreign Office made such a move, although it had already instructed its representative in Berlin to speak of the 'Political and Commercial Advantages' of Swiss railway development for Prussia.[21]

The extent of private British participation in Swiss railroad ventures is difficult to estimate, but various facts do point to considerable British investment in Swiss railroad projects. French financial companies are known to have been active in Swiss railroad investment and they in turn were undoubtedly supported in part by British capital, because the London and Paris money markets were so closely connected.[22] The Paris agent for one of the Swiss companies was in fact British, Sir Edward Blount, and Palmerston himself was reported to have invested in Swiss railway enterprises.[23] In 1854, when the British government was deciding whether to recruit Swiss for the Crimean army, Gordon reported that Swiss railway interests 'would much encourage the connivance in it of the Federal Council and cantonal governments ... if Her Majesty's Government should ... cause to be purchased ... a certain number of shares in some of these undertakings'.[24] Clarendon apparently paid no

[19] French pressure on the Swiss government to give equal legal rights to Jews can be traced to the House of Rothschild's desire to participate in Swiss railroad finance; see page 68. Buchanan to Malmesbury, 12 May 1852 (FO 100/72) and Walter A. Johr, *Schweizerische Kreditanstalt, 1856-1956* (Zurich, 1956), pp 41-2

[20] Palmerston to Christie, 29 July 1851 (FO 100/67)

[21] Palmerston to Westmorland, 24 June 1851 (FO 64/327)

[22] Leland H. Jenks, *The Migration of British Capital to 1875* (London, 1927), pp 164-5

[23] Ferd. Gubler, *Die Anfänge der schweizerischen Eisenbahnpolitik auf Grundlage der wirtschaftlichen Interessen, 1832-1852* (Zurich-Selnau, 1915), pp 330-31

[24] Gordon to Clarendon, 14 December 1854 (Clar. ms. c. 21)

attention to this suggestion, but the fact that it was made is significant. In general, the British government did favour overseas investment, although it would not always interfere on behalf of British investors.[25] The Foreign Office archives for 1856 contain some correspondence about the problems of British investors in the Swiss South-eastern Railway. When conflict between the Swiss and British stockholders – the latter owning half the capital of the enterprise – led the Grisons government to confiscate all the British shares, an appeal was made to the Foreign Office. No official interference was necessary in this case, however, because the matter was eventually settled 'amicably'.[26] The South-eastern Railway was not the largest Swiss railroad enterprise, but the high proportion of British shareholding is none the less remarkable. Another indication of the development of close commercial and financial ties between Britain and Switzerland is the attention given to the changes in the Bank of England's interest rate by the Swiss commercial journals. One article in the Swiss commercial press set forth the advantages of attracting British investment: in the writer's view it was a good omen for the success of an undertaking if it were patronized by British funds.[27]

Some evidence of British technical help is also available. When the Federal Assembly appointed a commission to explore the issue of railroads for Switzerland, it called on two English advisers, Robert Stephenson[28] and Mr Swinburne. Their recommendation of strong federal control of development was turned down, although it had much Swiss support, but their scheme of a main east-west line with branches was implemented. In 1852 Sir Charles Fox, of Fox, Henderson & Co., visited Switzerland to explore the possibilities of securing contracts. Buchanan, then British Minister in Berne, was instructed to 'afford [him] unofficially every assistance',[29] but his project there was unsuccessful. Earlier in the year, Buchanan had reported a rumour that another company, Williamson & Co., had been awarded some construction contracts and in December he heard that rival London companies were competing for the Geneva-Basle line. Unfortunately, the British diplo-

---

[25] While the government might interfere on behalf of holders of defaulted foreign bonds (R. C. Binkley, *Realism and Nationalism, 1852-1871*, New York and London, 1935, p167), it was against a general policy of interference on behalf of the dissatisfied or imprudent British investor (*Economist*, Vol. VII, 21 April 1849, p435)

[26] Gordon to Clarendon, 12 November 1856 (FO 100/104)

[27] *Schweizerische Handels- und Gewerbe-Zeitung*, 21 May 1853

[28] Son of George Stephenson, one of the founders of the British railway system

[29] Malmesbury to Buchanan, 27 November 1852 (FO 100/70)

matic records do not show to what extent British firms did in fact win the construction contracts, but a considerable increase in the number of British subjects in Switzerland in the early 1850s suggests that at least some of them were successful.

THE ANGLO-SWISS TREATY OF 1855

From 1852 on, the British consular and diplomatic dispatches from Berne are enlivened with a number of accounts of distressed British railroad workers who had been brought in for special jobs, met with some misfortune, and sought assistance from the British representative. As the number of British residents increased, the British Legation received more and more complaints that their Swiss taxes were higher than those of the French or Sardinian residents, because the latter two countries had treaties with the Swiss. When Christie brought the matter to the attention of the Foreign Office in 1854, he commented that because the Federal Council was not likely to take much notice of individual complaints, a treaty might be advisable.

Christie's suggestion of a treaty aroused interest and discussion in London. The Board of Trade was 'disposed to concur' with the idea, reasoning that the Swiss were not likely to turn it down if they already had similar treaties with France and Sardinia. The Board of Trade suggested that the proposed treaty might also include 'other objects of commercial importance'– specifically some reciprocal commercial provisions in the form of a most-favoured-nation clause. Also, it observed that the new and more centralized Swiss government showed some 'indications of a tendency to deviate ... from the system of entire commercial liberty ...'. Britain did not want to be placed in a disadvantageous trading position as a result of Swiss tariff reductions in their Sardinian trade.[30] The Foreign Office agreed to work on such a treaty.

In preparing a draft treaty during the summer of 1854, the Foreign Office was influenced by the course of treaty negotiations between Switzerland and the United States, which British representatives in Berne had followed in some detail since 1851. The Swiss had been quick to approve a draft treaty calling for reciprocal rights of establishment, extradition of criminals, and commercial agreements with a most-favoured-nation clause, but the United States Senate refused ratification on two occasions because the Swiss right of establishment was restricted to Christians. Although this treaty was important for the Swiss – many

[30] Board of Trade to Wodehouse, 17 May 1854 (FO 100/89)

Swiss were emigrating to the United States and Americans were buying many of their exports – they were unable to grant equal rights for Jews because of the cantonal sovereignty issue, as in negotiations with France. In 1854 the Federal Assembly delayed ratification of the treaty by raising questions about the right of foreigners to own land in the United States.

In September 1854 the British submitted their treaty draft to the Swiss government. They were optimistic about an early Swiss ratification, because the draft was based on portions of the American, Sardinian, and French treaties, but in this they miscalculated. They encountered more obstacles in their negotiations than the Americans had, although some of the problems were similar.

On the question of Jews, Britain was forewarned by the American and French experiences, and was therefore ready to compromise. Clarendon instructed Gordon to attempt to obtain Swiss agreement to the reciprocal right of establishment 'without any distinction whatever as to religious belief'; but if the Swiss refused to accept the amendment, however, Gordon was to withdraw it. The British government knew that the Federal Council favoured equal rights for Jews; therefore, since in fact little discrimination was practised in Switzerland, it raised the point as a matter of principle and to give the Federal Council arguments for amending both cantonal laws and the federal constitution. None the less, despite their sympathy for Swiss constitutional problems, the British made clear that if any difficulties for British Jews in Switzerland did arise, they would 'use every exertion in their power to attain equal privileges'.[31] Although the Federal Council could not accept the treaty provision, it did furnish the Foreign Office with a satisfactory written statement of the Swiss position. A decade later the Swiss amended their constitution to require equal treatment for Christians and Jews.

A second issue in the treaty negotiations was the legal status of mixed marriages. Swiss cantonal law, in many instances, would not admit the legality of marriages between British subjects and Swiss citizens if the marriage was performed under British law, and sometimes even if it was performed by Swiss without the permission of the British government. The influx of British subjects to work on railroad projects made an arrangement of the matter particularly desirable. Because some of the predominantly Catholic cantons had vetoed an earlier British proposal for a convention, Christie suggested that an article on the subject be included in the treaty. The Foreign Office had no objections, but it preferred spontaneous Swiss action; some cantons had changed their

[31] Clarendon to Gordon, 30 April 1855 (FO 100/90)

laws since the problem arose in 1852 and the Federal Council was likely to persist in urging the remaining cantons to do likewise. When the Swiss would not accept Christie's proposal, it too was dropped.

The British yielded to the Swiss on other issues also. They had wanted an article prohibiting any levy of forced loans on British subjects in Switzerland, but when it became evident that the Swiss understood something quite different about the meaning of the term, Britain agreed to omit the article. The Swiss suggestion of a guarantee of the right to expel paupers and law-breakers was accepted by Britain without much discussion. The Swiss were eager that the rights and privileges granted them by the treaty should extend to British colonies as well; Britain again agreed.

The Swiss too were forced to concede some points. Britain emphatically refused their suggestion of an article on extradition, because of parliamentary complications. Toward the end of the negotiations, the Swiss became excited by British and colonial laws against foreign ownership of property and argued that reciprocity required that they should be given the same rights as British subjects in Britain. The Board of Trade did not consider this issue negotiable. After the treaty was signed, a careful explanation of the British and colonial legal situations seems to have satisfied the Swiss on this point.

The British evinced some impatience as the negotiations dragged on. Their first draft was presented in October 1854, but the final draft was not signed until September 1855, and it was not ratified until February 1856.[32] The negotiations had been delayed by Britain for a few months during the winter of 1855, primarily waiting for an opinion from the Queen's Advocate. In mid-May 1855, with several points still outstanding, Gordon reported that the Swiss were anxious to conclude the negotiations; he added that the American treaty was likely to be ratified in the next Assembly session. By mid-June the Foreign Office wanted no time to be lost in putting the treaty into final form and in mid-July it requested ratification during the current Federal Assembly meetings, which were nearly over. Was there a trace of rivalry with the United States? The accuracy of the treaty translations had not yet been verified, nor had the question of property ownership been answered. Thus it is hardly surprising that the Federal Council was unable to recommend ratification before the end of the annual Assembly session in July. Yet when Gordon reported, at the end of July, that the treaty had not been signed, a Foreign Office clerk commented that 'the Swiss Gov't

[32] BPP 1856 [2041] LXI: 'Treaty of Friendship ... between Her Majesty and the Swiss Confederation ....'

have not behaved well in this affair'. Clarendon agreed and wrote of British 'surprize and regret', since the treaty 'contained no new principle'.[33] Perhaps the British were annoyed because the Swiss had suggested so many alterations and in fact had conceded very little themselves. In September the Foreign Office again expressed regret that the Swiss could not put the signed treaty into effect before ratification. Further discussion led the Federal Council to change its decision on this point, so that the special charges on British subjects in Switzerland were at last abolished.

Swiss opinion generally was favourable to the treaty, but even so, when the agreement was considered at a special session of the Federal Assembly in late January, Gordon had to use more persuasiveness to convince Herr von Gonzenbach, a key member of the committee concerned with the treaty, to recommend ratification. Von Gonzenbach objected to the prohibition of alien property ownership in British territories and to infringements of cantonal sovereignty in provisions regarding the right of search and exemption from military obligations. Gordon discovered that the French translation of British law dealing with aliens conveyed a very different meaning from the English, so that his explanations on this point were accepted. He also persuaded von Gonzenbach that the cantonal sovereignty questions were not serious. Later he remarked that if the Swiss rejected the treaty, the effect on the British government would be 'of a very disagreeable and undesirable nature'.[34] Such a threat was probably unnecessary, for the committee recommended ratification, noting nevertheless that Switzerland did allow aliens to hold property – 'in general [it is] advantageous to attract foreign capital ...'.[35] The Assembly approved the treaty with only one dissenting vote.

The treaty brought advantages to both parties. The Swiss gained easier access to British colonial markets. Their interest in clarifying the conditions for trade with the colonies and in the status of alien property ownership are indications of the commercial importance they attached to Britain's overseas possessions. Britain obtained more favourable treatment for British residents in Switzerland. That the Board of Trade initiated the idea of a commercial clause might signify a compliment to the economic potentials of the Swiss, but in fact the British were concerned in most quarters with safeguarding and developing their trading

[33] Note on Gordon to Clarendon, 25 July 1855 (FO 100/93) and Clarendon to Gordon, 31 July 1855 (FO 100/90)
[34] Gordon to Clarendon, 7 February 1856 (FO 100/100)
[35] Report to the Federal Council (SFA: EPD: 26)

interests on as free a basis as possible. When the new Swiss customs system had been in effect for a year, and the duties on some items were thought by the British to be rather high, Palmerston sent a Board of Trade statement of British trade figures to the Federal Council, as 'practical proof that a reduction of Import Duties is not always attended with a corresponding diminution of revenue'.[36] The British government was trying to guide the federal government away from any protectionist tendencies that might easily have made some headway in these formative years.

MEASUREMENT OF ANGLO-SWISS TRADE

When we turn to the measurement of Anglo-Swiss trade in this period, we are faced with serious statistical difficulties. Swiss commercial records do not show the trade with individual countries until 1892, and their classification system in the 1850s does not provide very specific information about the types of commodity, origin, or destination, as Table III indicates. The British records, while showing ports of origin and destination, do not distinguish the goods which came from or ultimately reached landlocked Switzerland.

However, in the absence of exact Swiss or British figures, some estimates of the volume and composition of Anglo-Swiss trade can be made, and, while these do not yield precise values, they can, by comparison and analysis, be used to establish some notion of the proportions of the trade. For this purpose, the French records can help us, since a large part of Swiss foreign trade was shipped through France in the 1850s and, fortunately, the French kept detailed records of their transit trade.

Calculations of the value of Anglo-Swiss trade were made by Mr Herries and by Mr Burnley, successive British Secretaries of Legation in Berne in the 1850s. Although both claimed to use French trade statistics, the information which each offers for 1855 is quite different.[37] Of the two, Herries reported the French statistics more accurately and his analysis of their meaning is more thoughtful. He assumed that all British imports from Switzerland were shipped through France and that about 80 per cent of all goods going in transit through France to Britain were from Switzerland. For Swiss imports from Britain, he

[36] He continued, '... on the contrary it is generally followed by an increased consumption which adds to the comforts and enjoyment of the People at large, while it affords at the lower Duty nearly the same amount of Revenue which was raised upon the smaller consumption by means of the preceding higher Duty'. Palmerston to Herries, 11 February 1851 (FO 192/11)
[37] See Appendix II

115

Table III. Course of Swiss

| | IMPORTS | | | EXPORTS |
Year	Class A (mill. head)	Class B (mill. francs)	Class C (mill. qtls.)	Class A (mill. head)
1850	·179	·039	4·553	·104
1851	·181	·071	5·257	·086
1852	·173	·170	9·203	·065
1853	·199	·220	9·418	·060
1854	·186	·332	10·197	·062
1855	·151	1·031	10·129	·088
1856	·167	·787	10·508	·109
1857	·193	1·477	11·192	·086
1858	·214	1·739	11·549	·084
1859	·214	·808	12·813	·088
1860	·218	·419	14·572	·090
Change between 1850 and 1860	+22%	+974%	+220%	−23%

Class A (head): Cattle and other livestock
Class B (francs): Manufactured goods, mostly related to transport
Class C (quintals): Raw materials, foodstuffs, and manufactured goods
(a) This reduction is due to a change in the classification system. Note

SOURCE: Switzerland, Département Fédéral des Douanes, *Rapports*

thought that of the goods from Britain in transit through France, again about 80 per cent were destined for Switzerland; to this he added 50 per cent, as the value of British goods shipped to Switzerland through Germany.[38] Applying Herries' reasoning and proportions to the French records on their transit trade for the years 1848 to 1860, we can construct some approximate annual values for the Anglo-Swiss trade through

[38] Herries' assumptions about different shipping patterns for Swiss imports are confirmed by other sources of information; see pages 121-4

		TRANSIT		
Class B (mill. francs)	Class C (mill. qtls.)	Class A (mill. head)	Class B (mill. francs)	Class C (mill. qtls.)
2·518	·559	·054	·240	·189
2·415	·606	·064	·144	·231
4·379	1·273	·065	·422	·386
5·627	1·166	·065	·891	·357
6·071	1·330	·069	·719	·395
5·164	1·490	·069	1·074	·530
6·967	1·558	·070	1·283	·597
5·670	1·618	·068	·602	·553
5·009	1·476	·080	·353	·655
4·251	1·435	·082	·405	·726
6·099	1·452	·091	·014 (a)	1·266
+142%	+160%	+68%	−94% (a)	+570%

development, and particularly to railways

that Class C transit is much higher in 1860 than in 1859

annuels de la Statistique du commerce suisse (Berne, 1850–60)

this period.[39] The results and, for comparison, the official Swiss data for 1892, are shown in Table IV.

[39] One modification of these proportions is called for, however, on the assumption that transportation patterns changed during this interval. Before 1855 probably equal amounts of Swiss imports were going through France and Germany; in the second half of the decade, as French railways were opened, the proportionate volume flowing through Germany had declined to the level of Herries' estimate, and then probably below it by 1860. This assumption is justified by information in French consular reports (see page 123) and by other statistics about the composi-

Table IV. Estimated Swiss Trade with Britain, 1848–60

| | Imports | | Exports | | Total |
	(mill. francs)	(A) (£ mill.)	(mill. francs)	(B) (£ mill.)	(C=A+B) (£ mill.)
1848	20	·8	20	·8	1·6
1849	40	1·6	27	1·1	2·7
1850	41	1·6	40	1·6	3·2
1851	25	1·0	54	2·2	3·2
1852	32	1·3	70	2·8	4·1
1853	31	1·2	110	4·4	5·6
1854	37	1·5	103	4·1	5·6
1855	60	2·4	79	3·2	5·6
1856	95	3·8	104	4·2	8·0
1857	105	4·2	99	4·0	8·2
1858	85	3·4	98	3·9	7·3
1859	105	4·2	132	5·3	9·5
1860	140	5·6	130	5·2	10·8
*	*	*	*	*	*
1892	42	1·6	117	4·7	6·3

SOURCES: France, Administration des Douanes, *Tableau général du Commerce de la France* (Paris) (to which Herries' method is applied); for 1892 (official Swiss figures), Waldvogel, p129. The French, Belgian, and Swiss francs had about the same value, 25 francs to the pound.[40]

The Anglo-Swiss trade shown by the estimates in Table IV was, of course, much more important for Switzerland than for Britain. In 1855 the total value of Swiss exports and imports was 750 million francs,[41] so that the British share (140 million francs) was nearly 19 per

tion of the French transit trade. The Swiss imported both raw cotton and iron (in various forms) from Britain throughout this period; the value of each going from Britain through France increased from 809,178 francs and (at least) 341,121 francs respectively in 1849 to 3,623,038 francs and (at least) 7,255,561 francs respectively in 1858, which by comparison with the figures in Table III gives a clear indication of shifting transport patterns

[40] Trevelyan to Hammond, October 1857 (FO 100/107)
[41] BPP 1857/58 [2444] p39

cent of it. In the same year, the Swiss trade was about 2·3 per cent of gross British foreign commerce (exports, net imports, re-exports, and transhipments). This was a very high share for such a small country.

Comparison of these estimates for the 1850s with the first Swiss accounts for trade with Britain in 1892 tends to support the estimates. In 1892, 4·8 per cent of all Swiss imports were from Britain, and 17 per cent of all Swiss exports went to Britain.[42] The Swiss proportion of the British total had fallen to less than 1 per cent, but this does not mean that the estimates of Anglo-Swiss trade were grossly excessive in the 1850s. In the thirty-five year interval, great changes in trade volumes and patterns had occurred, so that the Swiss were making greater use of continental mercantile services.

ORGANIZATION OF ANGLO-SWISS TRADE

In fact, a large part of Anglo-Swiss trade in the 1850s was overseas trade moving through Britain. Some was actually handled by Swiss or foreign merchants, and thus only transhipped through British ports, while some was actually re-exported by British merchants. The steadily increasing value of British re-exports and transhipments through the 1850s, indicated in Table V, correlates well with a rapidly growing Swiss overseas trade. In 1853 and 1857 the Federal Commercial Department reported that Swiss merchants preferred British shipping services, which offered all the advantages needed for Swiss trade: speed, safety, regularity, moderate prices, and activity in many parts of the world.[43] In 1856 the Swiss Consul in Liverpool wrote that, while he could not give details about the size of the Swiss imports into Britain, either for consumption, re-export, or transit, he did think that as much as 93 per cent of the Swiss goods passing through London might be destined for overseas.[44]

Even allowing for a little exaggeration by the Swiss Consul, his country's trade still played a significant part in British shipping and re-export activity. An approximation of its importance can be shown by some further calculations and comparisons with statistical information about the British re-export and transhipment trades. For this purpose, let us take 80 per cent of the estimated Swiss exports to Britain as perhaps nearer the mark than the Swiss Consul's 93 per cent for British re-export or transhipment of Swiss goods. British exports to Switzerland, on the other hand, were probably composed of a higher proportion

---

[42] Waldvogel, p129
[43] FF 1853, ii, 189; and BPP 1857/58 [2444], p49
[44] Zwilchenbart to the Federal Council, 1856 (SFA: EPD: KD: 1)

of products of domestic manufacture, such as iron in various forms for the machine industry and cotton goods for embroidery, so that it seems unlikely that the value of goods re-exported or transhipped from Britain to Switzerland exceeded 50 per cent of total Swiss imports from Britain. Applying these percentages to the figures for Anglo-Swiss trade suggested in Table IV, we can arrive at a clearer impression of the nature of Anglo-Swiss commercial ties. The results of these calculations, shown in Table V, indicate that the Swiss share of the British re-export and

Table V. Estimates of the Importance of Switzerland for
British Re-export and Transit Trades, 1848–60

	British re-exports (D) (£ mill.)	British tran-ship-ments (E) (£ mill.)	Estimated value of goods re-exported or transhipped			
			from U.K. to Switzerland (50% of A) (F) (£ mill.)	Swiss goods through U.K. (80% of B) (G) (£ mill.)	Total (H) (£ mill.)	H as % of D+E
1848	8·4		·4	·6	1·0	
1849	12·1		·8	·9	1·7	
1850	12·0		·8	1·3	1·2	
1851	12·5	3·0	·5	1·8	2·3	15
1852	13·0	3·7	·6	2·2	2·8	17
1853	16·8	5·3	·6	3·5	4·1	19
	18·6	5·0	·8	3·3	4·1	17
1855	21·0	3·6	1·2	2·5	3·7	15
1856	23·4	4·6	1·9	3·4	5·3	19
1857	24·1	4·5	2·1	3·2	5·3	19
1858	23·2	4·5	1·7	3·1	4·8	17
1859	25·3	6·6	2·1	4·2	6·3	20
1860	28·6	5·1	2·8	4·2	7·0	21

SOURCES: British re-exports: Albert H. Imlah, *Economic Elements in the Pax Britannica* (Cambridge, Massachusetts, 1958), p206; British transhipments: BPP 1861 [2825] LXII ('Statistical Abstract'); estimated values of Anglo-Swiss trade from Table IV.

transit trades in the years between 1851 and 1860 was between 15 per cent and 21 per cent. The proportions are remarkable for so small and landlocked a European country, and they provide a testimony to the importance of the British merchant marine and handling facilities at that time.

How much of the Swiss overseas trade that passed through Britain was handled by British merchants and how much was merely transit trade is not very certain, since several of the contemporary reports do not distinguish clearly between re-export and transit. Frequent advertising in a Swiss commercial journal by London merchants could point to British interest either in handling more Swiss overseas trade directly or simply in providing Swiss merchants with shipping services. The French transit trade statistics offer little help on this point; indeed, it is not clear whether they include re-exports.[45] Herries states that the great bulk of Swiss goods (primarily textiles) destined for South America, the United States, and for Australia, India, and other British possessions went first to Britain for 're-export'.[46] He may very well have used the term loosely, for a Swiss consular report from London in 1849 specifically mentioned the importance of the 'transit' trade in Swiss textiles.[47]

Comparisons of French and British statistical records on the transit trades, shown in Table VI, gives some firmer impressions about the auspices of Swiss overseas trade. Our attention turns first to possible patterns for Swiss exports. Between 66 per cent and 75 per cent of the British transit trade was from France, and over 90 per cent of this was in commodities which could have been produced in Switzerland. On the other hand, the commodities comprising the British re-export trade were overwhelmingly non-Swiss in origin so that, from this evidence alone, it seems that nearly all the Swiss commodities passing through Britain were in the transit category rather than re-exports. The French records do not show the destination of goods in transit from Switzerland, nor do they indicate the origin of all goods in transit to Britain,[48] but none the less we can draw some conclusions from the fact that, throughout the decade, the values of the principal Swiss export commodities in transit through France are far higher than the amounts which Britain is esti-

---

[45] 'Statistiques sur le commerce extérieur, 1828-1869' (AN: F¹²: 2714). Even if the French transit figures do include re-exports, it is unlikely that French re-exporters were active in much of the Anglo-Swiss trade; see pages 122-4
[46] BPP 1857/58 [2444], p49
[47] Prévost to the Federal Council, 24 May 1849 (SFA: EPD: KD: 1)
[48] Herries made allowances for this in making his estimates; see pages 115-6

mated to have received for transhipment. Some of these Swiss exports were shipped directly from France overseas, to the United States and, increasingly, to other parts of the world. Even of those Swiss goods which did not pass through Britain probably a small part was carried in British ships.[49] Thus it is clear that most of the Swiss export trade, much of which was sent in British ships, was none the less handled by Swiss merchants or foreign consignees, rather than by British merchants. The statistical evidence is corroborated by the British diplomatic record, which contains occasional promises of consular support for Swiss commercial agents in all parts of the world.

Swiss imports of foreign and colonial goods from Britain, on the other hand, were mainly re-exports handled by British merchants, rather than transhipments. The British re-export trade was composed largely of goods, such as raw cotton, coming in from across the high seas in great quantities for home as well as for foreign consumption, so the British could offer considerable 'economies of scale' for many commodities needed by the Swiss. Information about the British trade going to Switzerland indicates that the Swiss availed themselves of this economy. For example, as Table VI shows, the value of goods in transit through

Table VI. Statistics related to Swiss Trade
(values in millions of pounds)

	1853	1855	1857	1859
SWISS EXPORTS				
French transit:				
Total	14·5	15·5	19·6	21·5
Total goods to the United States	4·3	4·9	4·8	4·3
Total goods to Britain	5·5	3·9	4·9	6·6
Total goods from Switzerland	6·2	5·7	6·3	9·1
Swiss textiles and some manufactured goods (partial list)	5·4	5·2	5·7	8·2
Estimates:				
Total Swiss goods to Britain	4·4	3·2	4·0	5·3
Swiss goods transhipped or re-exported through Britain	3·5	2·5	3·2	4·2

[49] About 10 per cent of the ships sailing from France to Australia, India, and other possessions in the Far East were British. (France, Administration des Douanes, *Tableau général du Commerce de la France*, Paris)

British transhipments:	1853	1855	1857	1859
Total	5·3	3·6	4·5	6·6
Total from France	4·1	2·7	3·0	4·4
Silk, woollen, cotton, and leather manu-				
factures, and other manufactured goods				
(1) from France	4·0	2·5	2·8	4·2
(2) to the United States	3·7	1·9	2·1	3·5
SWISS IMPORTS				
French transit:				
Total from the United States	·4	·6	·8	·5
Total from Britain	1·0	2·0	3·6	4·1
Total goods to Switzerland	2·2	2·9	4·6	5·2
Raw cotton and silk, cotton textiles, and				
some iron and machines to Switzerland	1·0	1·8	2·8	3·1
Estimates:				
Total goods from Britain to Switzerland	1·2	2·4	4·2	4·2
Goods transhipped or re-exported by				
Britain to Switzerland	·6	1·2	2·1	2·1
British transhipments:				
Total to France, Holland, and Belgium	·1	·3	·3	·2

SOURCES: French transit trade: France, Administration des Douanes, *Tableau général* ... ; estimates from Tables IV and V; British transit trade: BPP 1854/55 [1890] LI; 1856 [2139] LVI; 1857/58 [2442] LIV; 1860 [2752] LXIV ('Annual Statement of Trade and Navigation of the United Kingdom')

France either from Britain or to Switzerland was many times the value of all British transhipments to France, Holland and Belgium; so, in comparison with her re-exports, British transhipments to the Continent, including Switzerland, were very small. The value of British tranship-ments to the Continent is also very small in comparison with our esti-mates of the value of goods transhipped or re-exported to Switzerland by Britain. Fénelon, in two 1858 consular reports, argued that France should capture some of the re-export trade in cotton, since the opening of new railway lines to Switzerland could make it cheaper for the Swiss in Havre than in Liverpool where they were known to be buying most of their raw materials. He states clearly that British re-exporters were doing good business selling to the Swiss in 1858.[50]

The fact that a high proportion of the Anglo-Swiss trade in the 1850s was actually overseas trade helps to explain the apparent decline of the trade between the two countries by 1892, when the Swiss first kept statistics on their trade with Britain. While the volume of trade for both Britain and Switzerland had greatly expanded, trading and shipping patterns had changed a good deal, increasingly by-passing Britain. The Rhine and the European railway network could carry Swiss goods to and from other ports for faster and more economical shipment to and from distant continents. What is equally notable, the Swiss had developed their own political and commercial organization to such an extent that by 1892 they were more independent in their overseas activities.[51]

Another interesting facet of Anglo-Swiss trade is the merchandise trade balance. According to the estimates in Table IV, from 1851 to 1856 the British appeared to run merchandise trade deficits with Switzerland. However, when estimates of the re-exports and transhipments by Britain are taken into account, the picture changes markedly, to a favourable balance for Britain throughout the period. As before 1848, the Swiss trade deficit was probably made up through British participation (mostly re-exports) in the handling of Swiss imports, through favourable balances with other countries, and through British investment in Switzerland.

Using the estimates in Tables IV and V, it is a simple matter to calculate the net Anglo-Swiss trade and its relation to British foreign trade. By subtracting estimates of the amount of Swiss trade which was only passing through Britain from the original estimates of Anglo-Swiss trade, we can construct Table VII, which shows the value of the Swiss goods consumed in Britain plus the Swiss imports originating in Britain. Comparing these estimates with figures for total British foreign trade in the 1850s, the ratios, between ·5 per cent in 1848 and 1·2 per cent in 1860, are much more reasonable than the proportion found earlier for 1855 by using values for gross trade. Furthermore, the sixfold increase in

[50] Salignac-Fénelon to Walewski, 17 July and 19 August 1858 (AAE: Berne: 5). Fénelon was also arguing for more competition with German transport facilities, which supports Herries's assumption about the shipping patterns for Swiss imports; see pages 115-6

[51] This is probably true of both imports and exports; in other words, the Swiss were using other shipping services and were buying less from British re-exporters. Partly through some British negligence, many more raw materials for Swiss industry were coming from Germany. (Waldvogel, pp 135-8)

Table VII. Comparison of the Anglo-Swiss Trade with
British Foreign Trade, 1848–60

	Estimate of net Anglo-Swiss Trade (C–H) (£ mill.)	British foreign trade (exports and net imports)	
		Total (£ mill.)	Swiss share (%)
1848	·6	132·7	·5
1849	1·0	152·9	·7
1850	1·1	162·4	·7
1851	·9	171·4	·5
1852	1·3	175·1	·7
1853	1·5	230·5	·7
1854	1·5	231·0	·6
1855	1·9	218·2	·9
1856	2·7	264·9	1·0
1857	2·9	285·8	1·0
1858	2·5	258·0	1·0
1859	3·2	284·3	1·1
1860	3·8	317·8	1·2

SOURCES: Swiss trade figures from Tables IV and V; British trade
figures from A. H. Imlah, *Economic Elements . . .* , p96

value between 1848 and 1860 is very remarkable, since it is much greater
than the rate of growth of British foreign trade as a whole. Rising British
incomes permitted much higher consumption of Swiss goods, even
though some Swiss products were directly competing with British
products.

IMPLICATIONS OF ANGLO-SWISS TRADE

It is clear that Britain was directly interested in a large part of Swiss
foreign trade and that Swiss trade was an important part of the British
re-export and transhipment businesses. The mid-nineteenth-century
British merchant cared not only about the exchange of British goods for
Swiss goods, but also about much of the trade between Switzerland
and the non-European world. An increasing British mercantile interest

125

in Swiss overseas trade is also indicated by the establishment, in the 1860s, of additional Swiss export industries, such as condensed milk and shoes, drawing a high proportion of British capital.

As in their foreign relations in the political sphere during the early 1850s, the Swiss were quite dependent on the British for carrying on their trade. Yet by the end of the decade, although relying as much as ever on British shipping, the Swiss economy had clearly become much stronger and had indeed already elicited the respect of many business-men. Swiss economic strength contributed in its turn to political viability and national spirit. The country was more able to defend its position among the Continental Powers and less in need of British diplomatic support.

Commercial relations between Britain and Switzerland were augmented by contacts in other spheres as well. For example, the British were increasingly attracted to the Swiss Alps, contributing to the growth of a great tourist industry later in the century. By the middle of the 1850s, the British public was better informed about Switzerland than in 1847 and hence more sympathetic to her political problems. Perhaps for this reason, if not because of an increased volume of Swiss trade handled by British merchants, the British government was forced to take a more active role in Swiss foreign relations in the second half of the decade.

CHAPTER EIGHT

The Neuchâtel Question:
Part II

REVIVAL OF THE PRUSSIAN CLAIM

WITHIN SIX months of the end of the Crimean war, the Neuchâtel question exploded into a major European issue. British diplomacy was again crucial in arranging the settlement for the Swiss. Although the primary motive for this diplomacy was still the political necessity of preserving an independent Switzerland in the heart of Europe, pressure from British public opinion on the government was now an increasing force. Contacts in the commercial sphere, better knowledge about Switzerland, and perhaps the relative success of the Swiss legion, contributed to much more widespread British sympathy for Switzerland in 1857 than in 1847.

When the Swiss refused to adhere to the Declaration of International Mediation in the summer of 1856, they had good reason for fearing that the Neuchâtel question would be raised again. Prussia had pressed the matter on several occasions since the protocol was signed in 1852. Indeed, one of her conditions for joining the western Powers in the Crimean war was a promise of restoration of Frederick William's right in Neuchâtel. To this, Britain and France could not agree.[1] At the Congress of Paris the Prussian Foreign Minister, Baron Manteuffel, was eager once more to have the Neuchâtel question discussed. Clarendon rejected his request, because the *de facto* Neuchâtel government seemed satisfactory and he deemed it imprudent to disturb the peace there.

Although the Swiss knew of Frederick William's eagerness to restore the Royalists in Neuchâtel, they were perhaps less aware that the Con-

[1] For a detailed account of some of the negotiations over this question see Jacques Petitpierre, *Neuchâtel et la Confédération suisse devant l'Europe* (Neuchâtel, 1957); Edgar Bonjour, *Englands Anteil an der Lösung des Neuenburger Konflikts 1856-57* (Basle, 1943); or Philippe de Vargas, *L'Affaire de Neuchâtel, 1856-1857; les négotiations diplomatiques* (Lausanne, 1913)

tinental Powers continued to worry about Radical infection spreading from the Swiss body politic to the rest of Europe. The French government had not openly challenged the Swiss since 1852, but it still received many reports of revolutionary activity and in 1856, according to Cowley, Napoleon was still 'frightened at the idea of Switzerland becoming the foyer of every revolution in Europe'.[2] In January 1857 the Russian Foreign Minister also considered Switzerland to be a 'nucleus of revolution in the centre of Europe'.[3] Frederick William believed so strongly in the righteousness of the monarchic principle that he could not comprehend the strength and national popularity of the new Swiss régime. As before the Crimean war, his interest in restoration was not limited to Neuchâtel, but extended to a hope of overthrowing federal political institutions. Because of the other European Powers' conservatism and reservations about Switzerland, it is not surprising that Prussia counted on their support. Indeed, some politicians in both Neuchâtel and Prussia were even counting on support from the British monarchy.

Since 1848 the Neuchâtel Royalists had lost ground steadily to the Republicans and during the Crimean war they felt threatened still more by the economic changes which railroad development would bring. Hence they decided to bring matters to a crisis in the late summer of 1856. They requested support for their plans from Frederick William, and he voiced no objections. On the night of 3 September they attacked government buildings in several parts of the canton; in the town of Neuchâtel itself they gained control of the castle and other important posts. It was a fleeting victory. Within twenty-four hours, and without calling for federal help, the Republicans recaptured all the temporarily Royalist territory, as well as nearly 700 Royalist prisoners.

Following the insurrection, in the opening phase of these negotiations over Neuchâtel, Prussia decided to pursue her claim, even though the unrealistic and poorly informed king had expected his adherents to gain control easily and had been poised to send them help. After their failure, his government protested again about the 1848 revolution and made a lame request to the Powers for support to restore the 'legal' government. When the dust began to settle in Neuchâtel itself, Sydow demanded that the federal government immediately release the prisoners and stop judicial action.

The insurrection took the Powers by surprise and they were not prepared to press the Prussian claim for restoration on the Swiss government. Gordon and Fénelon agreed to cooperate without apparent

[2] Cowley to Clarendon, 21 December 1856 (FO 519/220)
[3] Wodehouse to Clarendon, 24 January 1857 (FO 192/24)

reservation. Neither would do more than encourage the federal government in its moderate course and both attempted – vainly – to dissuade Sydow from making his extreme demands.

None the less, as before, the Powers' response to the Prussian claim was considerably conditioned by other international questions. The most important of these was disagreement over the interpretation of the provisions of the Treaty of Paris about the Russian frontier near the Black Sea. France supported the Russian claim about the location of Bolgrad, while Britain and Austria opposed it. The Neuchâtel question threw some confusion into this alignment because of its ideological and geographical implications; similarly the frontier question was to affect the subsequent manœuvring over Neuchâtel. In order to have their preferred frontier near the Black Sea, the Russians needed to weaken the Anglo-French alliance, and the Swiss question could serve very well for this. Russia had only to encourage the French to support Prussia, since the British were already known to oppose Prussian restoration. Austria's sympathy for the Prussian claim to Neuchâtel was reserved, because of her jealousy of Prussian influence in Switzerland and in the south German states. Napoleon held the crucial position. Wanting Prussian support on the frontier question and thinking ahead to his plans for Italy, he was eager to gain Prussian goodwill[4] and, for this reason, he was by no means as firm about Switzerland as Britain would have liked. Hatzfeldt, the skilful Prussian Ambassador in Paris, was able to elicit from Napoleon a promise that he would do all he could to help the Royalist prisoners. Napoleon did not dispute Frederick William's demand for the unconditional release of the prisoners before any discussions about the future of Neuchâtel might take place, nor did he even demur to the Prussian threat to use force.

Thus the lines were quickly drawn for several months of diplomatic wrangling. The French pressed the Swiss to release the prisoners, promising help and preservation against attack if they would cooperate, but avoiding any mention of specific conditions for the release. They asked Britain to follow their example, but Clarendon considered that such a demand would be 'little short of an attack upon the independence of the Confed[n] ...' and he 'felt that Switz[d] ought to refuse'.[5] In addition to the merits of the Swiss case, the British did not want France to take the lead in settling European policy, in regard to Bolgrad, Switzerland,

[4] Napoleon specifically discussed this interest in Prussian goodwill in a conversation reported by Bismarck in *The Man and the Statesman* (translated by A. J. Butler) (Leipzig, 1899), p240
[5] Clarendon to Cowley, 3 October 1856 (FO 519/174)

or any future question. Encouraged by Britain's confidence, the Swiss refused the vague French proposal, in this way preventing a Franco-Prussian *rapprochement* which would have strengthened Napoleon's bargaining position in the frontier question. The British and French governments now disagreed both about Swiss policy and about Bolgrad. Both questions strained the Anglo-French alliance severely – and neither could be solved without Anglo-French agreement.

THE BRITISH ATTEMPT TO FIND A SETTLEMENT

In the second phase of the negotiations, Britain initiated some realistic attempts to settle the dispute promptly. This was appropriate enough for several reasons. Because the 1852 protocol was signed in London, the British had some continuing responsibility for its enforcement. Britain enjoyed better relations with Switzerland than the other Powers, so that she was in a good position to wring concessions from the Swiss, if necessary. Furthermore, it was to Britain's advantage to find a solution to that question quickly, to prevent any further shifts in the delicate European power equilibrium.

The first British moves were made in Switzerland. Even before France asked Britain to join her to demand the release of the prisoners, Clarendon inquired, unofficially, whether, and on what terms, the Swiss would accept a joint Anglo-French mediation. In reply, Gordon reported that the Federal Council had growing national support for its 'unalterable determination' to insist on Prussian renunciation of sovereignty as a condition for granting an amnesty. The Swiss had made one conciliatory move, in releasing 634 prisoners, and they were quite ready to grant an amnesty to the rest, if Britain could obtain Frederick William's renunciation.[6]

To persuade the French government to mediate on this basis was more difficult. The British were well aware of their divergence from French policy. Clarendon had no sympathy for French frustration with Swiss firmness and he was unwilling to 'sacrifice *our reason on the altar of France [sic]*'.[7] He first tried an oblique kind of pressure; Gordon was to suggest to the Federal Council that it consider recalling the Swiss regiments in Naples and Rome. Unfortunately, this move brought no results. The Swiss had already discussed the possibility with Fénelon, with little effect other than an increase in Napoleon's irritation.

France and Britain did not go so far as to flaunt their disagreement

[6] Gordon to Clarendon, 5 October 1856 (FO 100/103)
[7] Clarendon to Cowley, 4 October 1856 (FO 519/174)

before all Europe, or even in Switzerland. To preserve appearances, Clarendon sent a note to the Swiss mentioning the possible unconditional release of the prisoners, but making no recommendations. The French apparently misunderstood the contents of this British message, since the Swiss President reported that when Fénelon repeated the French demand in mid-October, he claimed British support for it. After Gordon clarified his government's position, the Swiss again refused the French demand. At Fénelon's urging, Walewski did agree that this second French demand should be discussed with Gordon, so that the entente was at least shown some respect by the French in Berne. It is interesting that both Fénelon and Gordon noticed their Russian colleague's eagerness to foster Anglo-French disagreement. Unfortunately, Anglo-French cooperation in Berne – despite the Russian effort – was not reflected in London and Paris. In early October Clarendon proposed joint Anglo-French mediation, but the French postponed their reply, waiting for the results of their second demand of the Swiss.

Clarendon did not wait for an agreement with France to put pressure on the Prussian government. By the end of September he had sent several messages to Frederick William, attempting to make the reluctant monarch realize the necessity for renunciation. Unfortunately, as in 1852, lack of communication between the Prussian cabinet and the king's entourage added complications to the negotiations, so that many of the British messages may not even have reached the king. Clarendon specifically offered Britain's good offices to work out an arrangement with the Swiss, but he refused to call a conference until the broad terms of settlement were agreed upon. Since Napoleon had already offered his help on more favourable terms, the Prussian government was not, at first, inclined to accept the British proposal. The British then increased their barrage of arguments about the strength of the Swiss military, moral, and legal position, the danger for the peace of Europe from any Prussian military attack, and the realism of the British approach. When Manteuffel learned that the Swiss again refused the French demands, he was more amenable to the British proposal. He then managed to wring a highly confidential statement of terms of renunciation from Frederick William. On condition that the prisoners were released first, the king would renounce his sovereignty; however, he did insist on retaining his title and private property and on having a guarantee of certain religious and charitable institutions.[8] This Prussian concession, following the failure of the French effort to obtain the release of the prisoners, put Britain in a position to bring about a speedy settlement.

[8] Bloomfield to Clarendon, 15 October 1856 (FO 64/418)

Clarendon's next step was to ascertain whether the Swiss would accept the Prussian terms. They were presented unofficially to the Federal Council as a British suggestion. If Frederick William would accept these conditions of Anglo-French mediation, would the Swiss agree to release the prisoners? Clarendon warned the Swiss that a prolongation of the dispute might engender threats to their independence from 'Powers who are unfriendly to Switzerland and her form of government'.[9] The Swiss agreed to the British proposal.

It was more difficult to persuade France to join the British effort, and French cooperation was essential to obtain Prussian agreement. Already the sands had begun to shift again in Berlin and Paris. Manteuffel himself admitted that only the possibility of French opposition to Royalist restoration in Neuchâtel could persuade his government to renounce its claims. When told of the informal British communication to the federal government, Manteuffel would not affirm that Frederick William still held to the same conditions.

The French attitude seems to have changed even more in the week following Britain's joint mediation proposal. While Fénelon was displeased because the British did not support the French demand, he expected the Swiss to accept the British proposal and suggested that France associate herself with it. Fénelon's recommendation of cooperation with Britain was not, however, acceptable to his government. Immediately after the British proposal was presented to the Swiss, the undaunted Napoleon wrote to his old friend General Dufour, asking the general to persuade the Federal Council to accept the French proposal. Napoleon even threatened to allow Prussia to use force. Walewski claimed that if the British proposal had any chance of success, France would gladly support it; but since Prussia would certainly not agree to the British proposal, France would have nothing to do with it. Clarendon countered with a threat to continue without France, but even so the French would not revise their decision.

By the end of October, Prussia had taken steps to rally support among the German states, whose approval was necessary for any eventual military action against Switzerland. To counteract her efforts, the British took diplomatic action in that quarter also. They encouraged Austria to oppose Prussia in the German Diet and likewise urged France to resist discussion of the Neuchâtel question there, arguing that such a move, if supported by Austria, would 'probably lead to placing the Non-Germanic Provinces of Austria under the protection of the Germanic

[9] Clarendon to Gordon, 20 October 1856 (FO 100/99)

Confederation'.[10] Walewski admitted the validity of the argument, but promised nothing. French abstention from protest about Prussian pressure on the German Diet and her repeated demand to the Swiss in stronger form were tantamount to approval of Prussian insistence on unconditional release of the prisoners.

In view of French, and probably German, support for Prussia, it is not surprising that Manteuffel's attitude on the Neuchâtel question became less hopeful for the Swiss and that the king responded negatively to an informal report of the progress of British negotiations with the Swiss. Expecting that Prussia would now disavow her terms, Clarendon refrained from making an official proposal of mediation, in order not to emphasize the lack of Anglo-French concert.

Thus the French blocked an otherwise promising British policy in this phase of the negotiations. If France had agreed with the British proposals, the matter could probably have been settled quickly. French disagreement condemned the British attempt to failure. Clarendon was disgusted with the Powers' attitude that 'a king must be right and Democrats must be wrong, and that political axiom being settled, reason and common sense have little weight ...', but he was still willing to make British good offices available to Prussia.[11] Napoleon was irritated by British initiative and humiliated by the Swiss. He still wanted Prussian support on the Bolgrad question and those negotiations were making no progress either. Prussia was aware of this and, because of British reluctance to allow her participation in a conference to settle that issue, she was in no mood to cooperate with Britain on any other matter. Clearly, one or more of the Powers would have to make some concession before either of the questions could be settled.

BRITISH QUIESCENCE

The third phase of the discussions brought more semblance of understanding between France and England. Although Clarendon complained about the 'separate action' of France, he was quite willing to let France share the success of obtaining the release of the Royalist prisoners. Indeed, if the French were so sure that their scheme would work, Britain had no reason to object, but she would not be party to any attempt 'to ride rough shod' over the Swiss.[12] Clarendon judged that it was time for British 'retirement' from the Swiss question. For this there were two

[10] Clarendon to Cowley, 28 October 1856 (FO 27/1118)
[11] Clarendon to Bloomfield, 21 October 1856 (Clar. ms. c. 137)
[12] Clarendon to Cowley, 18 November 1856 (FO 519/174)

reasons. Britain needed French cooperation on other questions and this might be one way of getting it. Secondly, there was the possibility that the Swiss might try to shift responsibility for settlement to Britain – an uncomfortable prospect for the realistic Foreign Office.

The British failure in Berlin did not persuade the Swiss to agree to the French proposal. Swiss public opinion strongly supported the firm policy of the Federal Council, and the Council did not consider its position in any way weakened by continuing pressure from France and Prussia. Dufour answered Napoleon's message with an expression of his country's hope that the French government 'would not connive at an attack being made on the independence of Switzerland which acted like the keystone in the arch of the European Polity of Nations'.[13] Possibly the Swiss were beginning to have a slightly exaggerated view of their importance in Europe, but it was true that, as in 1847, their geographical position as a buffer state was of vital importance to all the Powers. When the federal government learned of the stalemate in British mediation, Dufour was sent to Paris to explain the Swiss position more carefully to his former student, Napoleon, and to try to elicit some more tangible assurance both from him and from Cowley about Prussian renunciation. The Swiss, and Fénelon, expected that settlement was now only a matter of form.

While Dufour was conferring fruitlessly in Paris, the Prussians made another move. In mid-November they presented the Swiss with a second demand for the release of the prisoners, advancing Frederick William's 'well-known moderation and absence of ambition' as assurance for a favourable settlement for the Swiss.[14] The Swiss again refused, but none the less the Prussians believed their anti-Swiss position to be stronger, on the basis of increasing German support. In Berne Austria and some south German states had indicated agreement with the latest Prussian demand and Bismarck, their representative in Frankfurt, had persuaded the Diet to approve the principles of Prussian policy about Neuchâtel. Bismarck also reported that the British representative in Frankfurt expected objections but not active opposition from the other Powers to the Prussian demands. In Bismarck's optimistic opinion, military measures would not be needed because the Swiss would sooner give in than spend money on defence.[15]

After ten weeks of diplomatic jockeying, the Prussian and Swiss posi-

[13] Gordon to Clarendon, 4 November 1856 (FO 100/104)
[14] Gordon to Clarendon, 18 November 1856 (*ibid*)
[15] Otto von Bismarck-Schoenhausen, *Correspondence diplomatique* (edited by Th. Funk-Brentano) (translated by L. Schmidt) (Paris, 1883), ii, p209

tions were further entrenched and the two potential mediating Powers remained in disagreement. Both France and Britain knew that the Swiss would agree to release the prisoners if they could be assured of a favourable outcome from subsequent negotiations. The French government pressed Cowley to recommend British support for the French proposal, but Cowley refused, because Britain 'could not blindly enter into engagements, which from their vagueness might lead to future misunderstandings'.[16] Furthermore, like Clarendon, he feared that the Swiss wanted to rely too much on Britain, for even Dufour did not deny that the Federal Assembly would require British approval in some form before voting for an amnesty for the prisoners. Napoleon was getting himself into a bad mess and would obviously need British help to extricate himself.

Because Britain would still not support the French proposal, Dufour's mission failed. He returned to Berne with no promise from Britain and only a very slightly strengthened promise from Napoleon, coupled with yet another repetition of the French demand.

THE THREAT OF WAR

Despite Britain's unwillingness to support the French approach to the Swiss question, the general diplomatic situation in mid-November seemed more favourable for a Neuchâtel settlement. Cowley was 'beginning to see daylight on the Bolgrad Question',[17] and better Anglo-French understanding on that issue permitted his government to indicate slightly more tolerance for French policy toward the Swiss. On both matters, Britain was resigned to helping Napoleon out of his 'self-made scrapes', as far as was consistent with British honour and policy.[18] On 25 November Clarendon sent another message to the Swiss: Britain was still unable to give any assurance that liberation of the prisoners would facilitate a solution of the question but, if the federal government decided to free the prisoners without trial, Britain would, with France, try to persuade Frederick William 'to arrange the Question about Neufchatel in accordance with the wishes of the Swiss ...'.[19] This slight British encouragement of Swiss cooperation with France had no immediate effect, however, since it reached Berne just after the Swiss had rejected French demands for the third time.

[16] Cowley to Clarendon, 20 November 1856 (FO 192/20)
[17] Cowley to Clarendon, 16 November 1856 (FO 519/220)
[18] Clarendon to Cowley, 11 December 1856 (FO 519/174)
[19] Clarendon to Gordon, 25 November 1856 (FO 100/99)

In early December the Prussians were moved by the evident failure of Napoleon's mediation efforts and other pressures to take some important decisions on the Neuchâtel question. On the 2nd, Prussian officials in Berlin recommended a combination of several moves; the king appears to have adopted all but one of them. The German Diet was informed of the latest Swiss refusal of Prussian demands; arrangements for the passage of troops, en route to Switzerland, were discussed with the south German states; and military preparations were started. On 8 December identical notes containing a summary of the Prussian position and a threat of military action were sent to the Powers and the German Diet. But Frederick William balked at the crucial recommendation of his more realistic advisers: in his message to Napoleon, he did not indicate any readiness to renounce Neuchâtel.[20] The British Ambassador in Berlin, Lord Bloomfield, considered the Prussian threats to be intended only to intimidate the Swiss, but he did not see how Prussia could retreat once mobilization, set for 1 January, was started. A week after sending her notes to the Powers, but before receiving their replies, Prussia broke diplomatic relations with the Swiss.

Because of these Prussian decisions, the question was discussed with more urgency in other European capitals. While official France still voiced support for Prussia, her ministers were privately increasingly worried about the situation. Concurrently with the Prussian diplomatic break with Switzerland, the *Moniteur*[21] published an article which was highly critical of Swiss obstinacy. Indeed, the French were apparently giving so much encouragement to Prussia that Cowley was not surprised at Barman's suspicion of French ambitions to occupy Neuchâtel themselves, if the affair reached a military showdown.[22] However, like Bismarck, the French government had expected the Swiss to be sufficiently intimidated to give in; it had not anticipated that Prussian military measures might actually be used. Although Napoleon spoke to Cowley at some length about the dangers from the Swiss right of asylum and free press, he was not at all pleased with the prospect of Prussian military action on the eastern frontier of France. While he had approved the public *Moniteur* article, in conversation with Cowley he claimed to have warned Prussia against war. Because much of French public opinion disagreed with an anti-Swiss policy and because of the real danger to

[20] Bismarck, *Correspondence diplomatique*, pp 213-19
[21] The *Moniteur* was an organ of French government opinion
[22] Cowley to Clarendon, 18 December 1856 (FO 192/20). The French would, incidentally, recover some of a prosperous watch industry which had been lost with the flight of the Huguenots from France

French security, the French government was under considerable pressure to obtain the release of the prisoners before Prussia mobilized.

The new Prussian moves also alarmed the Foreign Office, but Clarendon still refused to urge Switzerland to release the prisoners unconditionally. Since both France and Prussia seemed to be following policies dictated more by emotion than by reason, it was all the more important that the Foreign Office should keep the political realities of the situation in sharp focus. Yet to settle the matter, Britain needed French cooperation, and this in turn would demand much diplomatic subtlety. Before replying to the Prussian note, Clarendon checked to be sure that his draft would not 'jar too much' with the French reply. He took the opportunity to point out again that if Britain and France acted together, there would be more chance of 'checking that doublebarrelled Donkey the King who has got into an unhandsome fix between a folly & a humiliation'.[23] The French did not disapprove of the British note, but this was no indication of Anglo-French cooperation either, since it was counterbalanced by Britain's lack of any enthusiasm about Walewski's idea of including Neuchâtel in the agenda for the Great Power conference on the frontier question.

In Switzerland, two rather different trends were gaining impetus. The Swiss government still had strong popular support for its opposition to any policy which might lead to Prussian restoration. The Swiss considered their position to be at least as strong as Prussia's and, because theirs was a democratic form of government, they expected some support from other European liberals, which would weaken their monarchic neighbours. The bullying attitude of France, most recently manifested in the *Moniteur* article, had served only to revive Swiss fears of France and Napoleon's aspirations for another protectorate over Switzerland. The enthusiastic young nation was more than ready to defend itself against Prussia and France.

The second, less public, tendency in Switzerland was to give increasing attention to the support which Prussia seemed to have amassed; the Federal Council did not want to close the door to a peaceful solution. When, in mid-December, the Council heard rumours that most of the Prussian Cabinet favoured renunciation, it made another proposal to Prussia for direct negotiation, but the Prussians refused. As the date for Prussian mobilization drew closer, the diplomatic corps in Berne became keenly aware of a Swiss desire to reach an agreement peacefully with Prussia.

[23] Clarendon to Cowley, 16 December 1856 (FO 519/174)

Gordon was particularly impressed with this second element in the Federal Council's deliberations and with desirability for quick action to prevent an armed confrontation. On 21 December Clarendon was surprised by a telegram from Gordon proposing, with the American Minister, that the Powers' representatives in Berne declare with 'collective and positive assurance' that after the trial of the prisoners was called off, their governments would use their good offices to obtain Frederick William's complete renunciation of rights in Neuchâtel.[24] The Federal Council would agree to such a proposal supported by both Britain and France. However, Gordon's idea was scarcely likely to succeed. Russia, having favoured Prussia since September, refused; Austria also declined; and Sardinia deferred to the British and French lead. Ever mindful of the importance of the alliance, Britain left the decision to France. The French, annoyed by American interference, rejected the proposal because it was similar to their own, which they promptly renewed, thinking that the Swiss might now be more agreeable. Clarendon became concerned, with this flurry, lest the situation get out of control through developments in Berne, and he tersely instructed Gordon to 'Do nothing without further instructions.'[25] The Swiss still refused to place themselves at the mercy of France alone, and they were disappointed that the Powers had not taken up their willingness to settle.

Time was growing short, and the momentum of Prussian policy was unabated. Prussian plans were based on very poor information about factors working against them: Bismarck expected the Swiss to offer no military resistance and Manteuffel was confident that Prussia could simply occupy parts of northern Switzerland as 'a pledge' until the Swiss capitulated, without declaring war.[26] In early January Napoleon strengthened the Prussian estimate of French support against Switzerland by conferring an order of the Legion of Honour on Frederick William. The Prussian press discussed mobilization with enthusiasm, and permission for troop passage through south Germany was obtained. None the less, Bloomfield noted that little was being done in Berlin

[24] Gordon to Clarendon, 21 December 1856 (FO 100/105)
[25] Clarendon to Gordon, 26 December 1856 (FO 192/20). The British government had been unenthusiastic about Gordon's appointment to Switzerland in the first place. [Aberdeen to Clarendon, 20 December 1853 (Clar. ms. c. 4)]. By 1856 he had become very sympathetic with the Swiss, as most of his reports show, and for this reason, Clarendon put little store by his dispatches [Clarendon to Cowley, 5 December 1856 (FO 519/174)]. Considering the gravity of the question, Clarendon's private correspondence with Gordon was quite sparse. He urged Gordon, as much as the Swiss, to be cautious
[26] Bloomfield to Clarendon, 10 January 1857 (FO 64/432)

itself, as mobilization was postponed first until 6 January, then until the 15th.

French vacillation between policies of trying to satisfy Prussia and cooperating with Britain was evident in their discussions with Cowley about plans for a conference. On Christmas Day Napoleon agreed to a joint Anglo-French note inviting the Swiss 'to put [France and Britain] in a position to make ... propositions by means of a conference', but within twenty four hours Walewski announced another change in policy, to a plan more favourable to Prussia.[27] Cowley insisted that the Swiss be consulted on plans for a Great Power conference. Britain would consent to a conference only if the aims of negotiation were clearly defined beforehand and if it were held in London. France would not agree to hold the conference in London because Britain so clearly opposed Prussia, nor would the French give Cowley a straightforward answer about their intentions if, after the prisoners were released, Prussia did not renounce. After one of the conversations in Paris, Walewski wrote to Fénelon that Gordon was instructed to support the French offer completely, omitting Cowley's qualification which put the responsibility on Switzerland. Gordon was in fact sent no such instructions. The misunderstanding was another symptom of the French need for British help. Cowley wrote, rather smugly, that 'nothing ... could be better calculated ... [to show that] the moral weight of France alone is powerless even in a country where her influence ought to predominate. Joined to that of England, it is irresistible. [sic]'[28]

Hitherto, Austria had tried to stay as much in the background as possible, but at the end of December she too was drawn into the discussions. She was apprehensive about a war between Prussia and Switzerland lest it 'prove the signal for a struggle between monarchical principles and those of self-government upon the widest basis ...',[29] about the real prospect of Prussian troops coming into her sphere of influence in the German Confederation, and about the possibility of increased French influence in Switzerland as a result of cooperation with Prussia. These factors, and encouragement from Britain, prompted her to oppose Prussia in the Diet. For the same reasons, a special Prussian mission to Vienna failed soon thereafter to enlist Austrian cooperation. Like France, Austria wanted a Great Power conference to discuss the question immediately. She did not insist on a Prussian promise of renunciation before the prisoners were released, reasoning that, if Napoleon's

[27] Cowley to Clarendon, 25 and 26 December 1856 (FO 27/1140)
[28] Cowley to Clarendon, 2 January 1857 (FO 27/1187)
[29] Seymour to Clarendon, 24 December 1856 (FO 192/20)

policy failed, a conference would ensure that the king would renounce 'his very unreal and unprofitable rights'.[30] With this Austrian move in the direction of British policy, European alignments were loosened and the prospects for a settlement of the Neuchâtel question improved. Not only the Swiss had seen the spectre of Napoleon I's aggression in French policy.

The Bolgrad question was resolved by an agreement signed on 6 January. This settlement permitted Britain to give more attention to the Swiss question and freed her somewhat from the necessity to concede to France. Indeed, the Foreign Office was under growing pressure from inside Britain to take a more active part in the discussions about Neuchâtel. In December the press evinced such 'great sympathy .. for the Swiss & great excitement agst the K of P' that Palmerston and Clarendon feared that British public opinion would force the government to support the Swiss more actively, and that Britain would become 'every day more divergent from [the policy] of France'.[31] Yet Clarendon still considered it important that Britain should not annoy France. British policy had to choose a careful course in order both to satisfy British public opinion and to avoid becoming a scapegoat for the probable failure of French policy. By early January the pressure in Britain had built up even more. Clarendon wrote 'the thermometer is rising here & no Gov^t cd stand an hour when Parl^t meets if it it cd justly be accused of having helped to coerce or to deceive the Swiss'; if war between Switzerland and Prussia were not prevented, Britain would at least have to blockade Prussian ports to help the Swiss.[32]

Thus by the New Year the British government was prodded by domestic opinion to assume a more active role. Clarendon offered to resume the October negotiations because, he asserted, if the Prussian army reached Neuchâtel, there would be 'such an explosion' of revolution in Europe that Prussia would deeply regret her present policy.[33] The British Cabinet agreed unanimously to give no support whatever to Frederick William if he actually tried to enforce his rights in Neuchâtel. On 14 January, the day before Prussian mobilization was to take place, Clarendon made a last effort at persuasion: Manteuffel was to be told that Prussia 'should not be entirely ignorant of the active part which this Country may determine to take in the defence of Switz^d, if attacked by Prussia'.[34] These were strong words.

[30] Seymour to Clarendon, 31 December 1856 (FO 192/24)
[31] Clarendon to Cowley, 22 December 1856 (FO 519/174)
[32] Clarendon to Cowley, 3 and 12 January 1857 (FO 519/175)
[33] Clarendon to Bloomfield, 30 December 1856 (Clar. ms. c. 137)
[34] Clarendon to Bloomfield, 14 January 1857 (Clar. ms. c. 138)

Meanwhile, the Swiss were optimistic about cooperation from south Germany if a military showdown was unavoidable. The Federal Assembly voted for immediate mobilization and the appointment of Dufour as general; yet it also unanimously approved the Federal Council's policy of continued negotiations, and several efforts to find a peaceful settlement were afoot. The American Minister, Theodore S. Fay, who had at one time been on good terms with Frederick William, set off for Berlin in a private capacity to try to bring back some kind of assurance about renunciation.[35] A professor of the University of Basle also went to Berlin to try to mediate.[36] When the Duke of Saxe-Coburg offered his mediation, a Federal Councillor was immediately sent to Frankfurt to discuss his terms. The Federal Council sent another representative, Dr Kern,[37] to Paris in another attempt to extract more positive assurance from both France and Britain to guarantee the independence of Neuchâtel from Prussia. If he was successful, the Swiss would release the prisoners. In their repeated attempts to enlist unqualified British support and in their encouragement of other mediation attempts, the Swiss desire to liberate the prisoners was abundantly clear.

In early January Cowley was thus under added pressure from the Swiss for a less reserved statement. He remarked to Clarendon, 'Inconvenient as this may be to Her Majesty's Government, Your Lordship cannot but feel gratified at the homage thus paid to the honour and good faith of England' – but neither the Foreign Secretary nor his Ambassador was deflected from the agreed position.[38] Barman gave the impression that his government now wanted Britain to decide whether to release the prisoners and to determine the conditions for a final settlement. Yet because Barman also tried to elicit similar assistance from the French, Cowley was on his guard more than ever against compromising the British position and against Barman's 'double game'.[39] The Swiss were told that they themselves must make the decision and, on 6 January, that Britain could do no more than repeat her readiness to help find a settlement, with the same reservations as before.

As 15 January approached, Swiss railway and manufacturing interests became anxious about the disruptive effects which war would have on their enterprises, and the Federal Council prepared to recommend an

[35] Edgar Bonjour, 'Ein amerikanischer Vermittlungsversuch im Neuenburger Konflikt' (*Zeitschrift für Schweizerische Geschichte*, Zurich, 1939)
[36] Karl Wall, 'Heinrich Gelzer (1813–1889) als Diplomat im Neuenburger Konflikt' (*Basler Zeitschrift für Geschichte und Altertumskunde*, Bd. 49, Basle, 1950)
[37] Kern was another former acquaintance of Napoleon
[38] Cowley to Clarendon, 2 January 1857 (Fo 192/24)
[39] Cowley to Clarendon, 5 January 1857 (Fo 519/220)

amnesty for the prisoners. Although none of the private mediation efforts had produced any tangible results, the would-be mediators were optimistic about Frederick William's intentions. Barman's reports from Paris were not specific, but they too were hopeful. To pave the way for an amnesty, the federal government publicized French statements which assured that Prussian hostilities against Switzerland would not be permitted and recognized the Swiss right to expel the Royalists until the question was settled. The official Swiss press also asserted that Britain was joining French assurances about helping to work out a favourable settlement. British support was clearly being claimed to justify the Federal Council's change in policy.

Both Clarendon and Cowley realized that the Swiss would probably concede, and consequently their attitude also seems to have undergone some modification in early January. Cowley had observed that '... all they want is to get our name as a security for the transaction. I think it can be managed ....'[40] But he did not say how. So that the Federal Council would not misunderstand the extent of British encouragement, Gordon gave the President copies of the British dispatches to correct, officially, the mistaken press reports. This would satisfy Parliament if the Foreign Office were later called to account. Then, on 15 January, Clarendon telegraphed that the British position need not be publicized in the Swiss press: 'We have reason to believe that if the Prisoners are liberated France will be firm with Prussia.'[41] This message implied approval of a Swiss decision to release the Royalists and assurance that a favourable settlement for Neuchâtel would follow. The official British position had been made clear to the Swiss government, but Clarendon did not object to an incorrect press report which would enable the Federal Council to gain necessary popular support for a change in its policy.

Several factors probably persuaded Clarendon to allow Swiss public opinion to be misled in this way. First, Austria had recently declared herself in favour of Prussian renunciation of Neuchâtel. More important, however, were developments in Prussia and France. Bloomfield reported from Berlin that the Austrian position and strong British protests had caused some uneasiness in the Prussian government and Clarendon might well have expected his message of the 14th to Manteuffel to be decisive in persuading it to make some concessions. In the French direction, the British had never known whether Napoleon actually had received any promise from Frederick William about re-

---

[40] Cowley to Gordon, 3 January 1857 (*ibid*)
[41] Clarendon to Gordon, 15 January 1857 (Fo 100/108)

nunciation, but by the 14th some positive assurance about this from Napoleon reached Queen Victoria.[42] This, combined with increasing French nervousness about Prussian military plans, gave Clarendon grounds to expect more French firmness with Prussia. Furthermore, Cowley reported that Hatzfeldt apparently regretted his very effective 'net of diplomacy' around Napoleon, and he at least recognized that his king should have abandoned Neuchâtel long ago.[43] A fifth and most important reason for this British move was the obvious determination of the Swiss government to avert hostilities; the Foreign Office did not want to take positive action to make difficulties for the Assembly approval of the decision.

On 16 January, after stormy debate, both houses of the Federal Assembly approved an amnesty for the Royalists by nearly unanimous votes. While members of the Assembly recognized that their decision involved some risk, an important argument used was British support for the move. On the night of the 17th, the prisoners were released and banished from Switzerland until the status of Neuchâtel could be settled. In this way the trials were stopped before the Royalist links with Prussia were brought out in court. The Swiss army was soon demobilized and the Prussian order for mobilization was never put into effect.[44] The fourth phase of the affair was over, with the removal of the imminent threat of war.

NEGOTIATION OF A SETTLEMENT

The final stage of the question – the negotiation of the details of a settlement – had in fact already begun. Cowley had been discussing arrangements for a conference ever since Christmas, but his progress was slow because fundamental questions about the status of Switzerland were raised again. During the earlier phases of the discussions, in anticipation of this problem, the Foreign Office had prepared a memorandum reviewing British policy toward Switzerland in the 1840s; it stated that the British aim had been 'to discourage every project of foreign interference except under circumstances of the most urgent necessity'.[45] At the end of January 1857 two more Foreign Office memoranda concluded

[42] Clarendon to Wodehouse, 14 January 1857 (Clar. ms. c. 138). It is a mystery why, in these circumstances, Napoleon did not give more definite promises to the Swiss
[43] Cowley to Clarendon, 1 January 1857 (FO 27/1187)
[44] The king did actually sign the order, however. Bloomfield to Clarendon, 17 January 1857 (FO 64/432)
[45] 'Communications between H.M.'s Govt. and Foreign Govts. on the subject of an intervention in the affairs of Switzerland' (FO 100/107)

that in 1815 the Powers had not intended to require Great Power consent for any changes in Swiss internal organization. However, as in the *Sonderbund* crisis, the British view was not shared by the other Powers. It was clear that Prussia wanted a change of government in Switzerland. Russia supported the Prussian aim, reasoning that Switzerland should not be protected by her neutrality when she violated the treaty rights of another Power and that the neutral status of Switzerland was intended simply to provide a buffer state between Austria and France in case of war. For the Russians, neutrality was unrelated to independence or political viability. The Austrian and French views were somewhere between the British and Russian positions. Thus, despite the hopeful signs visible before the prisoners were released, there was still a real danger that Frederick William, even if forced to renounce, might have support for conditions inconsistent with Swiss independence.

The Swiss, in strong contrast with the Prussians and the French, took diplomatic action immediately after granting the amnesty. They formally requested a Great Power conference to discuss a settlement; and, at Britain's request, they drew up a precise statement of their conditions for such a conference. Also, they again sent Kern to Paris for further negotiations with the French government and with Cowley. Since September France had tried to give the Swiss the impression that a settlement would quickly follow the release of the prisoners, but, even before the amnesty was granted, both Napoleon and Hatzfeldt expressed their doubts, to Cowley, that Prussia would be more cooperative after the prisoners were released. Napoleon still wanted some kind of entente with Prussia, so that he was reluctant to exert the pressure necessary to force Frederick William to renounce. Indeed, after the Swiss released the prisoners, Prussia claimed that by so doing Switzerland had fully recognized Frederick William's rights, although Manteuffel still said that the king would renounce. Bloomfield predicted that Prussia would delay any negotiations in the hope of getting better terms 'and perhaps of serving at the same time the Conservative Party in Switzerland'.[46]

In Paris Cowley moved gingerly, wanting the French to ask for British help. He skilfully cultivated French irritation about Prussian delay, and at last manœuvred Walewski into further discussion of conference terms. The two main points requiring Anglo-French agreement were the location of the conference and the aims of the negotiations. The Swiss wanted to have the conference in London because they distrusted France, while the Prussians wanted Paris because they distrusted Britain. Clarendon conceded this point, however, when Cowley came

[46] Bloomfield to Clarendon, 17 January 1857 (FO 64/432)

144

within sight of agreement with Walewski about conference aims, 'but we ought to have an assurance that no attempt will be made to meddle with Swiss institutions'.[47] To help the talks about the aims of the negotiations, Cowley prepared a memorandum which Napoleon approved verbally, after he was satisfied that Paris would be the conference site. British concessions did not quite bring the French to terms, for, unfortunately, after more detailed discussion between Cowley and Walewski, the memorandum was not signed.

'This infernal Swiss question'[48] hung fire for nearly two weeks of French delay. Because Walewski seemed to hope that Britain would persuade the Swiss to accept any terms which a conference might offer, Cowley gloomily predicted that France 'will throw [Switzerland] over if Prussia continues obstinate ...'.[49] However, once Kern had drawn up a second memorandum about the Swiss position, Walewski was ready to be more precise on details and more agreeable about preventing any pretext for Prussian intervention in the future. Meanwhile, Cowley also needed French support about a dispute in Persia and, to enlist French cooperation on this, he began lavishing flattery on Walewski. The flattery must have had a beneficial side-effect on the Neuchâtel question: Walewski at last sent out invitations to a conference and, on 16 February, an Anglo-French *note verbale* about Neuchâtel was signed.

The first meeting of the conference was further delayed because the Russian Ambassador was away from Paris and the Prussians were slow to instruct their delegate to the conference. In the interval, nervousness about Frederick William's intentions grew. His government kept a stony silence about its conditions for settlement, while giving out some hints of increasing stubbornness, such as more complaints about the injustices suffered by the banished Royalists, remarks about the king's obstinacy, and, again, rumours of a Prussian military attack on Switzerland. In Switzerland, the delay caused much annoyance, for, with elections approaching, the Federal Council was accused of betrayal and many worried that the extreme Radicals might gain power because of popular impatience for a settlement. The Federal Council itself even feared that the Royalists, in spite of their ostensible exile, were conniving with Frederick William to plan another insurrection in Neuchâtel. The Swiss still anticipated French deception and threatened to recall Kern. The French, too, became annoyed by indications of Prussian evasiveness,

[47] Clarendon to Cowley, 20 January 1857 (FO 27/1172)
[48] Cowley to Clarendon, 28 January 1857 (FO 519/221)
[49] Cowley to Gordon, 4 February 1857 (*ibid*)

and, stimulated by Cowley's remarks about the dangers inherent in Swiss impatience, Walewski protested about Prussian delay.

Finally, nearly two months after the Swiss had released the prisoners, the first session of the conference was assembled in Paris, attended only by Walewski and the ambassadors of the other three mediating Powers. Walewski proposed a protocol asking Frederick William to renounce his sovereignty. A stronger statement was urged by Cowley, but it was defeated by Austria and Russia. Because Napoleon and Walewski still hankered to settle agreeably to 'that most uninteresting of Potentates and of men, the K. of Prussia', and because of obvious Russian delays, Cowley expected prolonged negotiations and little support for the British position.[50]

Within a few days a second meeting was held, with Hatzfeldt. Cowley was disgusted with the proceedings because Hatzfeldt, like a 'great baby', objected to everything and Walewski, as chairman, made no attempt to keep order.[51] Even so, the conference did agree to ask Prussia for a prompt statement of conditions and it rejected Prussian objections to Swiss representation at subsequent meetings.

More waiting followed the second meeting. Although France and Britain were both impatient, eventual Prussian compliance with the mediating Powers' request for a statement was attributed to the Tsar, who wrote personally to Frederick William 'that his hesitations were ruining the credit of Prussia'.[52] On 24 March the Prussians gave their conditions to a third meeting of the conference. Cowley was relieved, first, because he found the terms 'susceptible of arrangement'[53] and, second, because some of the Prussian allegations brought criticism even from Austria and Russia. A fourth meeting communicated the conditions to Kern.

With both the disputants and the mediators in possession of specific material with which to bargain, Britain's job was twofold, to encourage the Swiss to be conciliatory and to persuade the other mediators to insist firmly on concessions from Prussia. The Swiss made a number of objections: to a guarantee of church property and charitable institutions, to an excessively large indemnity, to an explicit recognition of the title of Prince of Neuchâtel for Frederick William, and to any engagement about constitutional revision for the canton because it would violate the federal constitution. Cowley agreed with some of these points, but insisted that

[50] Cowley to Clarendon, 6 March 1857 (*ibid*)
[51] Cowley to Clarendon, 8 March 1857 (*ibid*)
[52] Cowley to Clarendon, 15 March 1857 (*ibid*)
[53] Cowley to Clarendon, 24 March 1857 (FO 27/1192)

the Swiss be ready to make concessions where vital interests were not at stake. In this vein, he asked Gordon to urge the federal government to agree to a reasonable indemnity; the Swiss would take a great risk of another crisis if they forfeited their chance for Great Power recognition of the new position of Neuchâtel.[54] At least twice, Gordon attempted to persuade the Federal Council to change its instructions to Kern, but without apparent success. In other capitals, however, Britain described the terms as 'onerous': the indemnity demanded was excessive and 'objectionable interference in the internal affairs of the canton was contemplated'.[55]

On 1 April the fifth conference was held, with many more hours of discussion, and the sixth took place the next day. The mediating Powers agreed that the Swiss should not object to the use of an empty title by Frederick William, or to the principle of an indemnity for the rights he was to cede, and that Prussia should give up hopes for constitutional revision in Neuchâtel. Kern conceded that the charitable institutions might be guaranteed in some way.

In the two-weeks interval before the next formal meeting, a draft treaty prepared by Walewski (at Cowley's suggestion) was discussed informally. Clarendon, probably anticipating more pressure from domestic public opinion, wrote that Britain must stand by the Swiss in resisting Prussian pretensions, but Cowley, closer to the scene of action and exasperated by Kern's wariness about a guarantee of the charitable and religious institutions, described the Swiss as 'dunderheaded & as obstinate as mules'.[56] None the less, he persisted. With the French now more cooperative during this bargaining period, he managed to persuade Walewski to revise the draft on several points which were important to the Swiss. At its seventh meeting the conference unanimously recommended that Prussia and Switzerland agree to the French draft. The proposed treaty did not mention Frederick William's title; it did require a Swiss indemnity of one million francs (half the amount originally demanded by Prussia) and a guaranteed income for the charitable institutions.[57]

The final hurdle was to persuade the Swiss and Prussian governments to accept the treaty. Kern was convinced that the draft was the best his government could hope for, and he returned to Berne to advocate

[54] Gordon was again warned about being 'more Swiss than the Swiss'. Cowley to Gordon, 27 March 1857 (FO 519/221)
[55] Clarendon to Bloomfield, 27 March 1857 (FO 64/428)
[56] Cowley to Clarendon, 13 April 1857 (FO 519/221)
[57] BPP 1857 [2222 Sess. 2] XLIII. ('Treaty ... relative to Neuchâtel ...')

Federal Council approval. Gordon also acted vigorously to explain Cowley's arguments in favour of the treaty. An important point was the probability that Prussia would ask for changes and could be best restrained if the Swiss had already given their acceptance. All the other mediating Powers expressed their support of the draft in discussion with the Federal Council. The Russian Minister even encouraged the Swiss to listen especially to the strong recommendations of Britain! The Federal Council hesitated for a few days before making its decision, then to the great relief of the Berne diplomatic corps announced acceptance on 30 April.

As before, the Prussian government responded much less promptly than the Swiss. Clarendon seems to have followed Cowley's suggestion that Britain should have as little as possible to do with persuading Prussia, but, without official instructions, the British Chargé d'Affaires in Berlin did make a few pointed remarks to Manteuffel. The Austrian and Russian representatives in Berlin were not instructed to do anything about the treaty either, and French exhortations were described to Clarendon as 'placid'.[58] Frederick William was still not reconciled to renunciation. Before the Prussian government learned of Swiss acceptance, it instructed Hatzfeldt to inquire whether, if it gave up the indemnity, France would agree to a concession over church property. This Prussian dilly-dallying was not appreciated in Paris. Walewski immediately sent a stronger note to Berlin, and his most important argument was the Swiss decision to accept the draft. Then the Swiss nearly upset the diplomatic apple-cart by publishing the draft treaty, a move which displeased the Powers, because the negotiations, still incomplete, were to have been secret. A very critical article about this Swiss mis-step appeared in the *Moniteur*, but, fortunately, the French did not retract their recommendation of Prussian acceptance. In fact, they planned more pressure on Frederick William through an imminent state visit of Prince Napoleon to Berlin. Finally, on 11 May, Frederick William, faced with the prospect of seeing Prince Napoleon, whom he did not like, authorized acceptance of the draft treaty. The issue was at last settled.

Formal signature of the treaty took place in Paris on 26 May. As soon as the treaty was ratified by all the parties, in mid-June, the Royalists were allowed to return to Neuchâtel. Frederick William duly issued a proclamation releasing his Swiss subjects from his sovereignty; this was his last important act before he succumbed to mental illness. The Prussians complained that the Swiss were violating the treaty in July and again at the time of the Orsini incident the following January, but

[58] Loftus to Clarendon, 18 April 1857 (FO 64/435)

148

neither the French nor the British would give the Prussian case any sympathy.

REFLECTIONS ABOUT THE NEUCHÂTEL QUESTION

Several points of similarity may be found between the resolution of the Neuchâtel question and the diplomacy of the *Sonderbund* crisis. But there are differences also, and it can be argued that the settlement of the Neuchâtel question dissipated the last remnants of the fundamental issue involved in the *Sonderbund* – namely, the nature of Swiss independence and neutrality. Again in 1857 the British Foreign Office examined the reasons for maintaining the Swiss position in Europe and found them as important as ever. The other Powers were also brought to realize this, so that the alignment of the 1847-48 crisis was at last broken. While France supported Prussia on other grounds and as far as possible, Austria came to support a final settlement of the Neuchâtel question, so that the democratic Swiss institutions survived unscathed.

As in 1847, French diplomacy suffered a defeat, although over Neuchâtel it was a more subtle one. For both questions, French rulers had wanted to play the role of mediator without having a clear evaluation of the ingredients of their own position. Napoleon was in principle a supporter of liberal government and an ally of Britain, but in fact, in this case, he was strongly tempted to cooperate with absolutism and even to help perpetuate it. The biased reports of both Bois-le-Comte and Fénelon[59] clearly gave their government little appreciation of the strength and stability of Swiss institutions. In both situations, the French government put itself into a position where it could only be defeated. Wanting the credit for successful mediation favourable to the conservative Powers, it was forced to help humiliate them.

Another similarity is the misrepresentation of the British position by the Swiss press, which in both cases falsely claimed official British support. In 1847 Palmerston had wanted to restrain the Diet, but he had no time to object to the misrepresentation before the Diet made its critical decision. In 1857 the Swiss had more support in Europe and in Britain, so that, while Clarendon had time to clarify the British position in the Swiss press, he was satisfied merely to make formal objections to the

[59] Although Fénelon worked closely with Gordon in the early phases of the Neuchâtel dispute, his dispatches show increasing obsession with Swiss revolutionary activity in the later stages. Gordon wrote, in early 1857, that all members of the French Legation were confidently expecting Prussian decorations for their parts in the affair. Gordon to Clarendon, 26 February 1857 (Clar. ms. c. 77)

Federal Council, to meet subsequent parliamentary criticism in case the policy failed. In both international crises over vital Swiss interests, the federal government needed to claim British support for its policy in order to win public approval for it in Switzerland.

The state of the Anglo-French alliance was an important element of both crises, but here some differences are also apparent. In 1847 it had already been seriously weakened by previous issues, such as the Spanish marriages, whereas in 1856-57 France and Britain had cooperated successfully in the Crimean war and, although the alliance was strained by the Bolgrad, Neuchâtel, and other questions, both countries recognized its importance and were unwilling to jeopardize it seriously. Hence, both allies made some concessions, Britain in the earlier phases and the French particularly during the conferences in Paris. In fact, Walewski confided to Bismarck that it was impossible to make demands of Switzerland which she would refuse with certain British support, because none of the Powers would risk a disagreement with Britain.[60]

Another point of difference is the speed of the negotiations, once the crisis came to a head, which in turn is related to the issues involved. In 1847 the discussion was about the right of the Swiss to determine their own form of government, a point not provided for in the 1815 treaty. This was partly an internal matter which the Swiss could settle for themselves, thanks to the fact that most of the Powers' attentions were required elsewhere. In 1856-57 the issue involved a change in an explicit provision of the 1815 treaty, so that the settlement required agreement by the Powers. Hence the main discussion of the Neuchâtel question took place outside Switzerland and, because of the diverse interests and needs of the Powers, agreement was delayed.

The responsibility for prolonging the negotiations is divided. Napoleon's flirtation with the idea of an entente with Prussia was a primary cause; he surely gave both Prussia and Russia reason to hope and work for a break in the Anglo-French alliance. Toward the end of the negotiations, in conversation with Cowley, Bismarck commented that the question 'would have been terminated long ago if Moustier [the French Minister in Berlin] had had an ounce of pluck'.[61] Moustier's lack of pluck could have been ordained from Paris, but it was more likely a personal characteristic; he probably could have urged Walewski to take a stronger line. Frederick William's irrational character was another delaying element. Britain also must share in the responsibility for delay, although Clarendon probably had little choice. In the first stage, British

[60] Bismarck, *Correspondance diplomatique*, p245
[61] Cowley to Clarendon, 9 April 1857 (FO 519/221)

activity may have alienated France, so that quiescence was inevitable in the second phase.

Some Swiss, writing about the Neuchâtel question, have been carried away by their national pride. Schmid, for example, concludes that the episode proved his country's inviolability.[62] Another asserts that 'the proud and positive attitude of Switzerland created for herself an entirely new place in the consideration of Europe. From this moment nothing remained of the former protectorate.'[63] Relatively little space is devoted to the negotiations following the exile of the Royalist prisoners, in which Switzerland did not play a major role. Undoubtedly, the Prussian and, indeed, European threat did have a very beneficial effect on Swiss national life. The strong determination in all parts of the country and among all parties to defend their homeland was a big step away from foreign influences and toward real national unity. But the strength of Swiss military defences was never really tested, for the Prussian army was not sent against them. Their emergence unscathed from the dispute was intimately related to British support and sympathy. Perhaps their adoption of the melody of 'God Save the Queen' soon after this for the Swiss national anthem is testimony to the Anglo-Swiss relationship.

The Swiss were very dependent on Britain in the diplomatic realm. The little country needed the support of one of the Great Powers to have any hope of success, and the Federal Assembly recognized this when discussing ratification. The Swiss had no diplomatic corps in 1856 and their representatives in Paris and Vienna had little experience or training in diplomacy. Particularly at the critical time in early January, Cowley was frustrated by this lack of Swiss experience: 'I must say however that except for being in the right, the Swiss Gov.ᵗ, from their conduct, merit but little of our sympathy.'[64] Barman seemed increasingly unreliable and even the Federal Council expressed its doubts about Kern's firmness. Cowley inferred that the Federal Council expected him to guide Kern as a representative of Switzerland but, with Clarendon's concurrence, he refused to assume that much responsibility for Swiss policy. Fortunately, after the Paris conferences were over, Cowley was able to write that Kern had done his job well. The emergence of Switzerland from the protection of the Powers, including Britain, eventually required the development of a diplomatic corps, but in its early years,

[62] H. Schmid, 'Vor 75 Jahren: Der Neuenburger Handel 1856/7' (*Politische Rundschau*, Berne, 1932, Jg. 11), p144
[63] Paul Seippel, *La Suisse au dix-neuvième siècle* (Paris, 1899-1901), i, 295. (Section on 'L'histoire politique ...', written by Numa Droz)
[64] Cowley to Clarendon, 14 January 1857 (FO 519/220)

the federal government was generally recognized to be represented abroad by British diplomacy.

Clearly, by the signing of the Neuchâtel treaty in 1857, Switzerland had come a long way in ridding herself of the shackles of a dependent status, even if it was not entirely by her own efforts. Her growing economy had made a place in the world system and was a factor winning much respect. In the Neuchâtel negotiations, her representative sat at the conference table and signed the treaty along with the Great Powers. This was a real, legal recognition of Swiss independence and integrity as a viable state.

CHAPTER NINE

The Savoy Question

APPLICATION OF NEUTRALITY

THE CRISIS OVER Neuchâtel, the final direct challenge from the
Continental Powers to Swiss independence, served both to strengthen
Swiss national unity and to obtain an explicit Great Power recognition
of Switzerland as an independent state. Strains and dangers of a different
nature for Switzerland came between 1859 and 1861, with the unification of Italy. The Swiss were forced to react first to war between two
Great Powers near their southern frontier and then to changes of
sovereignty in that area. As a neutral nation, their response to war was
quickly and unanimously decided, and their positive neutrality was
supported by the Powers. But the anomalous 1815 treaty provisions for
the neutralization of North Savoy[1] meant that Swiss (and British) policy
in the aftermath of consolidation in northern and central Italy was less
easily formulated. Then, because the threat to Switzerland was hypothetical and the legal position subject to several interpretations, the very
concept of neutrality was confused with national independence, security,
and pride, and – more important – effective Great Power support for
Swiss demands was not forthcoming.

Discontent in Italy had made difficulties for the Swiss government on
several occasions, most recently during the Lombard insurrection in
1848 and following the abortive 1853 uprising in Milan. After the
Crimean war settlement, which recognized Sardinia as a growing Power,
Swiss anxiety about impending clashes in Italy increased. The Swiss
knew of the frantic negotiations to avert war between Austria and Sardinia in early 1859. Even before the outbreak of hostilities in the spring,
the Federal Council notified the Powers that it intended to stay neutral.
At the end of April, it began preparations for defence: Dufour was

[1] See page 8

153

again elected to command the army, troops were mobilized to protect the Ticino frontier, and a warning was issued that steamers on Lago Maggiore should be disarmed.

In this critical situation, questions about the nature of Swiss neutrality were again considered by the Powers. The British Minister in Berne, now Captain Harris, brother of the Earl of Malmesbury, suggested that the 1815 guarantors of Swiss neutrality should get a re-affirmation of it from the belligerents, since 'the sound political reasons which induced the eminent Statesmen of former days to guarantee [Swiss neutrality] ...' were still valid, namely, that Switzerland was 'a nucleus of Peace for conciliatory negotiations, an asylum for Commerce and Industry ... in which England has a large share [and] a Refuge for those who fly from the horrors of War ...'.[2] Malmesbury followed his brother's suggestion, but the idea needed to be pursued no further because the belligerents affirmed their respect for Switzerland by direct exchanges of notes. Swiss neutrality was now accepted by the Continental Powers as an element of European public law. In June the Swiss interned many soldiers who crossed the frontier, as well as the Austrian steamers on Lago Maggiore. Although at the time they were 'handsomely abused' by the press on both sides for such strict observance of neutrality,[3] the Powers implicitly expressed their appreciation of such a policy by holding the peace conference in Zurich.

While the enforcement of a neutral frontier in the Ticino was a relatively straightforward matter for the Swiss, arrangements for the frontier south of Lake Geneva were not. The 1815 treaty was not clear about the conditions under which Switzerland might occupy the neutralized zone. Austria would have liked the Swiss to control the area, because that would have hindered French communications with Sardinia, and the French of course urged the Swiss to decide against occupation. The simple fact that two of Switzerland's neighbours were at war might have justified occupation but, since the area had been neutralized in 1815 to assure the Swiss an efficient military frontier, and since the belligerents were not using North Savoy as the scene of their hostilities, the Federal Council made no move to occupy the area, nor did it object to the passage of French troops through Savoy. The Swiss and Sardinian governments did discuss details of an occupation plan, in case it became necessary, but they could not reach agreement.

[2] Harris to Malmesbury, 30 April 1859 (FO 100/120)
[3] Harris to Malmesbury, 17 June 1859 (FO 100/121)

The question of the legal status of North Savoy was raised neither for the first nor the last time in the course of the 1859 war. Because of its strong commercial ties with North Savoy, Geneva particularly was eager to protect its special relationship with the area. The Swiss had been tempted by the prospect of an increase in territory there in the spring of 1848; Palmerston had then argued against annexation by Switzerland because it would arouse French jealousy. Rumours of French annexation schemes, fed by French pressures about the refugee question and by a small unsettled border question north of the lake, persisted throughout the 1850s. As early as 1851 Napoleon disclaimed any intention to annex Savoy as a reward for French help to Sardinia in Italy, describing such a scheme as a 'strange mode of supporting an Ally'; clearly the idea was already in his mind.[4] At the time of the Paris peace conference in 1856, Barman assured his government that rumours of French annexation were pure invention. In October 1858 the Swiss President was worried by rumours about the meeting at Plombières, when France and Sardinia had made a secret agreement giving Savoy to France if France helped Sardinia to obtain Lombardy. Harris reassured the President that such a transaction was unthinkable because it would upset the balance of power so seriously, and no further action was taken. In July 1859 the same rumour was not so quickly dismissed by the Foreign Office: even before the Treaty of Villafranca, Cowley and Russell (now Foreign Secretary) successfully put pressure on the French government to disavow any ideas of annexation.

By September 1859 an expansionist element reappeared in Switzerland. Dramatic Swiss development in the 1850s, and particularly since the Crimean war, bolstered national self-confidence in both the economic and political spheres. Some members of the Federal Council, still worried about French plans, suggested that if Switzerland could obtain a better defensive frontier in North Savoy, she would willingly give up some other provisions of the 1815 treaty, such as the right to stop troop passage through the neutralized area. Two months later, in November, on the basis of their treaty rights in North Savoy, the Swiss claimed the right to participate in a proposed congress on Italian affairs; because the congress was never held, the claim was never rejected or confirmed. By the New Year exponents of territorial expansion were more vocal, but they were still in the minority.

Aside from the implications of the question of composition of a

4 Normanby to Palmerston, 13 March 1851 (FO 27/899)

congress on Italy, rumours of French annexation plans were again rife by the beginning of 1860. Kern was far from reassured by vague French promises of 'due regard to those provisions of the Treaties of 1815 ...'. He wanted this reported to the British government and implicitly appealed for its help.[5] The Foreign Office received other evidence of French plans, from Prince Napoleon's comment that Britain should not object to any little annexation which France considered necessary, and from Prince Albert, who heard of a claim made by Napoleon, to the French army, that he had obtained Savoy. Thus Russell was warned that something was brewing, but he was not prepared to protest officially to France. He stated simply that his arguments of the previous July still held and 'I do not wish, at present, to do battle in argument upon the question.'[6] The Cobden commercial treaty between France and Britain had just been signed, and to raise public suspicion about France might endanger the government's position. Yet in private correspondence with Cowley he wrote that Savoy was most important, that Napoleon should avoid jeopardizing European peace and that 'that scheme may surely be cast aside, to give confidence to Germany & England'.[7] Despite such private profession of concern, other factors seemed to require an outwardly passive British policy toward rumours of French expansion.

Meanwhile, as Swiss anxiety grew, the Federal Council initiated more diplomatic discussions about the status of Savoy, even though Harris tried to encourage the Council to rely instead on Britain. Abraham Tourte was sent to Turin to persuade the Sardinian government to maintain the *status quo* and to urge Hudson, the British Minister there, to take the same line. This mission seemed to achieve some success when Cavour assured both Hudson and Tourte that cession was not planned. In Paris, too, the outlook was still hopeful; Kern believed that he had received 'satisfactory assurance' from the Powers about Swiss interests.[8]

However, in February the situation became more complicated as the French made their true intentions known. Thouvenel, the French Foreign Minister, at last admitted that annexation was being considered. Promising that France had no thought of violating the guarantee to Switzerland, he suggested to Cowley that the Chablais and Faucigny

[5] Grey to Russell, 9 January 1860 (BPP 1860 [2624] LXVII, pp 9-10). For a detailed account of the Savoy question, see Luc Monnier, *L'Annexion de la Savoie à la France et la politique suisse, 1860* (Geneva, 1932)
[6] Russell to Cowley, 28 January 1860 (BPP 1860 [2624], p19)
[7] Russell to Cowley, 31 January 1860 (FO 519/198)
[8] Cowley to Russell, 25 January 1860 (BPP 1860 [2624], pp 12-13)

(the area along the south side of Lake Geneva in North Savoy) 'should be united permanently to Switzerland'.[9] He discussed his proposal with Kern also, and authorized his Chargé d'Affaires in Berne to make it known to the Swiss President, confidentially, as a gesture of French loyalty and friendliness to Switzerland.

The British were not pleased with this development, since both Cowley and Hudson believed that the Swiss were encouraging the French scheme in order to have part of the area for themselves. Consequently, on Cowley's advice, Russell informed the Federal Council that Britain was insisting on Great Power consent for any such transfer, an attempt to stop Swiss diplomatic activity. In response, the Council professed not to be encouraging the movement in favour of annexation; it had instructed Kern only to advocate the *status quo* but, if annexation was inevitable, to watch out for Swiss interests. In fact, this was the attitude which the French found the Swiss to be taking. The Swiss had not accepted the French offer, and the French were annoyed by such 'ingratitude,' which they attributed to British ill will.[10] The Swiss, as in previous international difficulties, were ready to rely on British advice, and the British discouraged them in Turin, in Paris, and in Berne, from following a self-interested policy. As a result, the French were again angry that British counsel seemed to carry more weight than their own in Berne.

The British government of 1860 was not as clear-sighted in its Swiss policy as previous governments had been. Indeed, Russell's policy on this question provides a strong contrast with the Foreign Office approach to Swiss affairs under Clarendon. The latter possessed an extraordinary ability to assess situations and to anticipate results, always setting reason above emotion in his analysis. He exercised a strong control over the conduct of British foreign policy. On the other hand, Russell was a weak Foreign Secretary, lacking Clarendon's analytic powers and being very much influenced by the opinions of those around him.[11] Palmerston, as Prime Minister at the age of eighty, had passed the high point of his career and was not able to provide Russell with much realistic guidance in foreign affairs. Although in October 1859 Russell wrote to Cowley that he would 'not dislike very much the addition of Chambéry to France, provided the road by the Lake of Geneva were made Swiss ...';[12]

[9] Cowley to Russell, 5 February 1860 (*ibid*, pp 27-8)
[10] Tillos to Thouvenel, 7 and 18 February 1860 (AEE: Suisse: 588)
[11] In September 1859 he wrote pleadingly to Palmerston, 'I know not how to cook my dishes to suit my neighbors palate.' (PRO 30/22/30)
[12] Russell to Cowley, 25 October 1859 (FO 519/197)

the following February he objected to a Swiss policy based on this kind of realism. He involved many people in the discussions about the Savoy question, and most of them considered that the prime policy aim should be the prevention of any precedent for French expansion. They assumed, mistakenly, that the 1815 alliance could be revived easily and effectively against France.

At the end of February the British government embarked on a policy of protest. Russell objected officially to the French project, while Cowley and Hudson disapproved Swiss discussions with the French about arrangements to ensure their security. Russell also tried to ascertain that the other Powers would protest against the probable French move as an unwise precedent in European politics. Yet concurrently with these official protests, in his private correspondence he seemed to accept Napoleon's determination to go through with the scheme. Palmerston reinforced Russell's inconsistency. In a conversation with the Sardinian Ambassador, he strongly urged opposition to the annexation scheme, but, writing privately to his Foreign Secretary, he acknowledged the idea of a change in the Swiss frontier as a realistic solution.[13]

Unfortunately, the Sardinian report of the British plan of protest was not put in cipher for transmission to Turin, and the French learned its contents.[14] This French discovery of such a strong British position led to a second serious turn in the February discussions. The French were irritated by the depth of British opposition and by apparent British connivance with both the Sardinian and Swiss governments. In contrast, the other Powers seemed little disposed to protest.[15] The French had no way of knowing that Russell and Palmerston had also expressed themselves, privately, as reconciled to the idea of some cession to Switzerland. To them, the British government appeared uncompromising and the Swiss too willing to follow British advice. In addition the French heard from Berne that the Protestant cantons of Switzerland were beginning to worry about the possible unbalancing effect in their confederation if more Catholics were added to the population. Within France, public opinion was running high in favour of annexation and all the government Ministers supported a policy demanding compensation for Sar-

---

[13] 'I do not see any difficulty in plainly telling France that we consider a good defensible Frontier for Switzerland a necessary adjunct to the European guarantee & France has no Right to take such a statement amiss ...'. Palmerston to Russell, 19 February 1860 (PRO 30/22/21)

[14] William R. Thayer, *The Life and Times of Cavour* (London, 1911), p201

[15] Persigny specifically gave this reason in conversation with Kern a year later in describing and explaining the change of policy. Knüsel to de la Rive, 19 January 1861 (Geneva: Savoie 47: III)

dinian annexations in Italy. For these reasons, the French withdrew their proposal of cession to Switzerland and sent a negotiator to Turin to demand all of Savoy and Nice.

FRENCH PERSISTENCE AND THE EUROPEAN RESPONSES

In March the developments were tangible and irreversible. On the first day of the month Napoleon made public his interest in reclaiming Savoy and Nice. On the 12th came the announcement of a plan to conduct a plebiscite in Savoy and Nice to decide the annexation question. On the 24th the Treaty of Turin was signed by France and Sardinia: Savoy and Nice were to be ceded to France if a plebiscite favoured the transfer, and (Article II) the neutralization of North Savoy was to be assured in consultation with the other signatories of the 1815 treaty.[16]

As the French had noticed in February, Swiss opinion about the situation was divided. The Geneva press reported a strong movement in North Savoy favouring annexation to Switzerland and advocates of Swiss annexation could cite petitions received by the Federal Council from over 12,000 citizens of the Chablais and Faucigny, but none the less the Swiss President was not sure that North Savoy would vote for annexation if the chance were offered. When, at the end of March, a few Swiss fanatics tried to invade a town (Thonon) in the disputed territory, the Swiss case was damaged. Fortunately both the federal and Geneva governments quickly took stern measures to quell the disturbance. After their initial irritation, the French did not take the attack very seriously, perhaps because the incident had a sobering effect on Swiss annexationist ambitions.

When French intentions were publicized the Swiss intensified their diplomatic efforts to press their claim for better security. Kern tried to wring from the French a written promise for cession of the neutralized area in Switzerland, but Thouvenel delayed replying for a week and then announced that the Chablais and Faucigny should 'share the fate of the rest of Savoy'.[17] At this, the Swiss protested about lack of French consideration for their neutrality, but Thouvenel was adamant. Toward the end of the month, Dufour was sent to Paris again to try to influence Napoleon, but again without success. The Emperor asserted that the popular will in North Savoy, which he claimed to favour France, and strong French feeling against Switzerland, prevented cession to the

[16] 'Treaty of Annexation of Savoy and Nice to France' (BPP 1860 [2656] LXVII, pp 26-8)
[17] Cowley to Russell, 12 March 1860 (FO 27/1334)

159

Swiss. In Turin, an embarrassed Cavour first encouraged the Swiss to press France for a clear statement about the Chablais and Faucigny and then, later, said that the neutralization question should be discussed with the Powers rather than bilaterally. Hudson also advised the Swiss to concentrate their efforts elsewhere, in Paris and London. Indeed, the Swiss needed little encouragement to turn to Britain, whom they believed to be their staunch supporter, as in previous crises. Through Russell's private correspondence with August de la Rive, a professor of physics in Geneva, the Federal Council learned that Cowley was dissatisfied with Kern.[18] Therefore, although the Swiss Consul in London had been reporting on developments in the Savoy question, the Federal Council decided in mid-March to send de la Rive himself to London.

The British government also took steps in March to thwart the French plan. True, in early March, Russell hoped that he could leave the defence of the *status quo* in Savoy to Cavour 'who is skilful enough at his weapons',[19] but he did extract from the French a vague promise to consult the Powers. He also discussed the problem with diplomats of the other Powers. To them, he readily admitted that French possession of Savoy had no immediate bearing on British interests. He justified his concern first by the dangerous concept of natural frontiers which the French might someday apply to the Rhineland, thus threatening Germany, and, second, by the diminished security for Switzerland. The Austrian, Prussian, and Russian representatives agreed with Russell that French annexation of Savoy and Nice was a poor precedent, but they could do no more.

After the French announcement of plebiscite plans, Russell changed his tack. Realizing that the French were unlikely to give up their annexation scheme, he sent strong notes to Prussia, Russia, and Austria, arguing against the annexation but at the same time suggesting that the Powers, in independent notes to France, should urge the cession of North Savoy to Switzerland in order to safeguard European security. Even though Swiss neutrality had proved a viable concept in 1859, Russell was convinced that Swiss (and European) security would be jeopardized by the annexation. Cowley warned the French against trouble if they did not reconsider cession of the Chablais and Faucigny to Switzerland, but when the French refused to reconsider, Russell, instead of making the trouble he had threatened, could only write plain-

[18] Ed. Rossier, 'L'Affaire de Savoie en 1860 et l'intervention anglaise' (*Revue Historique*, Paris, 1906, Vol. 90), p35; and de la Rive to the Federal Council, 8 March 1860 (SFA: Neutralität von Nord Savoyen: 4)

[19] Russell to Cowley, 6 March 1860 (FO 519/198)

tively that 'they have no business to disturb the balance of power in Europe',[20] since the other Continental Powers offered no effective support for British policy. None the less, British and Swiss pressure in both Paris and Turin probably played a part in the addition of Article II to the 24 March treaty, calling for consultation with the Powers.

In addition to Russell's lack of subtlety in formulating policy, Cowley, in Paris, was not at this time an entirely pliant instrument of the Foreign Office. Cowley was probably apprehensive about the new British government. In fact Clarendon had advised, in 1859, that he (Cowley) 'should not accept the *obiter dicta* (he has no principle of action) of Lord John without protest and without making him aware of the evil consequences they may entail'.[21] Cowley was deeply committed to the importance of the Anglo-French entente for the maintenance of European peace and, naturally, he was more sympathetic to French attitudes than were his colleagues in London. In his view, British support for Swiss objections to the annexation scheme posed a serious threat to good Anglo-French relations. Hence he criticized both Swiss policy and the Cabinet's decision to protest against the annexation, a course which he considered undignified. But he was hardly in a position to recommend general lines of policy to his government and, however capable he was as a diplomat, he still needed clear instructions from London. Since these were not forthcoming, he, like Russell, vacillated between a realistic approach aimed at compromise and a strong objection based on principle. The Queen herself was distressed with the lack of a 'firm, high, fearless tone' in his dispatches,[22] which were probably a fairly accurate reflection of British government thinking on the question. While Thouvenel's retraction of the French promise of cession to Switzerland was a disappointment, Cowley was even more 'disgusted with the Swiss, who now that they have failed in their selfish policy, want Europe to do battle for them on the general question'.[23] Cowley shared French annoyance at an active diplomatic effort by little Switzerland. Yet, in an official dispatch, he reported giving assurance to Kern that Britain would eventually want Swiss interests satisfied. While he maintained that the Swiss should leave the question for the guaranteeing Powers to settle, he was fully aware that an understanding between the Powers on the subject was unlikely.

[20] Russell to Cowley, 22 March 1860 (FO 519/198)
[21] F. A. Wellesley, *The Paris Embassy during the Second Empire* (London, 1928), pp 183-4
[22] Brian Connell, *Regina v. Palmerston* (London, 1962), p283
[23] Cowley to Russell, 16 March 1860 (FO 519/227)

On 19 March, before de la Rive's arrival in London, the Federal Council addressed the first of a series of formal appeals for help to the British government and to the other guaranteeing Powers. The Swiss request, news of the Treaty of Turin, and several reports from Cowley were considered by the Queen and the Cabinet as a Foreign Office dispatch box was circulated on the 25th. The Queen proposed that Britain immediately call a conference in London, to take the question out of Napoleon's hands. Neither Palmerston nor Russell agreed with her suggestion. Although both men still thought that North Savoy should go to Switzerland, Russell was beginning to assess the political realities of the situation: 'But is there any one Power prepared to enforce this arrangement? Not one of them has said so. Without some previous agreement I see no use, & much danger of discredit in a meeting of the nature proposed.' Palmerston suggested that Britain should encourage the other Powers to exert pressure on Napoleon, but he did not want needless offence to France 'especially as France knows that she may incur our displeasure without Danger of war'. After all, the French had not yet violated Swiss neutrality and, with encouragement, they might actually follow the good faith they were professing.[24] Too late, Palmerston and Russell were thinking soberly about the problem. They believed the situation still to be relatively fluid, although in fact the time for exerting pressure on France had long since passed.

Unfortunately, the flickers of realism evoked by the news of the 25th did not immediately bring about more restrained government policy. Palmerston recognized the risk of offending France, yet both he and Russell were still tempted to brandish threats as a means of persuading France. With the French representative, Palmerston discussed growing Anglo-French irritation and threatened that Britain would 'rise and rally as one man' if the two countries came to war.[25] In Parliament, on the 27th, Russell gave a major speech which was highly critical of French policy and which he hoped would bring Napoleon to his senses. Yet both Palmerston and Russell, in talks with de la Rive, counselled a moderate Swiss policy in order to placate French 'national vanity'.[26] Perhaps Russell and Palmerston thought that, because of the alliance, France would tolerate attacks on her 'national vanity' from Britain but not from Switzerland.

After this interlude of bluster, the British turned to the search for a

[24] Cabinet Memoranda, 25 March 1860 (PRO 30/22/27)
[25] Evelyn Ashley, *The Life and Correspondence of Henry John Temple, Viscount Palmerston* (London, 1879), ii, 392
[26] Palmerston to Russell, 25 March 1860 (PRO 30/22/21)

negotiated settlement. Another Swiss message to the Powers, requesting a conference, surprised the Foreign Office. None the less the British proceeded with their next step, notes to Austria, Russia, and Prussia suggesting independent notes from each to France, but taking care not to be 'as a Coalition' or 'of an offensive attitude towards France'.[27]

None of the other three Continental Powers was ready to oppose the French annexation plan. Austria and Prussia agreed in principle with the British arguments, but at that time Prussia was not in a position to exert much influence in Europe and Austria was satisfied that the annexation was exceptional. Austria would object only because of the international guarantee for North Savoy, and vaguely professed readiness to help to ensure Swiss neutrality for the future. Russia scarcely agreed even in principle with the British view. As during the Neuchâtel crisis she was courting French support on questions in the east and was therefore not disposed to criticize French policy in Europe. In fact, the Russians criticized the British proposal as being too anti-French.[28] Looking ahead, Russia may have anticipated that it would be easier to force modification of the 1856 treaty if France were allowed to make changes in the 1815 settlement. Meanwhile, Russia was far enough from the scene of action to feel no threat from potential French expansionism. She wanted Swiss neutrality maintained, but argued that French assumption of the Sardinian obligations would provide sufficient insurance. The French had clearly estimated the reactions of the Powers better than the British, so that the British note came far short of attaining its desired effect.

This British move did not engender a more conciliatory attitude in France because Napoleon was given little inkling of any actual change in British policy. He and his government were antagonized by British bluster and they accused their would-be ally of an attempt to form a coalition against them. Thouvenel vigorously contested Russell's arguments against the annexation, and refused to consult the guaranteeing Powers until after the plebiscite at the end of April. He threw in a red herring by claiming that North Savoy had been neutralized not to protect the Swiss, but rather for the benefit of Sardinia, a claim which the Swiss later proved conclusively to be wrong. Yet the French press did report a slight concession, in the form of a plan for establishing a

[27] Palmerston to Russell, 27 March 1860 (PRO 30/22/21) and Russell to Loftus, Bloomfield, and Crampton, 31 March 1860 (BPP 1860 [2702] pp 70-2)
[28] On 23 March 1860, Cowley wrote that Russia was hoping for a break between France and England (FO 519/227), so the Foreign Office was warned of the probable Russian response

special commercial zone for North Savoy to allow the continuation of its commercial relations with Geneva.

Although the French evinced strong determination to effect the annexation on their own terms, drastic action by the Swiss at this stage might have been successful. Swiss expansionists wanted military occupation of the disputed zone and they received some encouragement from Britain when Hudson told Tourte 'that there is only one remedy and that is gunpowder';[29] Palmerston thought that 'Hudson's advice is dangerous if adopted, but I am not sure it might not succeed if the Swiss were in great Force'.[30] It is not surprising that the French were nervous that this might happen. Before signing the treaty, Thouvenel telegraphed to find out whether the Swiss were ready to occupy North Savoy. Only after he was assured that no such orders had been given – although preparations were being made – did he proceed with the treaty. Directly after the Thonon incident, which served to strengthen Swiss arguments for a more conciliatory policy, the French were partly reassured by a Federal Assembly decision to withhold permission for military operations. On several occasions in April and May the French complained of a Swiss military build-up in Geneva, while the Swiss made the same complaint about French activity on the other side of the border. Because of the jealousies between the Great Powers, the Swiss might well have been able to carry off an occupation of North Savoy, but they could not be confident of much positive support from the Powers and they would have risked losing the guarantee of their neutrality.

The Federal Assembly insisted that the Federal Council should use only diplomatic channels to obtain a conference and, more immediately, to persuade the French to conduct the plebiscite in a fairer way. Both parts of this policy failed. The fruitless negotiations over the convening of a conference were long and drawn out, partly because of failures in communication between the personalities concerned and partly because of the current power alignments which did not particularly favour the Swiss. Regarding the more immediate question of the plebiscite, the Sardinian government listened sympathetically to the Swiss request, but was forced to submit to heavy French pressure not to offer the inhabitants of any of the districts of North Savoy the choice of joining Switzerland: the French feared that such an offer would jeopardize a strong vote favourable to their annexation. The Swiss vainly protested about the activity of French agents in Savoy before the vote, and the plebiscite, which took place on 20 April, was nearly unanimous for

[29] Hudson to Russell, 24 March 1860 (PRO 30/22/66)
[30] Palmerston to Russell, 27 March 1860 (PRO 30/22/21)

the annexation. Although the British and Swiss were highly sceptical of the apparent unanimity of the vote, in view of the way it was conducted, it does seem clear that the majority preferred France.

Despite the increase in her own diplomatic activity, Switzerland was still dependent on British diplomacy. Officially, the British aimed to make the question a European one, by means of a conference, but in private there were several bilateral attempts to find a compromise before the conference, or perhaps to avoid one.[31] Although Cowley could not persuade the French government to promise more for Swiss security, Persigny, the French Ambassador in London, wrote (in 1861) that, before 24 March, he had offered Russell a French promise to let the Swiss have the Chablais and Faucigny if Britain would stop criticizing the principle of annexation. Russell did not agree, because he still believed that the French could be forced to abandon the whole scheme and because information from Berne indicated that the Swiss were uncertain about wanting the area.[32] Just before the treaty was signed, and when the French were worried about Swiss occupation plans, Cowley telegraphed to Russell asking that presentation of some Savoy papers to Parliament be delayed because Thouvenel seemed to be 'seriously desirous of doing something to meet our wishes in regard to the neutral districts'.[33] This opportunity for settlement was also allowed to pass because the British government still opposed the scheme as a whole. On 10 April Persigny discussed the question with de la Rive and Russell and he then agreed that Switzerland should have a better strategic frontier which would include most of the Chablais and Faucigny. Russell was optimistic about Persigny's attitude, but noted that he had not pledged his government to anything. De la Rive reported this development to the Federal Council but without enthusiasm, since he was astounded when Persigny mentioned a 50 million franc debt to be paid before the Swiss might acquire the territory.

In the course of this attempt to find a compromise satisfactory for Switzerland, the disagreements between Russell and Cowley, and be-

[31] Palmerston was pleased by the possibility of settling the question out of conference, since he thought that such an arrangement would be better than most of the Powers were willing to insist on. Palmerston to Russell, 12 April 1860 (PRO 30/22/21)
[32] Monnier, pp 141-3, and Knüsel to de la Rive, 19 January 1861 (Geneva: Savoie 47: III). The report of this exchange is probably correct, although the offer was probably a private suggestion. It is not mentioned in Russell's papers, but it probably explains Thouvenel's hesitation, the second week in March, about giving Kern a written promise to cede the Chablais and Faucigny
[33] Cowley to Russell, 23 March 1860 (FO 27/1335)

tween Thouvenel and Persigny, who tended to favour British opinion, played an important part. Cowley was kept informed of the talks in London, but he was not to tell Thouvenel 'anything which may tend to bring on a refusal & complicate matters'.[34] From the British point of view, sensitive French government was more likely to be persuaded to compromise through Persigny than through Cowley, but for the French it was advantageous to keep the discussions in Paris. After Persigny's discussion on 10 April, Thouvenel countered, in conversation with Cowley, with an offer of some land for Switzerland on the south bank of Lake Geneva. This was a significant departure from his argument, two weeks before, that renewal of the Sardinian obligations would be sufficient security for Switzerland, but it was distinctly less than Persigny's suggestion. With Thouvenel in a more conciliatory mood, Cowley recommended that a deal be made quickly, because French feeling against Britain was growing. He wrote smugly of Thouvenel's great desire to maintain the Anglo-French entente, 'the only reason which induced him to make any concession whatever in the question of the neutral districts ...'.[35] Because he was sceptical about Swiss claims for better military security, Cowley wanted Russell to accept an only slightly better French offer. He argued that France could easily violate Swiss neutrality in other ways and could likewise find other routes to invade Italy; if the precedent of some concession by France were established, however small, it would be a limitation on 'the manner in which she sets Europe and treaties at defiance'.[36] Cowley surely did not press the French as hard as the Swiss would have liked. At this point he returned to London for a week to defend himself in the House of Lords against criticism of his activity on this question, which he did successfully, but when he returned to Paris, the propitious moment for striking a bargain had passed. By the end of April, the renewed negotiations were distinctly related to the basis for calling a conference, rather than being considered as a way of avoiding one. Persigny had wrung a somewhat better offer from Napoleon, but the Swiss were still dissatisfied.

The differences between the French and British governments were underlined by Swiss diplomatic efforts, which made the negotiations more dispersed. Whereas the British Embassy in Paris had been a pivotal point in discussions about previous crises for Switzerland, Russell could now hold talks with a Swiss representative in London, so that Anglo-Swiss communications by-passed Paris. Kern and de la Rive did

[34] Russell to Cowley, 10 April 1860 (FO 27/1324)
[35] Cowley to Russell, 15 April 1860 (FO 27/1337)
[36] Cowley to Russell, 15 April 1860 (FO 519/227)

write to each other about their activities, but that flow of information was haphazard. Kern does not appear to have seen de la Rive's official dispatches, a circumstance which probably emphasized differences between French and British officials.

In addition, British lines of communication with Switzerland were not clear. Russell relied on Harris to keep the Swiss from 'breaking bounds' and taking drastic action,[37] but he sent no instructions, public or private, for pressure on the federal government for concessions to France. In Paris, with Cowley increasingly sharp in his criticism of Kern, little Anglo-Swiss coordination was possible. Thus reports from de la Rive were the main source of information about British policy for the Federal Council. Even though he was scarcely an experienced diplomat, the Swiss envoy appears to have been quite clear-sighted in his initial appraisal of the London scene. He found Russell embarrassed because Britain could do very little about the Swiss cause. Since Anglo-French relations were very delicate and the Swiss were in fact isolated, he in turn recommended that the Federal Council should not have any illusions about the difficulties for Britain in supporting the Swiss position. None the less, he found British public opinion very much on the Swiss side. Indeed, it is reported that, following Russell's suggestion, he and other Swiss in London organized a crusade among members of Parliament and in the press to cultivate more British favour for the Swiss cause.[38] The press campaign was so successful that de la Rive himself became blinded to the realities of the situation and his dispatches became increasingly optimistic about the strength – and effectiveness – of British support. He reported Cowley's insistence on the need for Russian support, but he tripped up significantly in describing the last compromise offered by the French. His report of the offer is very different from the accounts given by Cowley and Russell, both of whom wrote that the Swiss would have to be satisfied with only a part of the Chablais and Faucigny.[39] Not until 8 May did de la Rive pass on to the Federal Council a British hint that the Swiss might consider a frontier somewhat nearer the lake. Although de la Rive wrote of continuing British support for the Swiss demands, Russell, in correspondence with others, had for at least three weeks recognized the necessity that the Swiss should accept less than the entire neutralized zone. Some of the weak-

---

[37] Russell to Harris, 26 March 1860 (PRO 30/22/107)
[38] Monnier, pp 347-8
[39] De la Rive to Frey-Herosée, 21 April 1860 (Geneva: Savoie 47: VI); Cowley to Russell, 14 April 1860 (FO 27/1336); Russell to Cowley, 16 and 18 April 1860 (FO 27/1324) and 24 April 1860 (BPP 1860 [2702], pp 202-4)

ness of de la Rive's reporting may be attributed to poor comprehension on his part, but much of the responsibility must lie in Russell's explanations to him, since Russell admitted his wariness of any French terms which might not be acceptable to the Federal Council.[40] In any case, de la Rive's mission certainly did not bring about Swiss understanding of the necessity for compromise.

FAILURE OF ANGLO-SWISS POLICY

In early May Cowley still feared a future threat from French expansionism,[41] but none of the other Powers was alive enough to this danger, nor was any of them in a strong enough position, to force France to accept a settlement which might be the least bit humiliating. Austria, who on previous occasions had reacted to French pressure on Switzerland, was more worried now about her remaining influence in Italy in the face of Sardinian expansion, and now adamantly refused to attend the conference if Sardinia was included. European governments generally became more absorbed by developments in the Middle East and by Garibaldi's expedition to Sicily. Consequently, the Savoy question slipped to a secondary level and the French, British, and Swiss positions became even less flexible.

Many of the reasons for French intransigence were the same as in late February. Napoleon and his government were annoyed by continuing Swiss protests and appeals to the other Powers, and by British support for Switzerland. By May the results of the plebiscite had further strengthened their case. France preferred to deal directly with Switzerland if possible, to avoid making concessions. While she could not refuse to consult the Powers, she could postpone consultation with argument after argument until the international climate was favourable to her point of view. By the time the plebiscite was over, she did not have long to wait. Thouvenel then refused to consult the Powers until after the treaty ratifications had been exchanged and France had actually occupied the disputed territory. This was delayed until 14 June.

The British government was immobilized by Russell's indecisiveness. While Russell retreated from some of his earlier conditions for a con-

[40] On 1 May Russell wrote to Cowley that 'At all events it would not do for us to be godfathers to a plan which would be received with indignation in Switzerland.' (FO 519/198)

[41] Cowley wrote to Russell on 2 May that 'We must be prepared for hints given to Prussia that she may extend her territories in the North, provided that France obtains compensation on the Rhine, and the future danger, to my mind, lies in these hints being inattended to ...'. (FO 519/227)

ference, in the expectation that the Powers could reach some agreement, he did not concede enough. Cowley recommended acceptance of the latest French offer, which the other Powers would probably support, but no action was taken before the French retracted even that. Privately, Russell was inclined to agree with Cowley, in mid-May, that a stalemate had been reached and the conference should be abandoned: '... if the Swiss understand that France will not advance a step further, & that we none of us mean to push her on with the bayonet, they will readily give up the Conference. De la Rive spoke to me in that sense this morning ... For my part I no longer see any good in it, & shall not be sorry to let it drop.'[42] But a few days later he confessed that 'while the Swiss ask for a conference, I think we cannot properly take any step that may have the effect of preventing the meeting'.[43] Russell was apparently very much swayed by de la Rive's arguments and by public pressure, so that he probably did not make clear to de la Rive the same thoughts which he had written to Cowley. Indeed, his private opinion about a conference did reach the Federal Council, not through de la Rive, but by way of Cowley and Kern. Palmerston's insistence on a conference was stronger. To Cowley, he wrote that Thouvenel's or Napoleon's words were not to be taken 'as ordinances from the Book of Fate. It is an old established manœuvre to represent as settled and inevitable that which one desires to accomplish ...'.[44] Palmerston did not want Britain to appear to fear France and he thought that Thouvenel could be forced to yield more. He and Russell knew that Cowley was more sympathetic to the French position than they, but in trying to counterbalance his bias, they put far too much weight on opposite, and sometimes irrelevant, considerations.

The inflexibility of the Federal Council is less surprising, since both the Council and its agents were new at the diplomatic game. The Swiss government erred both in the evaluation of the reports it received and in the representation of its own case abroad. While it heard of unflagging support in London, accounts from other quarters were less encouraging. At the end of April it sent a special envoy to Berlin and St Petersburg. He reported that the Swiss cause generally aroused sympathy but no effective support. In Berlin Bloomfield told him that Switzerland was likely to receive little more than nice words even from Britain. The Swiss Chargé d'Affaires in Vienna described the British representative as pessimistic about the success of a conference because the Powers disagreed. Kern wrote that Austria urged Switzerland to agree to the French

[42] Russell to Cowley, 15 May 1860 (FO 519/198)
[43] Russell to Cowley, 19 May 1860 (ibid)
[44] Palmerston to Cowley, 4 May 1860 (FO 519/292)

proposals. Within the country, some Swiss still pressed for military occupation of North Savoy, while many others wanted a conciliatory policy. The Swiss President interpreted many of these dispatches optimistically and the Federal Council, reflecting national differences of opinion, was unable to arrive at a firm policy decision. In turn, its diplomatic agents, without clear instructions, tended to express personal opinion rather than a national position. Thus in mid-May, while de la Rive clung to the demand for territorial change, Cowley reported Kern's account of the Swiss aims for a conference to be reaffirmation of its neutrality and a statement that North Savoy was neutralized for the protection not of Sardinia but of Switzerland – in other words, much less than his counterpart in London insisted on.

On 20 June the French government at last declared its readiness to discuss the neutralization of North Savoy with the guaranteeing Powers by the exchange of identical notes, by conference, or by direct negotiations with Switzerland. By giving the Powers a choice, Thouvenel exploited their differences and ensured that nothing would happen.

While formulating his reply to the French message, Russell still felt hounded by public opinion and by de la Rive. In mid-June, before the French note appeared, he wrote pleadingly to Cowley asking what the current French intentions were, because a question was to be asked in the House of Commons. After 20 June he and Palmerston agreed to press the other Powers for a conference because, 'in fact, as the Swiss continue to wish for it, we should appear to be deserting them if we rejected it'.[45] The British public had shown such an interest in the Swiss cause that perhaps no other course seemed safe if the government was to stay in office. In early July Russell instructed Cowley not to recommend a direct settlement between France and Switzerland: 'She is small & weak & ought to be heard in the Supreme Court of Europe.'[46] Harris produced a memorandum which might have provided the basis for settlement, with compromises on both sides, but Cowley did not broach it for fear of prejudicing its success in conference by having a prior refusal by the French.

By 13 July it was known in Paris that even Prussia did not think that a conference on Savoy was necessary at that time. Nervous about the Rhineland, Prussia wanted to do nothing to endanger good relations with France. With summer holidays approaching, with more important questions needing solutions, and with Austria, Russia, and Prussia singularly unenthusiastic, the conference idea died. Russell had been

[45] Palmerston to Russell, 23 June 1860 (PRO 30/22/21)
[46] Russell to Cowley, 5 July 1860 (FO 519/198)

warned weeks before that 'neither Conference nor anything else will induce the F.G. to give better terms to Switzerland'.[47] Early in July he must have received a report written for Cowley about the opinion of a Swiss colonel, then visiting Paris, whose point of view was entirely different from what the Foreign Office had been subjected to previously. He deplored the Swiss agitation over North Savoy and did not consider the area to be important strategically for Switzerland. He also remarked that de la Rive was a bitter enemy of France.[48] This information must have given Russell pause. On the 19th he officially – but very cautiously – began his retreat, writing to the French government of British pleasure in having confirmation of French interest in strengthening Switzerland, in knowing that France intended to take the initiative in calling a conference to renew the guarantee of Swiss neutrality, and in receiving French assurances of no intentions of further annexations. None the less, he still wanted a conference to consider a better frontier for Switzerland.

Thus, by the end of July, North Savoy was no longer a European issue, and the discussions between Britain and France had ceased. On 28 July de la Rive was informed that the conference would probably not take place, so that his presence was not needed in London. But his reports to the Federal Council gave a slightly different cast to the situation. He first wrote that the conference was adjourned for a long time and that any Swiss action would be inopportune, and then, within a week, that Palmerston and Russell promised to continue to work for a conference.[49]

Swiss resentment against France persisted for a long time, but the unsettled questions were never permitted to reach major proportions again. During the next few months, several anti-French incidents occurred in Switzerland, but fortunately French protests were moderate. Swiss irritation with France prevented the government from proposing any new project for a solution of the Savoy question for the time being and, in early December, the Federal Assembly approved the Federal Council's policy of discouraging further debate on the matter. Privately, Harris wrote of continuing agitation. He himself was careful not to

---

[47] Cowley to Russell, 1 June 1860 (FO 519/227)
[48] Claremont to Cowley, 2 July 1860 (PRO 30/22/55). The colonel's last observation is confirmed by de la Rive himself, who threatened that Switzerland would be obliged to turn to Germany to be secure against the dangers of the cession. De la Rive to Kern, 14 May 1860 (Geneva: Savoie 47: VI). De la Rive's threat of turning to Germany is also reported in Count Charles Frederick Vitzthum von Eckstädt's *St Petersburg and London in the Years 1852-1864* (London, 1887), ii, 59
[49] De la Rive to the Federal Council, 28 July and 4 August 1860 (SFA: Neutralität ... : 7)

entangle the British government in 'a Question which after all more nearly concerns those Continental Powers who withheld their assistance at the moment when alone it could be practically useful ...'.[50] Russell supported Harris publicly, writing that Britain would 'not take the initiative in any proposition respecting the neutral territory, but will be happy to concur in any proposal that is likely to be acceptable to Switzerland, and to have a fair chance of success at Paris'.[51] 1861 witnessed a few flickers of public discussion of the question in Britain, but officially Britain simply recommended conciliatory Swiss conduct toward the French. Not until 1881 did France and Switzerland make an agreement about commercial policy for North Savoy, and a final settlement came only after the First World War.

RECONSIDERATION OF THE SAVOY QUESTION

Many Swiss felt that failure of a policy aimed at joining part of North Savoy to Switzerland was due to Britain. The Federal Council, in its report for 1860, stated that absolute British opposition to the annexation had caused France to withdraw her promise to cede the Chablais and Faucigny. When Harris objected strongly to this explanation, the Council quickly expressed a belief that Britain had used every effort on behalf of Swiss interests, and it later pleaded that that part of the report only repeated French assertions. Indeed, we have seen that explanation of the fact that Switzerland did not obtain a more satisfactory arrangement is more complicated. The responsibility lies in several quarters.

One writer has suggested that the British government, in order to satisfy public opinion, merely used Switzerland as a tool for protesting strongly to France about the annexation, and that when public opposition had died down, Swiss interests were dropped.[52] This interpretation does not bear close scrutiny. Although the emphasis of the published Foreign Office dispatches differs perceptibly from attitudes reflected in the unpublished correspondence, official and unofficial,[53] both records show the British efforts to be sincere. The published material shows Russell persisting doggedly with legal, moral, historical, and military objections to the French annexation, with reference to Switzerland,

[50] Harris to Russell, 26 November 1860 (PRO 30/22/78)
[51] Russell to Harris, 17 December 1860 (FO 100/124)
[52] Rossier, p58
[53] Most analyses of the British side of the negotiations have been based only on the published documents

172

while the French were shifty and uncooperative. In fact, we have seen that compromises were put forward and considered by both sides and that discussion was not limited to the theoretical and high-principled realm seen by the public. Furthermore, diplomatic consideration of the question had ceased well before the public opposition in Britain subsided.

One reason for failure lies rather in the imprecision of British policy than in a Machiavellian intent to use Switzerland. Russell and Palmerston allowed themselves to be directed to an incredible extent by de la Rive's wishes and by public opinion, neglecting more emphatic steps, *vis-à-vis* Switzerland, which might have brought about a settlement. Either Russell did not formulate a rational, decisive policy, or he failed completely to communicate it. While the Swiss were confident of British agreement with their view, the French also, at one point (early May), thought that Russell agreed entirely with them. It was a paradoxical situation that British leaders considered themselves prevented from taking a more realistic line by public opinion which was, in turn, whipped up with their own encouragement by the Swiss. A stronger Foreign Secretary would have tried to steer public opinion in a direction dictated by the facts of the situation. As it was, Russell and Palmerston were under the illusion that British public opinion was almost as important to the French government as to their own. Clarendon, no longer in the government, criticized Palmerston's policy in early June as 'feminine', writing to Cowley that the Prime Minister was angry 'at finding that Louis Napoleon is a more artful dodger than himself, and that an irresponsible gentleman [Napoleon] with five hundred thousand bayonets at his disposal is not to be scared from his purpose by a sour dispatch or a House of Commons barking peacefully'.[54]

Another reason for the poor showing of British policy on this question may lie in the current European power alignments. After 1856 the European treaty system was oriented primarily toward restraining Russia rather than France. It had been only with some difficulty that the Powers were able to force Prussia to yield to the European interest over Neuchâtel in 1857. In 1860, with Anglo-French entente on other questions as a fundamental element in the European equilibrium, Britain could not enlist support from the eastern European governments against the French.

This British failure might be described as the beginning of a tendency – more marked later in the decade – to withdraw from European politics. By 1860 the Permanent Under Secretary at the Foreign Office was

[54] Wellesley, p206

an increasingly important figure in the formulation of British policy. His outlook was strongly influenced by a 'simple faith in retributive justice',[55] and Russell shared this faith at a crucial stage in his thinking about the Savoy question, naively believing that because the British attitude was just, it would prevail. Rational estimates of the probable responses of the other Powers to French and British policies would have led to a different stand by Britain. The balance of power did not operate on abstract principles and, consequently, reliance on principle alone presaged British isolation.

The Swiss must also bear some responsibility. Their inexperience in diplomacy was clearly a disadvantage. The Federal Council did not control its well-meaning but untrained agents who tended to allow personal feelings to influence their activities and reports. Cowley exaggerated only a little when he wrote to Harris, in mid-April, that 'Kern has been playing a very foolish game here ... He has been all along endeavouring to play the game off his own bat without ref[ce] to Europe ... he thought himself cleverer than Europe, and has only found out the contrary when it is too late. He has evidently not told his Govt the whole truth as to his proceedings, or else they do not tell the truth either, but my conviction is that it is to Switzerland alone that we owe our difficulties today.'[56] Certainly an experienced diplomat would not tell Hudson, as Tourte did, that he had little confidence in the government he was representing. De la Rive's performance in London also bore the stamp of inexperience. His unbounded enthusiasm for what he personally believed to be right prevented him from analysing the situation objectively. In addition to poor diplomatic reporting, divisions within the country and a lack of strong leadership had a paralysing effect on the Federal Council. Not unjustly, the Council has been criticized for an inconsistent policy, on the one hand asking for French goodwill, to be manifested in the cession of the Chablais and Faucigny, and on the other hand enlisting British support for an essentially anti-French policy.[57] The inconsistency is perhaps more apparent in the reports from Kern and de la Rive than in their instructions, but none the less the Federal Council might have foreseen that by attempting to move in both these directions at once the result would be no progress at all.

[55] M. A. Anderson, *Edmund Hammond, Permanent Under Secretary of State for Foreign Affairs, 1854-1873* (unpublished Ph.D. thesis, University of London, 1956), p86
[56] Cowley to Harris, 11 April 1860 (FO 519/227)
[57] Victor Bérard, *Genève, la France et la Suisse* (Paris, 1927), i, 413

Because neither Swiss nor British policy was carefully controlled at the centre, the personalities of all those concerned played an important role. Indeed, it is remarkable that so many of the representatives involved in the story were overpartial to the positions of the governments to which they were accredited. Of the British agents, Hudson was very sympathetic to Cavour, Cowley adopted many of the biases of the French government, and even Harris, whose dispatches had previously been brief and objective, waxed eloquent about the injustices suffered by Switzerland. Of the Swiss, Tourte was an old friend of Cavour, Kern was a former acquaintance of Napoleon, and de la Rive had many connections in Britain. Persigny exhibited more sympathy with the British government than Thouvenel, or even Napoleon, must have liked. The personal feelings of these men hindered good communication between governments and were another reason for the failure to find a solution to the Savoy question.

Having referred to the unsettled status of North Savoy at the end of 1860 as a failure for British and Swiss policy, we may question whether this was, in fact, precisely the case. Ostensibly the Swiss were worried about the security of their guaranteed neutrality, but implicitly the guarantee had been renewed in 1857 with the signature of the treaty for Neuchâtel. Swiss policy during the Austro-Sardinian war had strengthened their independent position considerably, and the Powers then had supported Swiss neutrality without reservations. The concept of a neutral Switzerland was never in question in 1860; rather the discussion was over the security necessary for an effective guarantee. Strong protests in Britain against French policy, and the weaker, but none the less recorded, objections of the other Powers did serve as a brake on France. Harris summed up the situation succinctly in late April, when he wrote privately to Russell that the failure of a conference was not likely to cause 'serious mischief ... At any rate France has not been allowed to walk over the course ...'.[58]

With the neutrality of Switzerland assured, and with no actual threat to Switzerland, the reason for a conference was hypothetical. The Powers might have consented to it had there been a real threat to the balance of power, but the Savoy question did not arouse them to action merely to prevent a danger which might occur sometime in the future. Furthermore, the hypothetical nature of the danger was clear to a majority of the Swiss who opposed a policy of military occupation of the disputed zone. The lack of unanimity in Switzerland was clear evidence that the *de facto* situation was not intolerable.

[58] Harris to Russell, 30 April 1860 (PRO 30/22/78)

CHAPTER TEN

Conclusion

WHEN THE FURORE over the annexation of Savoy subsided in 1860, the existence of Switzerland ceased to be considered a question in European politics. In fact, Great Power recognition of Switzerland came before the Savoy question. From a legal standpoint, the 1815 treaty provisions were implicity renewed with the Neuchâtel settlement of 1857. Moreover, both politically and military Swiss conduct during the 1859 war justified the Powers' decision to respect Swiss independence. In subsequent years the Swiss could begin to fulfil their modern role in the European system as a neutral state with strong interests in international peace. The Red Cross was founded in 1863 by a Swiss, with permanent headquarters in Geneva. Not without encouragement from the federal government, other international agencies established later also chose the relative calm of Swiss soil for the centre of their activities. None the less, as the Swiss could not rely on the Powers' continuing respect for their independence, despite its proven value, they have worked to improve their defensive strategy, and the Powers, however tempted in time of war, have not invaded Swiss territory. When war threatened to spill over their frontier in 1870, the Swiss followed the practice established in 1849 (Büsingen) and in 1859, disarming the French before allowing them to cross the Swiss frontier.

Thus the mid-nineteenth-century years were critical ones for the establishment of Switzerland as a modern state and, for this reason, our examination of Swiss relations with Britain in this period yields some general ideas about the relations between states, as well as some more specific impressions about the Anglo-Swiss relationship. In the questions about the *Sonderbund*, refugees, Neuchâtel, and North Savoy, poor information and faulty communication between governments contributed to the development of international tension. This was related in most cases to the personalities of diplomatic representatives; some were extremely critical of the governments to which they were accredited, while others were too sympathetic. It is also clear that the Powers concerned with the development of Switzerland were motivated by many factors, both internal and external, but not always directly related to Switzerland.

During this period when Switzerland was coming to maturity as a nation, she depended a great deal on British help in both the political and commercial spheres. The major threats to Swiss independence all brought some degree of British diplomatic support. In 1847 British reluctance to interfere in Swiss internal affairs caused a crucial delay in the plans of the Continental Powers and kept the European peace. When the conservative Powers appeared to be seriously threatening Swiss independence over the question of refugees and the status of Neuchâtel, Britain took decisive action. In 1860 the British government was sympathetic to Swiss policy objectives, if not completely effective in helping to attain them. In the commercial sphere the Swiss used British services extensively and occasionally asked for consular help too, as their salesmen ventured into new areas. On several occasions the Swiss sought British help on minor questions. For example, in 1850, when Austria required the withdrawal of all foreign consulates from Milan, the Swiss asked British opinion before complying. When relations between Switzerland and Prussia were about to be reopened in 1857, the Swiss relied on Britain to persuade Prussia not to send back an unwelcome diplomat. In 1859 and 1860 the good offices of the British representative in Naples were invaluable for the Swiss in negotiations about the termination of the mercenary service there.

Although 'dislike of foreign interference was a cardinal principle of Swiss policy',[1] the Swiss recognized their need for British support. In fact, this need probably helped to hold them to moderate policies which would not displease their guardian angel. In March 1860 de la Rive acknowledged that Swiss moderation was necessary to retain British support, and during the Crimean war, when the Swiss needed western support against Austrian pressure, they could not object to British demands which might otherwise have been considered compromising to their neutrality.

That the British government apparently wanted to have the confidence of the small country during this period shows in several ways. British representatives in Switzerland were sensitive about Swiss re-

[1] Christie to Clarendon, 9 August 1854 (FO 100/86)

luctance to consult them on the refugee questions in 1852 and 1853 – on the latter occasion their sensibility amounted to indignation. In 1855 the Foreign Office was exasperated when the treaty was not ratified as quickly as they wished. In many instances Britain took the initiative in acting as a diplomatic go-between, giving the continental governments reliable information about conditions in Switzerland. Britain's protective attitude also shows in her lack of enthusiasm for increases in Swiss diplomatic representation abroad. During the Neuchâtel crisis Gordon took it upon himself to encourage the Federal Council to consider increasing its diplomatic corps; he was quickly and curtly informed that Her Majesty's Government was 'not aware of any necessity' for more Swiss representation.[2] Even in 1860 the British government evinced little initial enthusiasm for de la Rive's special mission. This was perhaps because the British simply did not consider increased representation to be necessary for such a small country – but it is equally possible that the Foreign Office did not want Swiss diplomatic activity to get out of hand.

Basic reasons for a British policy which aimed at the preservation of an independent Switzerland are easy to discover. As Canning and others recognized, the geographical position of Switzerland in Europe required that she be an independent buffer state. After the unification of Italy, Swiss independence was more essential than in 1815. If any one of the Continental Powers had gained a dominant control over Switzerland, such jealousy would have been aroused among the others that a serious war would probably have been inevitable. In this event, Britain would have lost her special relations with Switzerland and, more important, the cost of a general European war would have been very high for all the Powers. This realistic line of thought about the importance of preventing war was fundamental to British policy. Because the Swiss were a small and liberal nation, Britain could not help but have some sympathy for their struggles but on the government's part, at least until 1860, sympathy was moderated by the reality of the landlocked Swiss geographical position. By the mid-1850s, increased Anglo-Swiss communication in many spheres had aroused more interest in Switzerland, so that public opinion was another pressure in Britain favouring the Swiss, although it was by no means decisive.

Switzerland was important for the balance of power, serving as a sort of pivot around which the Powers manœuvred. The maintenance of an independent Switzerland was just as valuable for the Continental Powers as for Britain, but because of their proximity to the potential

2 Clarendon to Gordon, 12 February 1857 (FO 100/108)

scene of conflict and because of the many other sources of tension between them, alone they were unable to keep the equilibrium. Britain often provided the essential element. Sometimes even British support was not enough: in the two series of negotiations over Neuchâtel, the voice of Russia, the other Power removed geographically from Switzerland, brought the final stimulus for settlement.

Obviously, the balance of power was important for Switzerland. Between the codification of European public law regarding Switzerland in 1815 and 1860, an interval which covered some critical stages in Swiss national growth, each of the neighbouring Powers wanted more influence in Switzerland but was prevented from making serious infringements on Swiss independence by the continual jockeying among the Powers on that and other issues. Because the Powers had conflicting interests in Switzerland, they were forced to agree not to interfere there – in other words, to desist from challenging the law. The state of Anglo-French relations was also of great importance. When France and Britain firmly opposed Austrian or Prussian policy toward Switzerland, Austria and Prussia were likely to fail; when Britain opposed French policy to Switzerland, the result was more dependent than ever on other circumstances, as in the *Sonderbund* crisis and the Savoy question. Thus, the situations of crisis in Swiss foreign relations during this fifteen-year period reflect many changes in the European political scene. With their growing national spirit, the Swiss of course played a part in forcing Austria, France, and Prussia to respect their independence, but it is clear that the external factors, particularly the interactions of the Great Powers, had a decisive bearing on the settlement of the disputes involving Switzerland at this period.

In these discussions among the Powers over the status of Switzerland, we have found several lessons about the settlement of international questions. When the issue involved a serious threat to the European peace, it was dealt with. When the peace was not endangered, in other words, when Swiss independence was judged to be secure, the Powers would pay little heed to Swiss complaints. The predominant procedure was bilateral negotiation and much of that was secret, so that the results depended to a great extent on the judgment and skill of the negotiators. Even when the issue was ostensibly to be settled by a conference, as was the Neuchâtel question, the essential discussions took place outside the conference room. To have any hope of success, little Switzerland had to have the active support of at least one of the Great Powers – and that Power was always Britain.

Although until now we have been discussing the maintenance of Switzerland in terms of her independence, the nineteenth century concepts of independence and neutrality were often used interchangeably for Switzerland. In fact, by abandoning her neutrality, Switzerland would have surrendered some independence. For Swiss internal politics, neutrality came to be an expression of a national purpose which made Switzerland distinct from her neighbours and which helped to rally the country to a national policy in times of crisis. Internationally, neutrality was the only possible course for a small country wanting to maintain its identity in the midst of several large Powers. By urging the Swiss to carry out their obligations as a neutral, Britain simply encouraged them to follow the course of survival. By insisting that the Powers accept Switzerland with her unique political institutions, Britain tried to preserve the non-aligned buffer state as a fundamental element in the European system at a time when European states were tempted to expand and when conservative continental governments were insecure.

To return to our initial question about the factors shaping Swiss neutrality in the period of development of the modern state system, neutrality seems clearly to have been dictated to a considerable degree by the exigencies of international politics. In the mid-nineteenth century, the Swiss position was hardly secure and on many occasions pressure was exerted from the outside on the Swiss to remind them of their unique obligations; similar pressure was exerted by one outside Power on another to preserve an independent Switzerland. However, pressures from the Powers would have been fruitless had the Swiss themselves not wanted to follow a neutral path. In 1815 Switzerland was neutralized. By 1860 she had demonstrated her capacity to follow, of her own independent will, a course of neutrality.

APPENDIX I

Canning to Palmerston, 12 November 1847 (private note) (FO 100/54), enclosing a memorandum, which he describes as a result of 'our conversation of Wednesday Evening'. Canning writes that his memory on some points may be at fault; that Palmerston's thinking probably by now has advanced 'beyond the stage to which it applies'.

MEMORANDUM

The question of trying to settle the affairs of Switzerland by a mediation of the Five Powers may be resolved in one of three ways. England may decline, accept simply, or accept with amendments and conditions. Of these several courses not one is wholly free from objection. With a view to adopting the least objectionable it is requisite to consider the nature of the points at issue between the Diet and the League, the character of the Federal Compact, the relations established between the Swiss Confederacy and the Allied Powers, the probable results of civil war, and their eventual effect on the policy of Great Britain and the interests of Europe at large.

The points ostensibly at issue are the removal of the Jesuits, and the dissolution of the Sonderbund. Behind these, less clearly avowed, but not less resolutely entertained, is the project of introducing a fundamental republican change into the Federal Compact.

Looking to the character of this Compact we find that it constitutes a solemn spontaneous agreement among the Cantons, as Sovereign States, for jointly maintaining their independence and internal order. It further appears that the federal Constitution, though tacitly left open to amendment, and not distinctly guaranteed, was in principle part and parcel of the general arrangement made in 1815 under the sanction and with the assistance of the Allied Powers.

Now, the recognition of Swiss neutrality and the territorial integrity of Switzerland within its new limits were made to depend upon the acceptance of that arrangement by the Cantons. The acceptance and the recognition form together the basis of those relations in which the country, as a whole, has hitherto stood towards the rest of Europe. It may indeed be said, and said truly, that the same Cantonal Sovereignty, which limits the powers of the Diet, retains for every integral part of Switzerland, notwithstanding a dissolution of the Federal Compact, the rights of neutrality and territorial independence enjoyed by the whole Confederacy. But it is equally true that such a state of things was not the one contemplated by the European Powers and the Swiss themselves in 1815, and that the common interest of Switzerland and Europe requires the maintenance of these relations, which, dating from the Congress of Vienna, must still be held to subsist between them.

In calculating the probable results of a civil war in Switzerland we must distinguish those which are too certain to occur within the Country from those which may come from without.

If the Cantons engaged in hostilities be left to themselves, it is clear that either one of the two parties will shortly overpower the other, or the struggle will continue indefinitely, each party maintaining its own system, and both perhaps ultimately acquiescing in a permanent separation. In any of these cases humanity will have much to deplore. Besides the ordinary evils of war, the country, by nature poor, will be hopelessly exhausted for a long series of years, and the malignant passions let loose throughout its whole extent will make the reconstruction of the Confederacy all but impossible.

Should the Diet prevail by force of arms, the first object of the dominant party would be the establishment of a Republic more or less similar to that which failed signally under LaHarpe in 1800, and which would be too expensive, too vexatious, and too much at variance with the habits of the internal Cantons ever to make the Swiss a contented people, or Switzerland a good neighbour.

Were fortune to decide in favor [sic] of the Catholics, their league would have either to maintain a general ascendancy by effecting a counter-revolution in the larger and more popular cantons, or to carry out its own system of exaggerated Sovereignty to the prejudice of many general interests, and more especially of the national union and strength. The democratic members of the league would probably strain every nerve to recover the possession of their alienated dependencies. Supposing the present division to continue after the cessation of hostilities, not only would the unity of Switzerland, of the body politic acknowledged by that name be destroyed, but whether we look to the interests of the Country or to those of Europe, – political, social, and commercial, – there would be everything, save actual war, to regret, and much for the future to apprehend.

182

The importance of Switzerland is not to be measured by the extent of its territory, the resources of its industry, or the amount of its population. Its position in the heart of civilized Europe, its command of the main channels of communication between Italy, France, and Germany, the hardy character of its inhabitants, and its capacity for defensive operations would alone make it an object of deep interest even if the features of the country were less remarkable, its institutions less free, and its early records less glorious and affecting. It cannot long suffer even by its own fault without enlisting the sympathies of every kindred state and generous mind. It cannot be enfeebled, convulsed, or mutilated without imparting a shock to the present system of peace, – without suggesting dangerous fears or guilty hopes to the great military monarchies which nearly surround it.

An immense boon was, no doubt, conferred upon Switzerland by the formal recognition of its neutrality. The partial improvement of its frontier, the demolition of Huninguen, and the more compact form of its federal relations were also real benefits simultaneously obtained for it from the neighbouring powers. But Europe also had a beneficial interest in these arrangements, and while the Swiss Cantons rejoiced in the prospect of maintaining their independence and neutrality without the burthen of a large military establishment, it was matter of general congratulation that the Alpine barriers were at the same time closed against the operations of war, and rendered emphatically subservient to the demands of peaceful intercourse. To the bordering states it must have been satisfactory to find the elements of disturbance & political contagion reduced to order along the line of an extensive frontier.

To withdraw that moral safeguard from the Swiss Cantons while they are plunged into war among themselves, is in effect to nullify their usefulness in the system of European policy, and to furnish very plausible pretexts for an intervention dangerous to their independence, and anything but european [sic] in its spirit and direction.

There is surely no power to which an issue of this character would be more distasteful and disparaging than to Great Britain. The nation would impatiently inquire by what fatality it had occurred, and the Government would find itself strangely embarrassed either to resist with effect, or to acquiesce with decency. Already in more than one instance the bulwarks erected at the close of the last general war by the united efforts of Europe against the encroachments of any one preponderant power have been violently overthrown, and if Switzerland be destined to draw a similar lot, there is no denying that a fatal shock will be given to what remains of the general settlement, and a new opening made for

183

those continental struggles which England can never witness with indifference nor share without sacrifices of a perilous magnitude.

But however strong & numerous the motives which engage the British Government to join in the proposed mediation, as the only available chance of arresting civil war and preventing an armed intervention by France and Austria, it is most essential to provide for the consequences of failure, in case of the worst, for keeping all the parties to the mediation, if possible, under the control of a strictly European principle.

The mediation may fail in the outset by the refusal of one or both of the hostile parties. It may also fail from want of means to enforce the decision of the mediators, with the temporary advantage, however, of a postponement or suspension of hostilities. The difficulty consists in finding sufficient motives for the Swiss to consent, without violating their independence or playing the game of any interested power.

On neither side can the Swiss be said to cherish an abstract affection for civil war. They will naturally incline to peace in proportion as the objects of a sanguinary struggle become faint, as a peaceful way is opened for the adjustment of their differences, and as the consequences of rejecting the proposals of the mediation take a more settled and imposing aspect.

If this be true, it is manifest that the Five Powers would produce a most powerful impression by taking their stand on the principles consecrated in the settlement of 1815. They might declare to the Diet, with the proffer of their mediation, that while they are ready to assist in promoting an amicable revision of the Federal Compact with the view of establishing a more uniform system for mutual convenience, they would regard any *organic* change of that solemn instrument without the unanimous consent of the Cantons as a violent departure from the reciprocal engagements, of which their joint recognition of Swiss neutrality was a conditional part, and they might call simultaneously upon the seven Catholic Cantons to join with them in obtaining the arbitration of the Court of Rome as to the retirement of the Jesuits, their separate league terminating naturally with that question.

So far the pressure would be stronger upon the Diet than upon the Sonderbund. To adjust the balance it should be distinctly agreed that none of the Five Powers will under any circumstances directly or indirectly assist the contending parties, and that although the reference to Rome will be made on grounds of humanity in the name of all, the Courts of Paris and Vienna will specially pledge themselves to exert their utmost influence to overcome any obstacle to the recall of the Jesuits and the consequent dissolution of the League.

It remains to provide against the danger of a separate armed intervention in case of failure, without entirely losing the advantage of bringing that strongest object of apprehension to bear upon the Swiss Counsels. This, it would seem, could only be done by reserving the further determination of the Powers, under an agreement among themselves that no such measure shall be adopted without the consent of all, and a special recorded understanding as to the mode, the time, the object, the instruments and other leading points of the operation.

In this manner, whether France and Austria accede to the British Counter-proposal, or not, Her Majesty's Government will have taken a position consistent alike with considerations of humanity and the best interests of Europe, reserving all their rights in case of disagreement, and combining, in that of acceptance, as much efficiency of action, and security from dangerous contingencies as the difficult nature of the question will allow.

Table VIII. Anglo-Swiss Trade for 1855:
Estimates and Reports related to them
(in millions of francs)

| | BRITISH | | SWISS | |
	Imports	Exports	Imports	Exports
French statistics:				
General minus special trade:[1]				
with Switzerland	—	—	78·5	148·4
with Britain	141·0	79·6	—	—
Transit: [2]				
with Switzerland	—	—	73·8	143·4
with Britain	98·5	49·6	—	—
Herries's report of French transit to and from Britain[3]	98·5	49·6	—	—
Herries's estimate of total Swiss trade with Britain	80·0	60·0	60·0	80·0
Burnley's report of transit through France[4]	—	—	73·4	246·6

SOURCES: (1) France, *Annales du commerce extérieur* ... (No. 49, 'Faits commerciaux') (Paris, 1862), pp 28–35. The special trade consisted of goods whose origin or ultimate destination was France, while the general trade included transit, re-exports, temporary admissions, and so on.

(2) France, Administration des Douanes, *Tableau général* ...

(3) BPP 1857–58, p48. Note that these figures are the same as the official French figures for transit. Herries used these as the basis for estimating the Anglo-Swiss trade; for his method of calculation, see pages 115–6.

(4) BPP 1859, p58. It is noticeable that Burnley's figure for Swiss exports via France is much larger than the official French figure, although his report on Swiss imports through France corresponds almost exactly. Burnley made little attempt to analyse his information, except to say that most of this trade, in transit through France, was with Britain.

1. Unpublished Documents

A. IN GREAT BRITAIN

1. AT THE PUBLIC RECORD OFFICE IN LONDON:

Board of Trade Documents:

BT 1/512/642/54 ⎱ BT 1/529/1651/55 ⎰	Correspondence about the Swiss treaty
BT 1/545/2050/57	Correspondence about a proposal for a copyright agreement with Switzerland
BT 1/547/558/58	Correspondence about the Swiss complaint about duties on plumetis

Foreign Office Documents:

FO 7	Austria (1847-55)
FO 27	France (1847-60)
FO 30	Germany (1847-57)
FO 44	Italy, Earl of Minto's Mission (1847-48)
FO 64	Prussia (1848-57)
FO 67	Sardinia (1847 and 1860)
FO 74	Switzerland (1832)
FO 94	Ratifications of Treaties
FO 100	Switzerland (1844-62)
FO 192	Archives of the British Legation in Berne (1845-60)
FO 208	Archives of the British Legation in Frankfurt (1856)

Private Collections:

FO 352	Stratford Canning Papers
FO 356	Bloomfield Papers
FO 391	Hammond Papers
FO 519	Cowley Papers
PRO 30/22	Russell Papers

2. AT THE BRITISH MUSEUM:
   Peel Papers (40455 and 40597-40600)
   Aberdeen Papers (43134 and 43151)
   Palmerston Papers (48554, 48555, and 48578-48581)

3. AT THE BODLEIAN LIBRARY IN OXFORD:
   Clarendon Papers

B. IN SWITZERLAND

1. AT THE BUNDESARCHIV IN BERNE:

Tagsatzung:

1972	Auswärtiges: Handelskonsulate: Korrespondenz mit ... London, 1845-48
2090	Verhandlung ... mit den Bundesbehörden: Grossbritannien, Korrespondenz, 1845-48

Eidgenössisches Justiz- und Polizeidepartement:
   Flüchtlinge 14, 16, and 34 (1849-51)

Eidgenössisches Militär. Departement:
   Landes-Gefestigungen, Bd. 77 [Genf]

Eidgenössisches Politisches Departement:

26	Grossbritannien: Freundschafts-, Handels- und Niederlassungs-Vertrag vom 6 September 1855
123-44	Oester.-Tessin Konflikt 1852-1856
152	Krimkrieg
153-58	Neuenburger Angelegenheit
356-58	Schweiz. Gesandtschaft in Paris: Politische Berichte, 1848-58
499-500	British Legation in Berne
587	Fremden Militärdienst Grossbritannien
KD: 1	(Konsular Dienst) London, Allgemeine Korrespondenz, 1848-61
KD: 2	(Konsular Dienst) Handelsberichts, 1858-70 Missiven des Bundesraths, März, April 1854

Neutralität von Nord Savoyen:

3-7	1859-August 1860

2. AT THE ARCHIVES D'ETAT IN GENEVA:

Savoie 47: Mission d'Auguste de la Rive à Londres, 1859-1863

C. IN FRANCE

1. AT THE ARCHIVES OF THE MINISTÈRE DES AFFAIRES ÉTRANGÈRES IN PARIS:

Correspondance commerciale:
Berne 5 and 6 (1857-62)

Correspondance politique:
Suisse 556-589 (1847-1860)

2. AT THE ARCHIVES NATIONALES:

F^{12} (A series including documents on economic history)

2. Published Documents

A. IN GREAT BRITAIN

Parliamentary Papers:

1836 [60] XLV	Report on Commerce and Manufactures of Switzerland, by John Bowring
1847 [771] LXX	Communications between the Representatives of Austria, Prussia and Russia in Switzerland, and the President and the Executive Council of Berne, on the occasion of the assumption by the latter of the Functions of Federal Directory
1847/48 [897] LXV	Correspondence relative to the Affairs of Switzerland
1854/55 [1890] LI	Annual Statement of Trade and Navigation of the United Kingdom
1856 [2041] LXI	Treaty of friendship, commerce and reciprocal establishment between Her Majesty and the Swiss Confederation, signed at Berne, September 6, 1855
[2055] LV	Statistical Abstract
[2139] LVI	Annual Statement of Trade and Navigation of the United Kingdom

1857 (Sess. 2) [2222] XLIII	Treaty between Her Majesty, the Emperor of Austria, the Emperor of the French, the King of Prussia, the Emperor of Russia, and the Swiss Confederation, relative to Neuchâtel; signed at Paris, 26 May 1857
1857/58 [2442] LIV	Annual Statement of Trade and Navigation of the United Kingdom
[2444] LV	Report by Mr Herries, Her Majesty's Secretary of Legation, on the Manufactures and Commerce of Switzerland
1859 (Sess. 2) [2570] XXX	Report by Mr Burnley, Her Majesty's Secretary of Legation, on the Manufactures and Commerce of Switzerland
1860 [2624] LXVII	Correspondence respecting the proposed Annexation of Savoy and Nice to France
[2630] LXVII	Despatch from Earl Cowley to Lord John Russell of 24th January, referred to in Earl Cowley's Despatch of 25th January, Savoy and Nice Papers
[2636] LXVII	Further Correspondence relating to the Affairs of Italy (Part II)
[2638] LXVII	Further Correspondence relating to the Affairs of Italy (Part III)
[2650] LXVII	Mémoire sur les rapports entre la Suisse at la Savoie neutralisée
[2656] LXVII	Further Correspondence relating to the Affairs of Italy (Part IV)
[2702] LXVII	Correspondence relating to the Affairs of Italy, Savoy and Switzerland (Part VI)
[2716] LXVI	Report by Mr Burnley, Her Majesty's Secretary of Legation, on the Manufactures and Commerce of Switzerland
[2717] LXVII	Letter addressed to the British Plenipotentiary at Vienna by the Deputies from Geneva, dated 7 February 1815
[2752] LXIV	Annual Statement of Trade and Navigation of the United Kingdom
1861 [2825] LXII	Statistical Abstract

1861 [2838] LXIII ⎫ Reports by Mr Burnley, Her Majesty's Secretary of
1863 [3222] LXXX ⎬ Legation, on the Manufactures and Commerce of
1864 [3392] LXI ⎭ Switzerland

Other Publications

Hansard, *Parliamentary Debates* (1847-61)

Sir Edward Hertslet, *The Map of Europe by Treaty
... since the General Peace of 1814* (London, 1875)

Royal Commission on the London Exhibition of
1851, *Reports by the Juries* (London, 1852)

B. IN FRANCE

Administration des Douanes, *Tableau général du
commerce de la France avec ses colonies et les puissances étrangères* (1849-61)

Direction des Affaires Commerciales, *Annales du
commerce extérieur* ('*Faits Commerciaux*') (Paris,
1860 and 1862)

Direction des Affaires Commerciales, *Un siècle de
commerce entre la France et le Royaume-Uni* (Paris,
1907)

Ministère des Affaires Étrangères,

Annuaire diplomatique de l'Empire Français (Paris,
1860 and 1865)

—*Documents diplomatiques, 1860* (Paris, 1861)

C. IN SWITZERLAND

Feuille Fédérale de la Confédération Suisse (Berne,
1849-61)

Département Fédéral des Douanes, *Rapports annuels de la statistique du commerce suisse* (Berne,
1850-60)

*Receuil Officiel des Lois et Ordinances de la Con-
fédération Suisse* (Berne, 1849-57)

3. Periodicals

The Economist (London, 1847-60)

Gentleman's Magazine (London, 1853)

Schweizerische Handels- und Gewerbe- Zeitung (Zurich, 1853-61)

The Times (London, 1847-60)

4. Contemporary Pamphlets

The Present Crisis in Switzerland and the Events which led to it, ed. E. Bickersteth (1848)

William de la Rive, *La Question de Savoie* (Geneva, 1860)

A. von Gonzenbach, *De la réforme du Tarif anglais et de ses conséquences probables pour le commerce suisse* (Zurich, 1846)

George Grote, *Seven Letters on the Recent Politics in Switzerland* (London, 1847)

Michel J. Mayers, *The Jesuit and the Sonderbund Contest in Switzerland* (London, 1847)

—*Notebook on the late Civil War in Switzerland* (London, 1848)

Sir Robert Peel, *France, Savoy and Switzerland* (London, 1898) (Excerpts from 1860 speeches in the House of Commons)

La Suisse dans la question de Savoie (Lausanne, 1860)

Saint-René Taillandier, 'Le Sonderbund et le Radicalisme Suisse' (*Revue des Deux Mondes*, Paris, nouv. sér., August 1847)

5. Published Memoirs and Private Correspondence

Otto von Bismarck-Schoenhausen, *Correspondance diplomatique*, edited by Th. Funck-Brentano and translated by L. Schmitt (Paris, 1883)

Otto von Bismarck-Schoenhausen, *Lettres politiques confidentielles*, edited by Henri de Poschinger and translated by E.-B. Lang (Paris, 1885)

—*Bismarck, the Man and the Statesman; being the Reflections and Reminiscences of Otto Prince von Bismarck*, translated by A. J. Butler (Leipzig, 1899)

Guillaume-Henri Dufour, *Campagne du Sonderbund* (Geneva, 1879)

Charles Greville, *The Greville Memoirs*, edited by Lytton Strachey and Roger Fulford (London, 1938), Volumes v to viii

James Edward Harris (Earl of Malmesbury), *Memoirs of an ex-Minister* (London, 1884)

Johann Conrad Kern, *Souvenirs Politiques*, edited and translated by Charles Dubois (Paris, 1887)

Lord Augustus Loftus, *The Diplomatic Reminiscences of Lord Augustus Loftus, 1837-1862* (London, 1892)

Prince Metternich-Winneburg, *Mémoires, documents et écrits divers*, edited by A. de Klinkowstroem (Paris, 1883), Volumes vii and viii

Lord John Russell, *The Later Correspondence of Lord John Russell, 1840-1878*, edited by G. P. Gooch (London, 1925)

Victoria, *The Letters of Queen Victoria, 1837-1861* (London, 1908)

Count Charles Frederick Vitzthum von Eckstädt, *St Petersburg and London in the years 1852-1864* (London, 1887)

F. A. Wellesley, *The Paris Embassy during the Second Empire; Selections from the Papers of Henry Richard Charles Wellesley, 1st Earl Cowley* (London, 1928)

Rosslyn Wemyss, *Memoirs and Letters of the Right Hon. Sir Robert Morier, G.C.B., from 1826 to 1876* (London, 1911)

6. Secondary Works

Willy Aeschlimann, 'L'Affaire de Savoie, en 1860, et l'expédition de Thonon' (*Almanach du Vieux Genève*, Geneva, 1947, Vol. 23)

M. A. Anderson, *Edmund Hammond, Permanent Under Secretary of State for Foreign Affairs, 1854-1873* (unpublished Ph.D. thesis, University of London, 1956)

Evelyn Ashley, *The Life and Correspondence of Henry John Temple, Viscount Palmerston* (London, 1879)

Bernard Bacot, *Des Neutralités Durables: origines, domaines et efficacité* (Paris, 1947)

P. Baillod, 'L'exil des royalistes après les mouvement insurrectionnel du 3 séptembre 1856' (*Musée Neuchâtelois*, Neuchâtel, 1930, Vol. 17)

Maurice Battelli, 'Genève et la neutralité suisse en 1848' (*Zeitschrift für Schweizerisches Recht*, Basle, 1959, Bd. 78)

Ed. Bauer, 'Deux documents sur le Sonderbund' (*Musée Neuchâtelois*, Neuchâtel, 1934, Vol. 21)

Marianne Bauer, *Die italienische Einigung im Spiegel der schweizerischen Oeffentlichkeit 1859-61* (Basle, 1944)

J. Baumgartner, *Schweizerspiegel; Drei Jahre unter der Bundesverfassung von 1848* (Zurich, 1851)

Derek Beales, *England and Italy, 1859-60* (London, 1961)

H. C. F. Bell, *Lord Palmerston* (London, 1936)

Victor Bérard, *Genève, la France et la Suisse* (Paris, 1927), Tome 1.

H. Bessler, *La France et la Suisse de 1848-1852* (Paris, 1931)

R. C. Binkley, *Realism and Nationalism, 1852-1871* (New York and London, 1935)

Werner Bleuler, *Studien über Aussenhandel und Handelspolitik der Schweiz* (Zurich, 1929)

Walter Bodmer, *Die Entwicklung der Schweizerischen Textilwirtschaft im Rahmen der übrigen Industrien und Wirtschaftszweige* (Zurich, 1960)

Edgar Bonjour, *L'Affaire de Neuchâtel sur le plan européen* (Neuchâtel, 1956)

—'Ein amerikanischer Vermittlungsversuch im Neuenburger Konflikt' (*Zeitschrift für Schweizerische Geschichte*, Zurich, 1939)

—*Englands Anteil an der Lösung des Neuenburger Konflikts 1856/57* (Basle, 1943)

—'Englands Einwirkung auf Preussen zu Gunsten der Schweiz 1856/57' (*Schweizer. Beiträge zur Allgemeinen Geschichte*, Aarau, 1943, Bd. 1)

—*Europäisches Gleichgewicht und Schweizerische Neutralität* (Basle, 1946)

—'Europäische Stimmen zum Neuenburger Konflikt' (*Schweizer. Beiträge zur Allgemeinen Geschichte*, Aarau, 1944, Bd. 2)

—*Geschichte der Schweizerischen Neutralität* (Basle, 1946)

—*Die Schweiz und England* (Berne, 1934)

—'Der Sonderbundskrieg' (*Schweizer Monatshefte*, Zurich, Nov. 1947)

—'Der Sonderbundswirren und das Ausland' (*Neue Schweiz. Rundschau*, 1948, Bd. xv)

—*Vorgeschichte des Neuenburger Konflikts* (Berne, 1932)

Edgar Bonjour, H. S. Offler and G. R. Potter, *A Short History of Switzerland* (Oxford, 1952)

Rondo E. Cameron, *France and the Economic Development of Europe* (Princeton, 1961)

François Cardis and Werner Rahm, *L'héritage économique suisse du XIXᵉ siècle* (Lausanne, 1959)

Edouard Chapuisat, *Le Général Dufour, 1787-1875* (Lausanne, 1942)

François Charles-Roux, *Alexandre II, Gortchakoff et Napoléon III* (Paris, 1913)

Brian Connell, *Regina v. Palmerston* (London, 1962)

Alfred Coville and Harold Temperley, *Studies in Anglo-French History* (Cambridge, 1935)

Emanuel Dejung, Alfred Stähli and Werner Ganz, *Jonas Furrer von Winterthur, 1805-1861, Erster Schweizerischer Bundespräsident* (Winterthur, 1948)

Delegation des Handels, *Der Schweizerische Grosshandel in Geschichte und Gegenwart* (Basle, 1944)

E. Dérobert, *La politique douanière de la Confédération suisse* (Geneva, 1926)

Johannes Dierauer, *Geschichte der Schweizerischen Eidgenossenschaft* (Gotha, 1922), Vol. 5 (1798-1848)

Carl Eckinger, *Lord Palmerston und der Schweizer Sonderbundskrieg* (Berlin, 1938)

Henri Fazy, *James Fazy, Sa vie et son œuvre* (Geneva, 1887)

Richard Feller, *Alfred Escher* (Berne, 1916)
—*Jakob Stämpfli* (Berne, 1921)

Fritz Fick, 'Das politische Asylrecht in der Schweiz' (*Schw. Juristenzeitung*, Zurich, 1908/9, Bd. v)

George Fischer, Ltd, *The Metallurgist, Johann Conrad Fischer, 1773-1854, and his Relations with Britain* (Schaffhausen, 1947)

Paul Flaad, *England und die Schweiz, 1848-1852* (Zurich, 1935)

Ernesto Gagliardi, *Histoire de la Suisse*, translated by August Reymond (Lausanne, 1925), Vol. 2

Henri Ganter, *Histoire du service militaire des Regiments suisses à la solde de l'Angleterre, de Naples et de Rome* (Geneva, 1901)

Lotti Genner, *Die diplomatischen Beziehungen zwischen England und der Schweiz von 1870 bis 1890* (Basle, 1956)

Philippe Godet, *La Caisse d'Epargne de Neuchâtel, 1812-1912* (Neuchâtel, 1912)

Donald M. Greer, *L'Angleterre, la France et la révolution de 1848* (Paris, 1925)

Ferd. Gubler, *Die Anfänge der schweizerischen Eisenbahnpolitik auf Grundlage der wirtschaftlichen Interessen, 1833-1852* (Zurich-Selnau, 1915)

Viscomte Eugène de Guichen, *Les grandes questions européennes et la diplomatie des puissances sous la seconde république française* (Paris, 1925-29)

—*La guerre de Crimée (1854-1856) et l'attitude des puissances européennes* (Paris, 1936)

Else Gutknecht, *Die Diplomatie des Auslandes in der Schweiz während des Sonderbundes* (Zurich-Selnau, 1917)

John Hall, *England and the Orleans Monarchy* (London, 1912)

H. Hearder, *The Foreign Policy of Lord Malmesbury, 1858-9* (unpublished Ph.D. thesis, University of London, 1954)

Rudolf A. Heimann, *Johann Ulrich Ochsenbein* (Berne, 1954)

Gavin B. Henderson, *Crimean War Diplomacy and other Historical Essays* (Glasgow, 1947)

W. O. Henderson, *Britain and Industrial Europe, 1750-1870* (Liverpool, 1954)

Edouard His, *Geschichte des neuern Schweizerischen Staatsrechts* (Basle, 1929 and 1938), Vols. II and III

Georg Hoffmann, 'Die grossbritannische Schweizer-Legion im Krimkrieg, Werbung und Schicksal' (*Zeitschrift für Schweizerische Geschichte*, Zurich, 1942, Bd. 22)

Albert H. Imlah, *Economic Elements in the Pax Britannica* (Cambridge, Massachusetts, 1958)

Alexander Isler, *Bundesrat Dr Jonas Furrer, 1805-1861* (Winterthur, 1907)

Leland H. Jenks, *The Migration of British Capital to 1875* (London, 1927)

Walter A. Johr, *Schweizerische Kreditanstalt, 1856-1956* (Zurich, 1956)

Stanley Lane-Poole, *The Life of the Right Honourable Stratford Canning, Viscount Stratford de Redcliffe* (London, 1888)

André Lefevre, *Sous le Second Empire: Chemins de fer et politique* (Paris, 1951)

Jean L. B. Leresche, *Biographe politique de Henri Druey* (Lausanne, 1857)

B. Lincke, *Die Schweizerische Maschinenindustrie und ihre Entwicklung in wirtschaftl. Beziehung* (Frauenfeld, 1911)

Theodore Martin, *The Life of His Royal Highness the Prince Consort* (London, 1875-80)

Paul Matter, 'Les missions de M. de Persigny à Berlin' (*Revue d'histoire diplomatique*, Paris, 1898)

Marguerite Mauerhofer, 'L'Affaire de Neuchâtel de 1856, d'après des documents français inédits' (*Musée Neuchâtelois*, Neuchâtel, 1950, Vol. 37)

Sir Herbert Maxwell, *The Life and Letters of George William Frederick, Fourth Earl of Clarendon* (London, 1913), Vol. II

Kurt B. Mayer, *The Population of Switzerland* (New York, 1952)

J. R. McCulloch, *A Dictionary ... of Commerce and Commercial Navigation* (London, 1859)

Luc Monnier, *L'Annexion de la Savoie à la France et la politique suisse, 1860* (Geneva, 1932)

Neue Helvetische Gesellschaft, *Neutralität und Mitverantwortung* (Berne, 1957)
—*Die Schweiz Hält Durch* (Zurich, 1948)

Wilhelm Oechsli, *History of Switzerland, 1499-1914*, translated by E. and C. Paul (Cambridge, 1922)

Hermann Oncken, *Napoleon III and the Rhine*, translated by Edwin H. Zeydal (New York, 1928)

Jacques Petitpierre, *Neuchâtel et la Confédération suisse devant l'Europe* (Neuchâtel, 1957)

Leopold von Ranke, *Aus dem Briefwechsel Wilhelms IV mit Bunsen* (Leipzig, 1873)

William E. Rappard, *Conditions de la prosperité helvétique* (Zurich, 1957)

—*L'évolution de la politique économique de la Suisse de 1848 à 1948* (Zurich, 1948)

—'*La Suisse et le marché du monde*' (in Handelshochschule St. Gallen, *Die Schweiz als Kleinstadt in der Weltwirtschaft* (St. Gallen, 1945)

Olivier Reverdin, *La Guerre du Sonderbund vue par le Général Dufour* (Geneva, 1948)

Gonzague de Reynold, 'Neutralisme et neutralité' (*La Revue*, Paris, June 1951)

Ed. Rossier, 'L'Affaire de Savoie en 1860 et l'intervention anglaise' (*Revue Historique*, Paris, 1906, Vol. 90)

Hans Rothfels, '1848 – One Hundred Years After' (*Journal of Modern History*, Chicago, 1948, Vol. xx)

Walther Rupli, *Zollreform und Bundesreform in der Schweiz, 1815-1848* (Zurich, 1949)

H. Schmid, 'Vor 75 Jahren: Der Neuenburger Handel 1856/7' (*Politische Rundschau*, Berne, 1932, Jg. 11)

Peter H. Schmidt, *Die Schweiz und die europäische Handelspolitik* (Zurich, 1914)

—*Die schweizerischen Industrien im internationalen Konkurrenzkampfe* (Zurich, 1912)

Hans Schneider, *Geschichte des Schweizerischen Bundesstaates 1848-1918* (Volume 6 of Johannes Dierauer, *Geschichte der schweizerische Eidgenossenschaft*, Stuttgart, 1931)

Paul Schweizer, *Geschichte der Schweizerischen Neutralität* (Frauenfeld, 1895)

Paul Seippel, ed., *La Suisse au dix-neuvième siècle* (Paris, 1899-1901)

R. W. Seton-Watson, *Britain in Europe, 1789-1914* (Cambridge, 1937)

George Soloveytchik, *Leu & Co., 1755-1955* (Zurich, 1955)

Léon E. Straessle, *Die Entwicklung der schweizerischen Neutralität* (Fribourg, 1951)

Eric Streiff, *Die Einflussnahme der europäischen Mächte auf die Entwicklungskämpfe in der Schweiz, 1839-1845* (Zurich, 1931)

Swiss Bank Corporation, *Swiss Merchant Bankers in London* (London, 1954)

Switzerland, Eidgenössisches Volkwirtschaftdepartement, *La Suisse économique et sociale* (Einsiedeln, 1927)

Saint-René Taillandier, 'Le Sonderbund et le radicalisme suisse' (*Revue des Deux Mondes*, Paris, nouv. série, 1847, Vol. xix)

William R. Thayer, *The Life and Times of Cavour* (London, 1911)

Andrew Ure, *The Cotton Manufacture of Great Britain* (London, 1861)

Philippe de Vargas, *L'Affaire de Neuchâtel, 1856-57; les négotiations diplomatiques* (Lausanne, 1913)

Auguste Vitu, *Guide Financier; répertoire général des valeurs financières et industrielles* (Paris, 1864)

Rudolf H. Vogeli, *Die schweizerische Regeneration von 1830-40 in der Beleuchtung englischer Gesandtschaftsberichte* (Weida i. Thur, 1924)

Hans A. Vögelin, *Die Grundung des schweizerischen Bundesstaates im Urteil der Engländer* (Basle, 1952)

Adolf Walcher, *Die Neutralität der Schweiz, spezial diejenige Hochsavoyens und des Pays de Gex* (Freiburg i. Br., 1939)

William Waldvogel, *Les Relations Economiques entre la Grande-Bretagne et la Suisse dans le passé et le présent* (Neuveville, 1922)

Karl Wall, 'Heinrich Gelzer (1813-1889) als Diplomat im Neuenburger Konflikt' (*Basler Zeitschrift für Geschichte und Altertumskunde*, Basle, 1950, Bd. 49)

E. Weinmann, 'Der Anteil des Tessins am italienischen Risorgimento und die schweizerische Neutralität 1848' (*Zeitschrift für Schweizerische Geschichte*, Zurich, 1932, Bd. 12)

Theodor Weiss, *Alfred Escher und Jacob Stämpfli* (Berne, 1927)

Karl Welter, *Die Exportgesellschaften und die assoziative Exportförderung in der Schweiz im 19. Jahrhundert* (Berne, 1915)

Index

Aargau, 13-15, 17
Aberdeen, Earl of, xi, 15-17, 22, 29, 38
Act of Mediation, 6
agriculture in Switzerland, 10
Albert, Prince, 58-59, 156
alliance, Anglo-French, 9, 14, 19, 27, 84, 87-88, 129, 131, 150, 161, 163, 166-167, 173, 179
alliance, proposed, between Switzerland and Sardinia, 42, 61, 77
alliance system of Europe, 87-88, 150, 158, 179; *see also* treaty system
Alsace, 28
Americas, 103, 106-107, 121
amnesty: and *Sonderbund*, 33, 35; and Neuchâtel settlement, 130, 135, 141-144
Anglo-French Circular, on rights and duties of neutrals, 91
Anglo-Swiss treaty, *see* Treaty between Britain and . . .
annexation of Savoy, *see* Savoy question
asylum in Switzerland, 40, 42, 45-46, 60, 136; *see also* refugee problems
Australia, 121
Austria, 25, 61
Austrian policy: to Baden, 69; to Britain, 14, 25, 76, 82-83, 87-88, 96-97; to France, 7-8, 14, 25-26, 31, 36-37, 52, 54, 71, 74, 80, 139, 168; to the German States, 79; in Italy, 25, 37, 84-85, 168; to Milan consulates, 177; to the Pope, 22; to Prussia, 47, 51, 54-55, 63, 139, 142; to Sardinia, 77, 168; to Switzerland, 8, 14-15, 19-20, 25, 30-33, 35-36, 43, 49, 58, 61-63, 69, 74-88, 95-96, 134, 154, 169, 177; *see also* Bolgrad; constitution; expansionism; independence; intervention; Neuchâtel; neutrality; refugees; Savoy; *Sonderbund*
Austro-Sardinian War, 153-154, 175
Austro-Swiss disputes, *see* refugees and Austrian policy

Baden, 28, 45-46, 54, 63, 69
balance of power, 4-5, 9-10, 24, 60, 74, 88, 91, 129, 155, 161, 173-175, 178-180
balance of trade, Swiss, with Britain, 101, 124
Bally, 108
Bank of England, 110
banks, Swiss, 12, 103, 108-109
Barman, Joseph-Hyacinthe, xi, 55, 65-66, 70, 73, 76-77, 80, 96, 136, 141-142, 151, 155
Basle, 15, 68, 80, 89-90, 98
Bavaria, 41
Belgium, 54, 70-71, 77
Berne, 8, 15, 17-18, 28, 31, 37, 40, 43, 53, 71; *see also* diplomatic corps
Bismarck-Schoenhausen, Prince Otto von, xi, 129, 134, 136, 138, 150
Black Sea, 129
blockade, 91; of Prussia, discussed, 140; of Switzerland, 62, 75, 78-79, 83, 85-86; threatened, 19-20, 33, 74

Bloomfield, Lord, xi, 54, 56, 136, 138, 142, 144, 169
Blount, Sir Edward, 109
Board of Trade, 92, 111, 113-115
Bois-le Comte, Count, xi, 20, 24-25, 29, 37, 149
Bolgrad question, 129-130, 133, 135, 137, 140, 150
boundary, Swiss, 86, 155
Bowring, John, 11, 100
British colonies, 114, 121
British missionaries, 34
British policy: to Austria, 19-20, 28, 30, 54, 61, 65, 76-77, 79-86, 88, 132, 139-140, 160, 163, 173, 177; to France: about Neuchâtel, 54-55, 129-135, 137-140, 142, 144-147, 150-151; about refugees, 54, 67-74, 77-87; about Savoy, 156, 158, 160-163, 165-166, 168-175; about the *Sonderbund*, 19-20, 26-31, 37-38; to the German States, 46, 51, 79-80, 109; to Prussia, 28, 30, 32, 44-45, 47, 52-59, 65, 109, 131, 133, 135, 137, 140, 147-149, 160, 163, 173, 177; to Russia, 19, 28, 30, 160, 163, 167, 173; to Sardinia, 158, 160-161; to Switzerland (general), 4-5, 7-8, 39, 42, 53, 66-67, 74-75, 87, 89-90, 98, 112, 126-127, 143-144, 151-152, 177-178; to the United States, 113; *see also* Bolgrad; commercial policy; competition; diplomacy of Switzerland; expansionism; independence; mercenary system; neutrality; Neuchâtel; railway development; refugees; Savoy; *Sonderbund*; treaty
British residents in Switzerland, 111-114
British Swiss Legion, 95-98, 109-110, 127, 177
British travellers to Switzerland, 89, 126
Buchanan, Sir Andrew, xi, 55-58, 110
buffer state concept, 5, 7-8, 134, 144, 178, 180
Bunsen, Christian Karl Josias, xi, 47-48, 54
Buol-Schauenstein, Count, xi, 79, 81, 83, 86
Burnley, Joseph Hume, xi, 115, 186
Büsingen incident, 46-48, 176

Cabinet, British, 20-21, 27, 140, 161-162
Cabinet, French, 28
Cabinet, Prussian, 44, 131, 137
Canning, Sir Stratford, xi, 26-27, 30-36, 39-41, 45, 178, 181-185
cantonal sovereignty, 6, 8, 10-11, 13, 19-22, 27, 30-36, 40, 42, 102, 112-114
cantons of Switzerland, 1-2, 6-7, 102; *see also* cantonal sovereignty
capital needs for Swiss development, 108-109, 114
capital resources of Switzerland, 5, 12
Capuchins, 75-76, 78, 82, 84-86
Catholics in Switzerland, 1, 13-18, 20-22, 26-29, 34, 68, 75-76, 78, 82, 84-86, 158
Cavour, Count Camillo Benso, xi, 156, 160, 175

202

centralization, Swiss, 7, 10-12; see also Federal Pact reform
Chablais and Faucigny, 156-157, 159-160, 165, 167, 174
Chambéry, 157
Chambre de Députés, 24
Chambre de Pairs, 36
cheese, Swiss, 101-102, 108
Christie, William Dougal, xi, 58, 67-68, 70, 82, 84, 111-113
civil war in Switzerland, see Sonderbund; war
Clarendon, Earl of, xii, 58, 76, 79-81, 84-88, 93-94, 109-110, 112-114, 127, 129-133, 135, 137-138, 140-144, 147-151, 157, 161, 173
clericalism in Switzerland, see Capuchins, Jesuits
clock industry, Swiss, see watch industry
cloth printing industry, Swiss, 106
Cobden commercial treaty, 156
commerce, European, 4
commerce, see also trade
commercial contacts, Swiss, 11
commercial interests, and war, 38, 92-93, 141
commercial policy: of Baden, 69; of Britain, 101, 107, 111, 114-115; of France, 71; of Switzerland, 11-12, 51, 69, 100-102, 114-115, 154; of Zollverein, 12, 51, 102
commercial ties between Britain and Switzerland, 101, 103, 106-111, 114-115, 119-127, 177
commercial treaty, see Treaty between Britain and . . .
Commons, House of, 170, 173; see also Parliament
communication: between governments, 25, 154, 166-168, 173, 175-178; between Swiss cantons, 1-2, 58; see also reporting
communication patterns in Europe, 4, 92; see also transportation
communism, alleged, in Switzerland, 47, 75, 86-87, 90
Como, Bishop of, 75, 86-87, 90
competition, between British and Swiss industries, 100-101, 103, 106-108, 122, 125, 177
Congress of Paris, 98-99, 127
Congress of Verona, 9
Congress of Vienna, 7-8
Congress (proposed) on Italy, 155
Constance, Lake of, 97
constitution, Swiss, 40; and Continental Powers' desire for change, 44, 46-47, 54, 59-60, 62, 64, 68-74, 78, 84, 86-87, 127-128, 132, 143-144; and economic development, 101-103;and the Neuchâtel settlement, 146-147; and the refugee problem, 45, 63; see also Federal Pact; independence; Jews
Consul, Swiss: in London, 27, 101, 106, 108, 160; in Liverpool, 119
Council of States, 40
Continental System, 6-7, 10
contraband, 92
convent question, see monasteries
corn, 51, 102
corps francs, see volunteer bands
cottage industry, Swiss, 6-7, 103

cotton industry, Swiss, 106, 108, 118-120, 122-123; see also textiles
coup d'état, by Louis-Napoleon, 69
Cowley, Earl of, xii, 53-56, 70-74, 76-77, 79-83, 86, 89, 95, 97, 128, 134-136, 139, 141-148, 151, 155-158, 160-162, 165-171, 173-175
Cracow Republic, 19
Crimean War, 87, 91-99, 127, 153, 177
culture, Swiss, 1-3
curtains, Swiss, 106-107
customs system, Swiss, 10-11, 19, 40, 102
customs unions, Swiss, 12

de la Harpe, 7
de la Rive, Auguste, xii, 160, 162, 165-171, 173-175, 177-178
de Redcliffe, see Canning
Declaration of International Mediation, 99, 127
Declaration of Maritime Law, 99
defence of Switzerland, 6-7, 40, 46-47, 98, 134, 137, 151, 153-154, 160, 165-166, 171, 175-176
Derby, Lord, 53, 58
Diet, German, 132, 134, 136, 139
Diet, Swiss, 8; and Neuchâtel, 32-33, 35; and the refugee problem, 45, 61-62; and the Sonderbund crisis, 12, 14-15, 17-23, 26-28, 30-37, 39-40, 42, 149; see also commercial policy; Swiss policy
diplomacy of Switzerland: and British policy, 5, 53, 151-152, 157, 165, 177-178; and the Savoy question, 166, 168-170, 174
diplomatic communications, see reporting
diplomatic corps in Berne, 18, 28, 30, 37, 42-43, 93-94, 137-138, 148
directing cantons, under Federal Pact, 8
disarmament: of foreign troops by Switzerland, 46, 154, 176; of Lago Maggiore steamers by Switzerland, 154
drawing instruments, Swiss, 108
Drouyn de Lhuys, Edouard, xii, 77, 79-81, 86
Dufour, Guillaume-Henri, xii, 22, 29, 31, 34, 132, 134-135, 141, 153-154, 159

Eastern Question, 58, 74, 76, 83-84, 86, 168
economic crisis in Europe, 19
economic development, British, 5
economic development, European, 24-25
economic development, Swiss, 5-6, 10-13, 42, 101-103, 124, 126, 152; see also population
Economist, 104, 107, 109
education, Swiss, 40, 103
electrical machinery, Swiss, 107
Elliot, see Minto
embroidered goods, Swiss, 101, 103, 106-107, 119-120
emigration, Swiss, 112
employment, Swiss, 6-7, 11, 96, 98, 101, 108
entente, see alliance
establishment, right of, 11, 68-69, 101, 111-112; see also labour
Europe, as market for Switzerland, 106-107
expansionism in Europe, 5, 180
expansionism, French: and Austrian policy, 154, 158, 160, 163, 168-170, 175; and

203

expansionism—*continued*
British policy, 52-55, 77, 87, 140, 158, 160-163, 165-166, 168-175; and Prussian policy, 163, 170; and Russian policy, 55, 163; *see also* Rhineland, Savoy
expansionism, Prussian, 55
expansionism, Sardinian, 155, 158-159, 168
expansionism, Swiss, 42, 74, 155, 158, 164
exports, British, 92-93, 100-101, 103, 114-116, 118-120, 122-125
exports, Swiss, 10-11, 92-93, 100-108, 112, 118-126, 177; *see also* markets
expulsion by Switzerland: of paupers, 113; of refugees, 46, 63-64, 69-73, 75, 89; *see also* Neuchâtel
extradition, 60, 86, 111, 113

Fane, *see* Westmorland
Far East, 103, 107
farming, Swiss, 6-7
Fay, Theodore S., 141
Federal Assembly, Swiss, 40, 50, 56, 81, 102, 110, 114, 135, 141, 143, 164, 171
Federal Council, Swiss, 40, 62-65, 70, 75-78, 82, 85-86, 88-90, 92; *see also* Jews; Neuchâtel; refugees; Savoy; Swiss policy
Federal Pact, Swiss, 8, 11, 13-14; and economic development, 10-13; reform movement, 9-10, 12-13, 15-18, 20-21, 26-28, 30, 32-36, 39-41
Fénelon (Salignac-), xiii, 69-72, 89, 94, 97, 123-124, 128-132, 134, 139, 149
food, Swiss imports of, 10, 102
Foreign Enlistment Act of 1854, 94-95
foreign investment, *see* investment
Foreign Office: communications with British diplomats, 16, 18, 30, 161; *see also* British policy
Fox, Sir Charles, 110
France, defeat in 1814, 7
Franco-Prussian War, 176
Frankfurt Parliament, 47
Frederick-William IV, *see* Prussia, King of
free trade, *see* commercial policy
Freischaren, see volunteer bands
freight rates, 102
French financial companies, 109
French policy: to Austria, 7-8, 17, 24-25, 65, 70, 72, 74, 77-78, 80; to Belgium, 54, 77; to Britain: about Neuchâtel, 54-55, 130, 132-135, 137, 139, 142, 144-145, 150; about refugees, 65-66, 69-73, 82, 87-89; about Savoy, 157-158, 160, 162-163, 165-168, 170, 173; about the *Sonderbund*, 17, 24-25, 27-31, 36-39; to the German States, 51, 69; to Italy, 20, 37, 74, 84-85, 129, 155; to the Pope, 14-15, 22; to Prussia, 43-44, 47, 49, 51, 54-55, 57, 65-66, 79, 81, 132-133, 136, 139, 143-146, 148-150; to Russia, 79, 81; to Sardinia, 72, 85, 155, 158-159; to Switzerland: about Neuchâtel, 43-44, 65, 129, 131-132, 134-137, 142, 144-150; about refugees, 43, 53, 64-74, 77-82, 87-90, 155; about Savoy, 154-157, 159, 161-162, 164-165, 167-168, 170-172; about the *Sonderbund*, 15-17, 26, 28, 33, 35-37; to the United States, 138; *see also* Bolgrad; boundary; British Swiss Legion; constitution; diplomatic corps; expansionism; indepen-

dence; intervention; Jews; Neuchâtel; neutrality; refugees; Savoy; *Sonderbund*
French Swiss Legion, 95, 97-98
Fribourg, 13, 27-29, 33, 67-68, 78-81
Fribourg, Bishop of, *see* Marilley
frontier question, *see* Bolgrad; boundary; defence
Furrer, Jonas, xii, 86

Garibaldi, 62, 168
Geneva, 7, 18, 35, 63-66, 69-70, 72, 80, 85, 88-89, 93, 159, 164, 172
Geneva-Basle railway, 110-111
Geneva, Lake, 8, 166
geography, Swiss, 2, 4–5, 59, 61, 73, 134, 178
German-Helvetic Legion, 63
German Confederation, 47, 79-80, 133; *see also* Neuchâtel
German States, 25, 43, 45-47, 49, 51, 63, 69, 79-80, 97, 160; *see also* Neuchâtel; Zollverein
Gladstone, William, 95
Gonzenbach, A. von, 114
Gordon, George John Robert, xii, 89-90, 95, 97, 112-114, 128-131, 138-139, 147-149, 178
government, Swiss, 6-8, 40; *see also*, constitution; Federal Pact
Gower, *see* Granville
Granville, Lord, xii, 52, 69-71
Great Exhibition of 1851, 104-108
Greece, 19
Grisons, 19-20, 38, 78, 110
Grote, George, 38
Guizot, François, xii, 17, 19-20, 24-28, 30-31, 36-39
gunpowder, Swiss, 92-93

Hall, John, 38
Harris, *see* Malmesbury
Harris, Captain E.A.J., xii, 155-156, 170-172, 174-175
Hammond, Edmund, 173-174
Hatzfeldt, Count, xii, 129, 143-144, 146, 148
Herries, Edward, xii, 115-118, 124, 186
Hessian troops, 46
Hudson, Sir James, xii, 156-158, 160, 164, 174-175
hydraulic machinery, 107

ideology, 4-5, 14, 19-20, 38-39, 60, 87, 149, 178; *see also* liberalism
imports, British, 100-101, 103, 106-108, 115, 118-120, 124-125
imports, Swiss, 10, 100-101, 103, 114-116, 118-125
incomes, British, 125
indemnity: and the Austro-Swiss dispute, 75, 82, 86; and the Neuchâtel settlement, 146-148
independence, Swiss: and Austrian policy, 77-78, 84, 144, 149, 175; and British policy, 4-5, 7-8, 15-16, 26-27, 39, 53, 73-75, 87-88, 90, 96, 98, 126-127, 143-144, 149, 151-152, 177-178; and European Powers' policies, 7-9, 37, 41-43, 69, 91, 151-153, 176, 179; and French policy, 65-66, 70-73, 144, 149; and neutrality, 1-4, 180; and Prussian

policy, 44, 56-57; and Russian policy, 92, 94, 144; and Swiss policy, 37, 132, 134; *see also* balance of power; constitution; economic development; international law; Neuchâtel; refugees; *Sonderbund*
India, 121
industry, Swiss, 5-7, 10-12, 100-103, 126, 154
intelligence collection, *see* reporting
international law, 31, 72, 99, 153-154, 179
international organizations, 2, 176
internment, Swiss: of belligerents, 46, 154, 176; of refugees, 45-46, 61, 67, 72-73, 75, 88-89
intervention in Switzerland: and Austrian policy, 9-10, 19, 21-23, 28, 37, 43, 46-47, 61, 72-73, 80, 87; and British policy, 21, 27-28, 37, 44, 50, 131, 143-144; and French policy, 19, 21-25, 28, 37, 43, 46-47, 65-66, 68, 70-71, 87, 132; and German States' policies, 46-47; and Prussian policy, 43-44, 46-47, 49, 51-52, 63, 73; and Russian policy, 46-47; and Swiss policy, 21, 177; *see also* invasion; Neuchâtel; refugees; *Sonderbund*
invasion of Italy, 166
invasion of North Savoy, threatened, 154, 164-165, 170, 175
invasion of Switzerland, by France, 6, 65
invasion of Switzerland, threatened, 33, 35, 46-47, 49, 61, 63, 65-66, 69, 80, 129, 132, 134, 136, 138-143, 145, 176
invasion of Thonon, 159
investment in Britain, by Swiss, 101
investment in Switzerland, 12, 101, 103, 108-110, 124, 126
iron, 51, 118-120, 123
Italy, 19-21, 24-25, 28, 37, 42, 61, 74, 84-85, 95, 98, 129-130, 153-155, 168, 177; *see also* Lombardy

Jesuits in Switzerland, 13-18, 20-22, 26-29, 68
Jews in Switzerland, 68-69, 111-112
July Revolution in France, 9
Jura mountains, 7

kidskin, 101
King of Prussia, *see* Prussia, King of
Kern, Johann Conrad, xii, 141, 144-151, 156-157, 159-161, 166-167, 169-170, 174-175
Klapka, General, 88

labour, Swiss, 11, 101; *see also* employment; establishment
La Chaud-de-Fonds, 89-90
Lago Maggiore, 154
Lake Geneva, 8, 154, 157
languages, Swiss, 1-2, 4, 13
law enforcement, Swiss, 40
Le Havre, 123
leather goods, Swiss, 108, 122-123, 126
Ledru-Rollin, 64
liberalism: and Austrian policy, 84; and British policy, 4-5, 18-19, 22, 38-39, 178; and French policy, 28, 37, 64, 79, 84, 149; and Prussian policy, 44, 46-47, 54, 59, 64, 137, 144; *see also* ideology

liberalism in Europe, 40-42, 60
liberalism, Swiss, 9-10, 13-14, 22, 28, 38, 40-42, 57, 60-61, 91, 100, 127-128, 140
licences, export, 92-93
liqueurs, Swiss, 108
Liverpool, 123-124
loans, forced, and Anglo-Swiss treaty, 113
Lombardy, 61-63, 75-78, 81-83, 85-86, 153, 155
London, and the Neuchâtel conference in 1857, 139, 144-145
London Protocol of 1852, 54-56, 58-59, 74, 130
Lords, House of, 166
Louis-Napoleon, 52, 64; *see also* Napoleon
Louis-Philippe, 24-25, 28, 31, 37
Lucerne, 8, 14-17, 21, 30, 33

machine goods, Swiss, 107, 119-120, 123
machine industry, Swiss, 7, 11, 103
machinery imports of Switzerland, 92
Magenis, Sir Arthur Charles, xii, 73
Malmesbury, Earl of, xii, 53-59, 71-73, 90, 154
manpower, Swiss, *see* employment; labour
Manteuffel, Baron Otto von, xii, 127, 131-133, 138, 140, 142, 144, 148
manufactured goods in Swiss trade, 92, 100, 108, 122-123
Marilley (Bishop of Fribourg), 67-68, 79, 81
markets for Switzerland, 10-11, 103, 108, 114, 177
marriages, Anglo-Swiss, 112-113
Mazzini, Guissepe, xii, 61-62, 64, 78
meat, 102
mechanization in Switzerland, 7, 103, 106
mercenary system, Swiss, 5, 11-12, 94-98, 130, 177
merchant marine; *see* shipping services
merchants, British, 101, 119, 121-126
merchants, Swiss, 119, 121-122, 124
Metternich-Winnebürg, Prince von, xii, 8-10, 15-17, 19, 25-26, 36
Milan, 61, 75, 78, 83, 85-86, 177; *see also* Lombardy
military intervention, *see* invasion
militarism in Europe, 4
milk (condensed) industry, Swiss, 125-126
Minto, Earl of, xiii, 20-22, 29, 34
missionaries, British, 38
mobilization, Prussian, against Switzerland, 136-143
mobilization, Swiss, 46, 81, 141, 143, 153-154
monasteries question, 13-14, 17
monetary system, Swiss, 11, 40, 101-102
money markets in Europe, 109
Moniteur, 136-137, 148
Moustier, 150
Morier, David R., xiii, 9, 12, 15-16, 18-19, 26, 37
Morier, Sir Robert, 9
most-favoured-nation clause, 102, 111, 114-115

Naples, 94-95, 97-98, 130, 177
Napoleon (III): and Italy, 85, 129, 155; and the Neuchâtel question, 52, 128-139, 142-146, 149-150; and the refugee problem, 50, 64, 66, 70, 88, 128; and Savoy,

Napoleon (III)—*continued*
  155-156, 158-159, 162-163, 166, 168-169,
  173, 175
Napoleon, Prince, 148, 156
Napoleonic conquest of Switzerland, 6-7,
  10, 65
National Council, 40
national anthem, British and Swiss, 151
nationalism in Europe, 4
nationalism, French, 162
nationalism, Swiss, 1-3, 12, 22-23, 49,
  56-57, 66, 74, 82, 98, 126, 128, 130, 137,
  151, 153, 155, 179-180
navy, British, 98
Near East, 103
Neuchâtel, 7-8, 25, 31-33, 36, 43, 46-47, 49,
  51-53, 58, 141, 149; *see also* Neuchâtel
  question; Republican; Royalist
Neuchâtel question: and Austrian policy,
  51, 54-55, 132, 134, 138-140, 142, 146,
  148-149; and British policy, 32-33, 44-45,
  47-50, 52-59, 65, 76, 88, 98, 100, 127,
  129-152, 177; and French policy, 43-44,
  49, 51, 54-55, 57, 65-66, 72, 78, 129-139,
  142-150; and the German Confederation,
  43, 51, 132-134, 136, 138-139; and
  Prussian policy, 25, 32, 35-36, 41, 43-59,
  63, 65, 75, 87, 127-129, 131-134, 136-148,
  150, 173, 179; and Russian policy, 32, 51,
  54-55, 57, 129, 163, 179; and Swiss
  policy, 48-51, 55-56, 59, 63, 99, 130-135,
  137-138, 141-145, 147-148, 150-151, 178;
  see also Bolgrad; London Protocol
neutrality, Swiss; and Austrian policy, 8,
  61-62, 75-76, 153-154, 163, 175; and
  British policy, 4, 10, 17, 27, 53, 66, 71,
  76, 88, 91-99, 149, 160, 162-164, 166, 171,
  177, 180; and French policy, 7-8, 71, 166,
  171; and German policy, 42, 45-46, 63;
  and Russian policy, 93-94, 97, 144, 163;
  and Sardinian policy, 153-154, 175; and
  Swiss policy, 2-4, 11, 37, 42, 45-46, 91-92,
  99, 153-154, 164, 170, 175-176, 180; *see
  also* constitution; independence; nationalism *Sonderbund;* Treaty of 1815
neutralization of North Savoy, *see* Savoy
  question
neutralization of Switzerland, 7-8
New Helvetian Society, 2-3
noodles, 102
Normanby, Marquis of, xiii, 24, 28, 36,
  65-66

occupation of North Savoy, *see* invasion;
  Savoy
Ochsenbein, Ulrich, xiii, 18-22, 32-34, 37,
  41, 97
October 1846 memorandum on Switzer-
  land, 18-19, 38-39
Orient, and Anglo-French rivalry, 37
Orsini incident, 88-90, 148

Palmerston, Viscount, xiii; and ideology,
  38-39; and Neuchâtel, 32, 36, 44-45,
  47-51, 59, 65, 140; and refugees, 45-47,
  65, 68, 87; and Savoy, 155, 157-158, 162,
  164, 169-171, 173; and the *Sonderbund,*
  18-22, 24-32, 34-40, 149; and Swiss
  commercial policy, 115; and Swiss constitutional reform, 10, 16, 36, 39; and
  Swiss interests in Italy, 42; and the Swiss
  mercenary system, 95; and Swiss railways, 109
Paris, and the Neuchâtel conference in
  1857, 139, 144-145
Parliament, 11, 94, 98, 142, 162, 165, 167
Peel, Robert, xiii, 18-21, 25, 27-30, 37-39,
  42, 46-48, 63-64
Peel, Sir Robert, 38
penal code, Swiss, 94
pensions for British Swiss Legion, 98
Persia, 145
Persigny, Count, xiii, 49, 165-166, 175
personality, and diplomatic relations,
  44-45, 56, 148, 150, 175-177
"philosophical instruments," Swiss, 108
Phipps, *see* Normanby
Piedmont, *see* Sardinia
plebiscite in Savoy, 159-160, 163-165, 168
plebiscite, proposed, for Neuchâtel, 56
Plombières, 155
political organization of Switzerland, 1, 8,
  40; *see also* cantons; constitution
political reporting, *see* reporting
Pope, 14-16, 20-22, 26-29, 34, 90
population, Swiss, 6-7, 10-11, 96, 98, 101,
  108, 158
postal system, Swiss, 11, 101
precision tools, Swiss, 108
Presidency, Swiss, 8; *see also* Federal
  Council
press, Austrian, 154; British, 38, 140, 167;
  French, 163-164; in Geneva, 159; in
  Milan, 78; Prussian, 50, 138; Sardinian,
  154; Swiss, 21, 96, 110, 121, 142, 149-150,
  159
Press and Aliens Conclusum, 9
prête-noms, 68
Prince Albert, *see* Albert
propaganda, 93
property ownership, and the Anglo-Swiss
  treaty, 113-114
protectionism, *see* commercial policy
Protestants, Swiss, 1, 158
Prussia, King of, 8, 32-33, 41, 43-46, 50-53,
  55-56, 58-59, 127-129, 136-148, 150
Prussia, Prince of, 47
Prussian policy: to Austria, 25, 47, 51, 69,
  79, 81, 139; to Baden, 69; to Britain,
  25-26, 32, 35-36, 47, 50-54, 56-59, 88,
  127, 131-133, 136, 142; to France, 25-26,
  36, 45, 51, 54-55, 127, 132, 144-146; to
  the German States, 132, 134, 136; to
  Russia, 47, 51; to Switzerland, 31-33, 36,
  41, 44, 46-48, 50, 53-55, 57, 63, 127-128,
  131-134, 136-137, 142, 144, 146-148; *see
  also* constitution; expansionism; independence; intervention; Neuchâtel; neutrality; refugees; Savoy; *Sonderbund*
public opinion, British, 28, 38, 126-127,
  140, 147, 167, 169-170, 172-173, 178
public opinion, French, 19-20, 28, 136-137,
  158-160, 166
public opinion in North Savoy, 159
public opinion, Swiss, 4-5, 69, 78, 92, 94,
  96, 98, 114, 134, 142, 150, 159, 170

Queen of Britain, *see* Victoria
Queen's Advocate, 113

206

Radetzky, Marshal, xiii, 61
Radical party, Swiss, 14-16, 18-21, 25-26, 30-31, 35-36, 39-41; *see also* Republican party; *Sonderbund*
railways, European, 124
railways, French, 117-118, 123
railways, Swiss, 12, 58, 92, 102, 108-111, 128
recruitment in Germany, 97
recruitment in Switzerland, 61, 95-98
Red Cross, 176
Redcliffe, *see* Canning
re-export trade, British, 119-125; French, 121, 123, 186
refugees: in France, 67-68; in Sardinia, 77; in Switzerland, 9, 11, 40-41, 43, 45-46, 49-50, 52, 60-67, 69-88; and Austrian policy, 43, 47, 49, 52-54, 58, 61-63, 69, 71, 74-88; and Baden policy, 45-46, 63, 69; and British policy, 40-41, 45-47, 54, 61, 63-64, 67-89, 100, 177; and French policy, 43, 47, 49-50, 52-53, 64-74, 77-90, 155; and German policy, 32, 43, 46-47, 49, 51, 63, 79-81; and Prussian policy, 43, 46-47, 49-52, 54, 63, 79, 81, 149; and Russian policy, 47, 52, 54, 71, 79, 84, 93 and Sardinian policy, 64, 77, 85; and Swiss policy, 45-46, 49, 61-78, 80-83, 85-86, 88-89, 177
"Regeneration," Swiss, 16
religion in Switzerland, 1, 13-14, 68-69, 75, 86-87, 90, 111-112, 158; *see also* Catholics
reporting, political, 176-177; and Austrian policy, 20, 43, 84, 87-88; and British policy, 16, 18, 29-30, 43, 64, 85, 161, 178; and French policy, 20, 24, 43, 66-67, 85, 87-90, 149; and papal policy, 21; and Prussian policy, 43, 50, 128, 138; and Swiss policy, 166-167, 169-170, 174
Republican party in Neuchâtel, 41, 43-44, 57, 128; *see also* Royalist party
revolutions of 1848, 37, 40-41, 43, 45-47
Revolution, French, 4
Revolution, French, of July 1830, 9
revolutions in Switzerland, 9, 15, 18, 41, 43, 128
revolution, *see also* liberalism
revolutionary societies in Switzerland, 46, 49
Rhine, 124
Rhineland, 49, 160, 170
rice, 102
right of establishment, *see* establishment
right of expulsion, *see* expulsion
Rome, 94, 98, 130
Royalist party in Neuchâtel, 32, 41, 43-47, 50-54, 56-58, 127-131, 133-135, 137-139, 141-146, 148, 151
Russell, Earl John, xiii, 52-53, 155-158, 160-163, 165-175
Russian, loan, 93
Russian policy: to Austria, 79, 84; to Britain, 93-94, 129, 131, 163; to France, 52, 54, 71, 129, 131, 163; to Prussia, 47, 51, 54-55, 57, 146; to Switzerland, 37, 92-94, 144; *see also* expansionism; Neuchâtel; neutrality; refugees; Savoy; *Sonderbund*

St Gall, 19
Salignac-Fénelon, Count, xiii, *see* Fénelon
saltpeter, 92-93
Sardinia, 64, 72, 153-154
Sardinian policy: to France, 85, 155, 159, 164; to the Pope, 22; to Switzerland, 42, 77, 102, 111, 154, 156, 160, 164; *see also* Neuchâtel; refugees; Savoy; *Sonderbund*
savings, Swiss, 12
Savoy, 8, 153-175; and Austrian policy, 154, 158, 160, 163, 168-170, 175; and British policy, 156-158, 160-164, 166-175, 177, 179; and French policy, 155-175, 179; and Prussian policy, 158, 160, 163, 170, 175; and Russian policy, 158, 160, 163, 170, 175; and Sardinian policy, 154-156, 159-160, 164; and Swiss policy, 155-157, 159-175
Saxe-Coburg, Duke of, 141
Schleswig-Holstein, 45, 49-50, 54
Schmid, H., 151
Schnepp affair, 66
Schwarzenberg, Prince, 35, 74
security, Swiss, *see* defence
Seton-Watson, R. W., 38
shipping patterns of Swiss trade, 92, 115-119, 121-126
shipping services, British, 103, 119, 121-126
shipping services, European, 119
shipping services, French, 122-124
shoe industry, Swiss, 108, 125-126
Sicily, 168
silk industry, Swiss, 101, 107-108, 122-123; *see also* textiles
smuggling, 35
socialism in Paris, 72
socialism in Switzerland, 72, 87; *see also* communism; reporting
Sonderbund crisis, 13-40, 61, 65, 67-69, 144, 149, 176-177, 179; and Austrian policy, 14-15, 19-20, 22-23, 25-26, 30-33, 35-37, 61; and British policy, 10, 14, 18-40, 100, 144, 149, 177, 179; and French policy, 9-10, 15-17, 19-20, 22-31, 33, 35-37, 39-40, 179; and Prussian policy, 25-26, 31-33, 35-36; and Russian policy, 32, 37 and Sardinian policy, 22; and Swiss policy, 18, 20-23, 25, 27, 29-35, 37, 67-68; *see also* Jesuits; Radical party; war
South-eastern Railway in Switzerland, 110
Spanish marriages, 19, 31, 37-38, 150
special league, *see Sonderbund*
Spectator, 38
Stephenson, Robert, 110
stock exchange, Swiss, 93
Strasbourg, 66
straw goods industry, Swiss, 101, 107
Swinburne, 110
Swiss policy, 50, 56, 81; to Austria, 37, 75-78, 81-82, 85-86, 162-163, 169; to Baden, 45-46, 63, 69; to Britain, 4-5, 25, 66-67, 80, 100, 109, 150-151, 157, 177; about Neuchâtel, 48-50, 55-56, 59, 127, 132, 134-135, 141, 143-144, 149; about refugees, 65-67, 76-77, 79, 82, 86-87; about Savoy, 155-157, 160, 162-163, 165-167, 169-170, 173-174; about the *Sonderbund*, 21-23, 25, 27, 29-31, 33-35, 149-150; to France, 55, 66, 176; about Neuchâtel, 55, 59, 130-131, 133-134,

Swiss Policy—*continued*
137-138, 141, 144; about refugees, 65,
67-68, 70, 72, 89-90; about Savoy, 157,
159, 161, 164-167, 171, 174; about the
Sonderbund, 25 37; to the German
States, 46, 141; to international agencies,
2, 176; to Italy, 42, 153; to Prussia, 33,
37, 48-51, 56, 137-138, 141, 143-144,
147-148, 162-163, 169; to Russia, 37,
93-94, 162-163, 169; to Sardinia, 42-43,
61, 77, 83, 156, 160-161, 164; to the
Zollverein, 51, 102; *see also* buffer state;
commercial policy; expansionism;
Federal Council; independence; intervention; investment; mercenary system;
Neuchâtel; neutrality; refugees; Savoy;
Sonderbund; war
Sydow, Rudolf von, xiii, 43, 46, 50, 58,
128-129

Tahiti incident, 16
tariffs, British, 100-101
tariffs, Swiss, 10-11, 102
tariffs, *see also* commercial policy; customs
system
taxes, Swiss, on British residents, 111, 114
technical assistance, British, to Switzerland,
100, 107, 110-111
Temple, *see* Palmerston
textile industry, Swiss, 6-7, 11, 101, 103,
106-108, 121-123
Thouvenel, Antoine-Edouard, xiii, 156-157,
159, 161, 163-166, 168-170, 175
Thonon, 159, 164
Ticino, 19-20, 61-63, 71, 75-78, 82-84,
86-87, 90, 154
Times, The, of London, 29
tolls, cantonal, 102
tourism in Switzerland, 126
Tourte, Abraham, xiii, 156, 164, 174-175
trade, Anglo-Swiss, 101, 115-125, 186;
British, 5, 101-108, 115, 118-126, 186;
French, 115, 117-118, 121-124, 186;
Swiss, 5, 11-12, 92, 100-108, 115-126, 177,
186; *see also* balance of trade; commercial policy
trade marks, 107
trade volume, between Britain and Switzerland, 101, 118-119, 124-125
transhipment trade, *see* transit trade
transit trade: through Britain, 106, 119-125;
through France, 115-118, 121-124, 186;
through Germany, 116-117, 124; through
Switzerland, 10-11
transportation, Swiss, 11, 102; *see also*
railways
transportation patterns of Anglo-Swiss
trade, 115-119, 121-126
Treaty of 1815, 7-8, 10, 15, 21, 36, 49, 51,
54-55, 78, 143-144, 150, 153-154, 156,
159, 163, 176

Treaty between Britain and Switzerland,
96, 111-115, 177-178
Treaty ". . . relative to Neuchâtel . . .",
147-149, 152, 175-176
Treaty of Paris, 129, 155, 163
Treaty between Sardinia and Switzerland,
102, 111
Treaty of Turin, 159, 161-162, 164-165
Treaty between the United States and
Switzerland, 111-113
Treaty of Villafranca, 155
treaty system of Europe, 52, 54-55, 163,
173; *see also* alliance system
Tsar of Russia, 7, 146
Turgot, Marquis Louis, xiii, 70-73, 78
Turin, *see* Treaty of

ultimatum, French, of 1852, 52, 69-74; *see
also* refugees and French policy
Ultramontanists, 13-14, 87
unification of Italy, 153-154, 168, 178
unification of Switzerland, 6; *see also*
Federal Pact reform
United States, 103, 106-107, 111-113,
121-123, 138
Ure, Andrew, 106

Valais, 7, 15, 33
Valengin, 56
Vaud, 17, 32, 34, 38, 43, 64
Vatican, 98; *see also* Pope
Verona, Congress of, 9
Victoria, Queen, 27, 32, 52, 143, 161-162
Vienna, Conference of 1855, 86
Vienna, Congress of, 7-8
Villafranca, *see* Treaty of
volunteer bands, 15-17, 45

Walewski, Count, xiii, 69-70, 72, 131-133,
137, 139, 144-148, 150
war, between Austria and Sardinia,
153-154, 176; declared on Russia, 91;
see also Crimean War; between France
and Prussia, 176
war, civil, in Switzerland, 22-25, 31-35, 39;
see also Sonderbund
war, threatened: about Neuchâtel, 136,
138-143; about Savoy, 162
watch industry, Swiss, 6-7, 101, 103,
107-108
water power, Swiss, 7
Wellesley, *see* Cowley
Westmorland, Earl of, xiii, 44, 76, 79-81,
86, 97
wheat, 51, 102
Williamson & Co., 110

Zollverein, 12, 51, 102
Zurich, 8, 12, 17-18, 92, 154